QUAGMIRE

QUAGMIRE

Personal Stories from Iraq and Afghanistan

EDITED BY **DONALD ANDERSON**
FOREWORD BY **PHILIP BEIDLER**

Potomac Books

AN IMPRINT OF THE UNIVERSITY OF NEBRASKA PRESS

All rights reserved. Potomac Books is an imprint of
the University of Nebraska Press.
Manufactured in the United States of America.

The story "Allawi" originally appeared in Patrick
Mondaca's *Adjustment Disorder: A Collection of
Maladjusted Essays* (Bauhan, 2021).

Library of Congress Cataloging-in-Publication Data
Names: Anderson, Donald, July 9, 1946, -editor.
Title: Quagmire: personal stories from Iraq and
Afghanistan / edited by Donald Anderson.
Other titles: Personal stories from Iraq and
Afghanistan
Description: [Lincoln, Nebraska]: Potomac Books,
an imprint of the University of Nebraska Press,
[2021] | Includes bibliographical references.
Identifiers: LCCN 2020057471
ISBN 9781640124523 (paperback)
ISBN 9781640124899 (epub)
ISBN 9781640124905 (pdf)
Subjects: LCSH: Iraq War, 2003–2011—
Personal narratives, American. | Afghan War,
2001—Personal narratives, American. | BISAC:
HISTORY / Military / Afghan War (2001–) |
HISTORY / Military / Iraq War (2003–2011)
Classification: LCC DS79.766.A1 Q34 2021 | DDC
956.7044/34092273—dc23
LC record available at https://lccn.loc.
gov/2020057471

Set in Questa by Laura Buis.

Look west at the hill of water: it is half the
planet: this dome, this half-globe, this
bulging Eyeball of water, arched over to Asia,
Australia and white Antarctica: those are the
eyelids that never close; this is the staring
unsleeping Eye of the earth; and what it watches
is not our wars.

—ROBINSON JEFFERS, from "The Eye"

Contents

Foreword

PHILIP BEIDLER

A reader of this collection of personal narratives from the American wars in Iraq and Afghanistan—partaking also of the critical insights of Donald Anderson's prologue and of John Whittier-Ferguson's epilogue—will gain a new knowledge of what happened there; or, to be more precise, what horrific enterprises the Iraq and Afghanistan wars turned out to be over the years for a myriad of participants in a plethora of assignments, actions, duties, and locales. In this respect, one should begin by noting emphatically that the title, however ironically chosen, says exactly what it means: that a post–Vietnam War America, having extricated itself toward the end of the twentieth century from the morass of Indochina, at the beginning of the twenty-first actually found it possible to create a new military and geopolitical quagmire in the desert. I, for one, on the basis of reading these first-person narratives, feel that I actually may now at least begin to comprehend in very direct and concrete ways—as I never did before—what an incomprehensible, ghastly mess the whole decades-long endeavor turned out to be. Indeed, I should go so far as to say, the collection as a whole—studded, as one might expect with all the bizarre new acronyms and nomenclatures comprising the nation's latest glossary of war—Sandbox, Humvee, MRAP, IED, Hillybilly Armor, LN, TCN, TCP, MRE, Moondust, DFAC, Fobbit, T-man, Johnny Jihad—at many points makes me think that my own war fifty years ago in Vietnam was by comparison reasonably coherent. Twenty-four hours a day, for weeks at a time, we went out to find the enemy and kill him.

All the rear-area stuff and strategic confusion was just background noise to most of us. Yes, we heard about all kinds of strange, off-the-wall "missions." The LRRPs, the Green Berets, the secret SOG Cambodia stuff, and the Phoenix assassination teams. And, to be sure, we had our own superabundant supplies and varieties of housecats: clerks and jerks, we called them, Remington raiders, REMFs (rear-echelon motherfuckers). All over the country we built back-in-the-world installations: barracks, mess halls, PXs, Officers' and NCO and EM clubs packing plenty of beer and soda. By the end, MACV—with all its allegedly "advisory" and "assistance" program—had its own Pentagon West campus outside Saigon.

In contrast to even this prolonged military train wreck, what I get out of the *Quagmire* narratives is that there never really was anything resembling a mission to begin with and that the longer we stayed in Iraq and Afghanistan the more bizarre and incoherent it all became—no matter how or where one was deployed. And that, I must say, is to me the most concentrated composite effect of the essays: that there were nearly as many wars going on as there were different participants in different situations over a nearly interminable period of years. And, if anything, the differences themselves were breathtaking, again even for a Vietnam War veteran who thought he had seen the most of it. Here a roadblock, erupting into the latest shooting up of a carful of civilians, seemed to be an everyday occurrence. With the flick of a cellphone an incredibly powerful IED could turn any patrol into a bloodbath. Anyone on the street truly could be a suicide bomber. (Hence the mantra, "Be professional. Be polite. Be prepared to kill everybody you meet.") Weeks and months were spent on the most utterly exhausting missions of house-to-house fighting. Sometimes the city was Mosul or Kandahar. As often, a young American on his second or third tour would find himself assigned to the second or third retaking of Mosul or Kandahar.

The work included here is generally so powerful as to reduce one into appalled silence. We follow the globe-girdling flight of the B-2 bomber command pilot who initiates the war precisely on time by dropping its bomb directly down the shaft of Saddam Hussein's führerbunker. A young Marine at a roadblock relents at the last moment from opening fire on the automobile of a confused, frightened civilian trying not to be late for work, but then ponders whether he will go home scorned as the only U.S. Marine who has never killed anybody. A former Chinook pilot at an elegant Sunday brunch with old college friends tells a gruesome war story with every intention of spoiling his complacent, privileged companions' football weekend. Here then, ranging from the horrific to the banal, is a true literature of witness. Something changes radically in the lives of those who have looked upon the face of battle. To borrow from Donald Anderson, the phrasing "the voice that knows" says it all.

When War Becomes Personal

A Prologue

DONALD ANDERSON

> Well, about my experience, it illustrates how you can become something you never thought you would become, without being aware of the transformation. That there is evil in you, or violence in you, or both—which you're not fully aware of—and that it can sneak up and in effect possess you, or snatch your soul.
>
> My old editor at the *National Geographic Adventure* magazine used to be a Golden Gloves fighter in Ohio, and he was talking about the young interns they had working at the magazine. He said, "You know the trouble with a lot of these people, a lot of them have never been cut."
>
> —PHILIP CAPUTO

As regards war literature, it feels defensible to suggest that we list more toward the authority of experience than we do to the authority of imagination. We accept, don't we, that *The Red Badge of Courage* provides insight into the American Civil War even though Stephen Crane himself did not participate in that war? But does Tim O'Brien's service in Vietnam add weight to *The Things They Carried*? Or Elliot Ackerman's service to his accounts of Iraq? Benjamin Busch's and Brian Turner's service certainly reinforces the accuracy and legitimacy of their Iraq War memoirs, does it not? Of course all writers draw on the power of imagination when they write their best. So the effect's blurry. Nonetheless, there is a kind of insider/outsider phenomenon at work when we encounter war literature. When it is an insider writing we perk up as we do in the movie theater seeing "Based on a True Story" scroll across the screen. I admit I'm a sucker for it.

But I can be fooled. Perhaps like you, I was stunned when I encountered Cynthia Ozick's 1980 *New Yorker* short story "The Shawl." The story, a strafing account of a death camp murder of a stick-limbed child, felt entirely authentic. I knew Ozick was Jewish; I knew she was of an age to have been interned in a death camp. But she wasn't. She was, at the story's fictional time, a cheerleader in high school in New Jersey, the story an altogether brilliant fabrication. That said, I must say that to find that Norman Mailer served in World War II invited me to read his long first novel *The Naked and the Dead*, in the way that James Jones's war experience led me to *The Thin Red Line*, to Kurt Vonnegut and *Slaughterhouse-Five*. And so it goes. . . . We do, if not privilege, at least muster a weighted respect for war experience. Tim O'Brien puts it this way: "True war stories don't generalize. They do not indulge in abstraction or analysis."

Experienced soldiers speak from an earned visceral location. But let's not restrict the term combatant to uniformed troops. Consider this "noncombatant" Nicaraguan mother from *Writing Between the Lines*:

> The three of us crouched in the corner of the house, trembling and crying all at once, thinking that surely we would die here as the bullets and shrapnel were destroying our small wooden home. We decided to leave and find a safe place to hide. So we went through the back, through the kitchen, my husband carrying our young daughter in his arms. A plane flew very low and seemed to be coming directly at us and firing rockets all over, striking my daughter in the back and my husband as he carried her. From where I was, only a few paces behind them, I saw only the heart and the entrails of my child. She seemed to have been blown apart. . . . My husband stumbled some thirty steps with his arms torn away, blood pouring out of him till he fell dead. There was a great hole in his chest. Part of it was still smoking, a smoking rocket was still in one leg. The other was stripped of all flesh to the bone. I wanted to pick up my daughter, but there

were only pieces of her. . . . I ran and found her arm and tried to put it back on her, tried to put back everything that had spilled out of her. But she was already dead. She was my only child and it was hard for me to have her. I dressed her myself for parties. Spoiled her. I don't know what I'm going to do.

What is this but moral authority?—a voice that merits and demands attention—a voice that *knows*. Felt threat is a constant for any person, near or on the front lines. To put it another way, in war there is the sense that one is available for death. War is for all soldiers, as it was for young Paul Fussell, an "introduction to the shakiness of civilization." The possibility of death is something that sticks. From an interview, Tim O'Brien:

> There's a passage where Paul Berlin is going to war and he looks at his own hands, "my hands, my hands." Love of one's limbs. Love of their presence, because in war there's always the proximate danger of their absence. No hands. No legs. No feet. No testicles. No head. That passage in *Cacciato* was written with a real purpose in mind: "my hands." Those are things we take for granted. We don't look at our hands and take a shower and say "my hands." But war teaches you to value those hands.

In *The Soldiers' Tale* Samuel Hynes takes on the issue of "truth problems"—he knows that any individual's perspective, especially in the carnage, chaos, and fog of war, is limited, not only by one's place in the field (a trench, a tank, a cockpit), but by the "infidelities of memory" and the "distortion of language." But, nonetheless, the individual's vision, confined or not, helps make up the larger, more accurate picture, the truth of war "being the sum of witnesses, the collective tale that soldiers tell":

> We don't need to call that convergence of witnesses historical truth, if that seems too confident; call it instead the recoverable past of war. Such recovery is possible; it is more than possible: it is imperative. What other route do we have to understanding the human experience of war—how it felt, what it was like—than the witness of [those] who were there?

These personal responses to war in Iraq and Afghanistan have been selected from *War, Literature & the Arts: An International Journal of the Humanities* to mark the thirtieth anniversary of its inaugural publication. The responses, written over the period of the last fifteen years, mirror, approximately, the lengths of these two Middle Eastern conflicts, and demonstrate, I believe, the fixed aftermath of war, the degreed ripples that extend beyond soldiers to families and friends, lovers, hometowns, even pets. For citizens there is an obligation—is there not?—as Neruda advised, to "Come and see the blood in the streets." To ignore what we do in war and what war does to us is to move willfully toward ignorance and pretense. To scorn such reminders carelessly imperils ourselves, our communities, and our nation.

QUAGMIRE

Things to Pack When You're Bound for Baghdad

JASON ARMAGOST

Missouri, 19 March 2003

The clock is punched for war in Mesopotamia. Six hours until midnight, the day before the sudden flourish of air combat. I am suited, armed, and briefed for a 20,000-mile flight. The middle 208 seconds of the journey will be over Baghdad. Tomorrow's strikes will compose the first salvos of "shock and awe."

Our warbirds are carbon-fiber and titanium stealth bombers. They idle, topped with fuel, preflight crews tending aircraft systems on the rain-damp tarmac of Whiteman Air Force Base. In the course of the next two days I will stiffen my backbone against exhaustion and battle with air force–issued amphetamines, a half-case of canned espresso drinks, and forty thousand pounds of steel and high explosive. And books.

The Northrop Grumman B-2a Spirit is a flying wing—a sixty-year old concept writ lethal in composites and computers. In profile it is racy—a falcon stooping on distant prey. From the front—a menacing winged whale; from overhead—wedge-shaped Euclidean study in parallel form. The plane carries aloft a crew of two pilots with the necessary life-support systems—oxygen, heating, air-conditioning, and cockpit pressurization. The pilots sit next to each other in twin ejection seats. The running joke is that the seats don't work because you'd rather be dead than face an accident board having crashed a $2.14 billion national asset.

Satiny charcoal in composition with a smooth, blended body, the B-2 is simultaneously rounded and angular. The skin is exotic and TOP SECRET. Wing span is 172 feet, two-and-a-half times its length of 69 feet nose to tail. It is rare—only twenty-one were built—but not endangered. It threads the 3-D envelopes of missile defense networks. Stealth has the same effect on defenses as speed, rendering reactions ineffective because they are too little, too late, if at all. This plane will bring us home.

The payload consists of sixteen weapons mounted on two eight-position rotating launchers in each of the three aircraft of our flight. My primary weapons are thirteen one-ton penetrator bombs for hardened targets and runways. The three remaining launcher stations carry the 4,617-pound GBU-37 "Bunker Buster." These two-and-a-half-ton monstrosities are targeted against deeply buried, steel-reinforced concrete command centers in a planned effort to "decapitate" Iraq's leadership. In the lingo of combat aviators, these bombs will "prosecute" targets. Rarely—unless in talk about Saddam or his sons—is killing mentioned. We are distanced. We make "inputs" into a network of flying computers. I manage the ghost in the machine.

Our enemies label us the "Great Satan"—moral descendants of the Paladins of Charlemagne, Protector of the One Church. I don't know if those we aim to liberate call us anything at all. We are armed to strike from the air, over the land, between the two rivers.

I have brought a bag of books and journals to pass the hours of tedium. I am bound for desert places.

Over Indiana at thirty-five thousand feet. Our wingmen in position 2 and 4 miles behind us, stacked up in altitude. We have settled into our roles and tasks. We have momentum. I boost out of the left seat and leave the colonel in the right to man the stick and throttles. A thick Bible is cradled in his lap.

The cockpit is brimming with electronics, maps, target photos, food, bottled water, and standardized military duffels containing "comfort items"—sleeping bags, air mattresses, pillows, black foam eye-masks to darken the day, noise cancellation headsets and extra earplugs to stifle the rhythmic thrum of the engines. I sort the mounds of bags to locate my combat survival vest. There it is, folded and resting for war against a circuit-breaker panel. It is choked with maps for evasion on the ground, water packets, radios, night-vision goggles, a fixed-blade knife, compass, firestarter, handheld global-positioning-system (GPS), and a nine-millimeter handgun with three full magazines. I pull the vest on—right arm, then left—zip it, and try to locate specific items with my eyes closed. It weighs twenty-eight pounds.

I have supplemented the standard equipment with my own essentials stashed throughout the seven pockets of my flight suit:

3 tubes of ChapStick, medicated

Toothbrush, floss, and travel toothpaste

1 oz. tin of Bag Balm—cow-udder salve for dry hands

Nail clippers

Aspirin, acetaminophen, ibuprofen, vitamin C, multivitamin, Immodium, iodine, Band-Aids, saline nasal spray, eyedrops

Baby wipes in a plastic sandwich bag

Sunglasses

Swiss army knife

Duct tape

In a stained and ratty helmet bag I have a small library of books and personal journals:

Heartsblood: Hunting, Spirituality, and Wildness in America—David Petersen

The Shape of the Journey: New and Collected Poems, and *Just Before Dark: Collected Nonfiction*—Jim Harrison

Winter Morning Walks—Ted Kooser

Nine Horses: Poems—Billy Collins

A Timbered Choir: The Sabbath Poems 1979–1997—Wendell Berry

West with the Night—Beryl Markham

Fire Road and *Aftermath: An Anthology of Post-Vietnam Fiction*—Donald Anderson

The Things They Carried—Tim O'Brien

Winter: Notes from Montana—Rick Bass

Burning the Days: Recollection and *Dusk and Other Stories*—James Salter

Blood Meridian, or The Evening Redness in the West—Cormac McCarthy

The Vintage Book of Contemporary American Short Stories—Edited by Tobias Wolff

A Voice Crying in the Wilderness—Edward Abbey

The Art of Living and Other Stories—John Gardner

Hunting the Osage Bow—Dean Torges

The Norton Book of Classical Literature—Edited by Bernard Knox

Don Quixote—Cervantes, Starkie translation

Gilgamesh—Translated by Herbert Mason

Thoughts of a Philosophical Fighter Pilot—Jim Stockdale

Wind, Sand, and Stars—Antoine de Saint-Exupéry

The Longest Silence: A Life in Fishing, and *Keep the Change*—Thomas McGuane

The Nick Adams Stories—Hemingway

Gray's Sporting Journal—August 2001 & November/December 2002

The *Iliad* and the *Odyssey*—Homer. Robert Fagles translations

Beowulf—Seamus Heaney translation

Four leatherbound journals in various states of wear

At the bottom of the bag, among the books:

Stainless-steel Colt 1911A1, .45 ACP with custom night-sights and four loaded magazines—in a nylon chest holster

Four pairs of wool socks, black silk long johns, three brown undershirts, two pairs of flannel boxer shorts

Blue fitted-wool logo baseball cap "Yale—*Lux et Veritas*"

Black & white photo of my wife, son, and daughter

These things, these books, are a measure of security. A redoubt in war. They bring me comfort in their many ways. The books have all been read. That is the point. In the middle of the Atlantic I won't be interested in the cheap plot twists of the latest bestseller. I'm in need of art—recklessness, patience, wisdom, passion, and largesse. I rifle through the titles, grab five, and return to the seat. We are over Ohio. Me, my books, and the colonel.

Much Later, the Med, Splitting the Strait of Gibraltar

To the north, Spain. From the library bag—Cervantes: "But all this must be suffered by those who profess the stern order of chivalry." And: "My judgment is now clear and unfettered, and that dark cloud of ignorance has disappeared, which the continual reading of those detestable books of knight-errantry had cast over my understanding."

Don Quixote was, and remains, redemption for a maimed veteran of the Battle of Lepanto and seven-year prisoner of the Saracens. Four hundred years later we are bestowed the unwisdom of the knight and the fidelity and candor of his man Sancho. I pray he squires me now.

To the south the Atlas Mountains heave up through the sands of North Africa. Over the water—low, scattered, vivid-white cumulus clouds. Time, distance, and history are crammed in the 14 kilometers severing continents. The sea below is a Homeric wine-dark against the early afternoon March sun. Our Mediterranean flight plan ushers us through international airspace to minimize the political complexities of trucking weapons to war.

Valencia.

Barcelona.

Marseilles. The lilting music of a female French air traffic controller's voice. She knows we are USAF bombers. Our documentation conceals nothing. I expect contempt in her voice, but hear none. Her warmth suggests a kind of condolence. A sadness floods me when she hands us off to the next controller.

Italian Controlled Airspace Over the Tyrrhenian Sea

Mindful of the *Iliad*'s great tactician and diplomat, Odysseus. Hunkered at the siege of Troy for ten years, he brokered the egos of Agamemnon and Achilles. With the deployment of his Trojan horse, he became the technological progenitor of the plane my enemies won't see. Unbeknownst to Odysseus, during his twenty-year absence his wife Penelope would weave a death shroud during daylight. In the eventide she would unweave this tapestry and forfeit her art more in fear than in hope. She gave twenty years of her life to a war at the eastern edge of the known world.

My wife is named Diane; the Roman conflation of Artemis, goddess of the hunt, daughter of Zeus and Leto, sister of Apollo. In seven hours, back in Missouri, she will press RECORD on a machine tuned to CNN's live coverage from Baghdad. One of my targets is Saddam's main presidential palace. It looms in the backdrop across the Tigris River from the hotel where journalists shoot their footage. At 11:04:25 a.m. Central Standard Time a long series of cracking explosions will send dust and fire into the sky in a televised close-up. Diane will cry when she sees antiaircraft artillery and missiles racing skyward. She will hide her tears from our young children. She will claim that I didn't warn her.

Eleven hours in—steering southbound 30 miles east of Sardinia toward the Strait of Messina between the toe of the Italian boot and Sicily. Odysseus's six-headed Scylla and devil-vortex Charybdis hunger 5 miles below the pregnant bellies of bombers. A couple of times an hour, someone in the formation offers a joke on our discrete radio frequency. We laugh and make smartass comments even when the joke isn't funny. We are all reluctant to resume the silence.

I snap open my fourth lukewarm Starbuck's Doubleshot. I can smell the coffee through my dry skin. In the preceding thirty-six hours I have "flown" the bomb runs four times on a computer simulator back in Missouri and hundreds of times since in my head. Two weeks ago we practiced the Baghdad portion of our bomb runs over Omaha at two o'clock in the morning. Method, repetition, and judgment. One human part of a vast system set in motion.

The colonel twists in a crouch over green computer displays. A technophile living a technophile's dream. The computers are his decorous armor against any debate over the consequences of our words and deeds. The colonel and I. We're different. We each need the other.

Ionian Sea, West of Greece

Again, Homer, the "blind poet." When this thirty-nine-hour mission is over I will have seen three "rosy-fingered dawns" and, like Apollo the Archer, I will have "come down like night" over the skies of an ancient city.

As Homer's prelude to Western history suggests, virtually everything revolved around honor and courage in battle for the warring Greeks in their *poleis*. Death and the horrors of war were acknowledged as tragic, but their constancy and proliferation paled in comparison to the everlasting honor gained through a display of fierce strategic genius, the first virtue. The *demos* elected and impeached the men who would lead them into battle. Generals—*Strategos*. The electorate rewarded skill, intellect, courage, compassion, and wisdom. They had their politics. They had their heroes. Both were accountable to the people.

I lift Stockdale's book from where it rests on the glareshield. Handwritten on the inside cover is a note I penned six years ago when I was living in rural northern Japan, flying "Wild Weasel" missions in the F-16. It is from Clausewitz's *On War*:

> The soldier's trade, if it is to mean anything at all, has to be anchored to an unshakeable code of honor. Otherwise, those of us who follow the drums become nothing more than a bunch of hired assassins walking around in gaudy clothes . . . a disgrace to God and mankind.

Admiral Stockdale survived seven-and-a-half years as the senior ranking officer in Vietnamese prisoner-of-war camps. Malnutrition. Torture. Fear. Guilt. *Four years of solitary confinement.* He had no books—nothing physical to anchor himself. In his mind he bore the great Stoic philosophers Marcus Aurelius and Epictetus. "Character is fate." After the war he received the Medal of Honor; but more than that, he was possessed of honor.

The colonel breaks the silence over the intercom. "I'll be heads down in the navigation systems for a while." I nod.

Ezra Pound once suggested Homer was an army doctor because of his keen descriptions of the honor displayed and the horror rendered in combat deaths. I seek honor in my posthistorical air war, but it is difficult to match deeds with the ancients. I am cloaked in the conceit of technology.

I look down at a map and figure angles and distances in my head based on our current heading. The Greek Peloponnese is off our nose, out of sight, over the horizon. Ancient Sparta. I look up and left, past the wingtip. Honor is, at best, diluted in the binary code of the most advanced airplane in the world. I place maps and mission papers in a lidded case behind the throttles to my left and pull out the *Norton Book of Classical Literature*. I linger on a highlighted section of Hesiod. By his description, the Olympian gods were petulant, arrogant, inhuman. When brilliant—yet inevitably flawed—mortal heroes approached the gods in deed, their deaths were tragically orchestrated. But they lived on in myth. They reflected great truths. Truths that were refined with the first spoken art. An art that began around campfires, in caves, in long halls, on wooden ships. The poems and stories we have always needed to bring meaning to random acts of man and nature that thwart our best plans.

Tonight I will shoot Apollo's silver bow that never misses. I will be miles above the Olympian mountaintops. The skin of the airplane that shields me from my enemies' eyes also shields me from renown. Popular stories of airmen are more often about machines pushing the limits of human capacity and endurance (I almost let the F-16 kill me numerous times) than about the nature of the individuals who pilot them. Technology trumps our shared human nature. I tell myself that my actions will help save the lives of soldiers who are racing north out of Kuwait. This is honorable. It is not honor.

Socrates. Sophocles. Aeschylus. Thucydides. Pericles. Xenophon. Demosthenes. All clarified their moral, physical, and intellectual courage on the fields of battle. The immediacy and closeness of war led them to believe that they would rather die fighting than live as another man's slave. As the ability to project power over great distances has advanced with technology, the question I must now ask is: will I *kill* to free another man's slave into a world that may be more chaotic, anarchic, and dangerous?

Aeschylus's epitaph mentioned nothing of his considerable poetic legacy, only of his having served as an Athenian officer at the battle of Marathon against the "longhaired" Persians. "In war," he wrote, "the first casualty is truth."

The radio hums and barks. I don't recognize a word the Greek air-traffic controller is saying. Apparently my wingman can translate his English, so I swallow the pride of a flight lead and let him have the radios until we get handed off, southbound, to the controller out of Cairo. The Cairene and I are talking over each other. Clipping transmissions. He orders our flight to climb above thirty-thousand feet. After we do, he no longer answers our queries. The radio silence is peculiar and I wonder if he is searching for a supervisor to turn us around and give us back to the Greeks. The coast looms. Southeast on the veiled horizon I can see a brown cloud of civilization mixing over the Nile delta from the pollution of Alexandria and Cairo, Egypt's two largest cities. The cloud trails off to the east as it rises and meets the lower reaches of the jet stream. The sky above fades to the deep blue of altitude.

Nineteen days past was my thirty-third birthday. Two months older than Alexander the Great when he died in Babylon. The age of Christ at crucifixion . . .

A handwritten fragment of Heraclitus from a small black notebook carried in the thigh pocket of my flight suit:

> Fire of all things
> is the judge and ravisher.

Egyptian Airspace—12 Miles Inbound

The coast that bears down is 30 miles west of El Alamein and another 30 miles from Ptolemy's Alexandria, where, according to Plutarch, arrogance and betrayal among Roman factions led to the destruction of the greatest library of the ancients. A fire at the Temple of the Muses. The most extensive collection of the genius of the Hellenes. Gone. Who can forgive Julius Caesar his "collateral damage" when Alexandria burned?

Nothing but sand in all directions now. The pressurized, treated air in the cockpit tastes coppery. The B-2, like every aircraft I've ever flown, blows hot air in your face while your feet are bitten by frost. I have learned. I am wearing merino wool socks so thick that I have been shoeless since shortly after takeoff. Quite probably this is against some regulation.

Ninety minutes later. Still only sand. Saint-Exupéry and the Sahara Desert country of *Wind, Sand, and Stars*. Somewhere east of our current position he crashed an old prop-driven airplane in 1935 while trying to set the speed record from Paris to Saigon. He made wonderful art from his ordeal in the desert that nearly consumed him. "It has become impossible to say whether love or hate plays the greater part in this setting forth of the warriors." My mission is not to establish speed or endurance records. I carry bombs.

I make safe the ejection seat and unbuckle the shoulder harness and lap belt. I tap the colonel's shoulder and gesture to the food in coolers behind us. He passes a thumbs-up and I press out to stand in the eighteen square feet of real estate between the chemical toilet and the port bulkhead of the cockpit. The cooler lid creaks as I lift it and pass a roast-beef-and-cheese sandwich forward. Needly pain in my lower back and legs. I dance a jig—elbows bent tight, fists clenched chest-high, feet bouncing heel-toe, Scottish war pipes ripping my imagination. I twist from the waist and jab-jab, right cross, dip duck, feint, left hook, combo uppercuts to the liver and chin. Arms raised in victory, I declare myself the undisputed welterweight champion above thirty thousand feet. I shake out, roll my head left, then right, and crumple to the nonskid rubberized floor. I build a "nest" with a camping air mattress and a drab canvas sleeping bag. I unwind into the bag and compel myself to relax. The lower third of my body rests on the closed interior door of the entry hatch. Even though it only opens inward, I imagine plunging through every time I step on it, disgorged from the aircraft. Wind-tossed terminal velocity. Shoeless death.

I roll up to a sit, reach around to the map case, and grab the last book I was reading. Cormac McCarthy's *Blood Meridian*. I fan the mangled and tabbed pages. Highlighted passages and penned marginalia flick past my eyes like a grade-school notebook cartoon. Without reading the words, I recall tempers and thoughts that came to me as I knew the book for the first time. Undistilled violence promoted to high art. Ares— god of war—come to the 1840s Southwest border country as the mercenary Judge Holden. He never sleeps and never dies.

He speaks all languages. Artist. Scientist. Shaman. Preacher. Liar. Killer of children. Eventually he will have us all.

A yellowed grocery-list bookmark falls from page 248, where orange highlighting burns the judge's explication of war into the page:

> It makes no difference what men think of war, said the judge. War endures. As well ask men what they think of stone. War was always here. Before man was, war waited for him. The ultimate trade awaiting its ultimate practitioner. That is the way it was and will be . . .
>
> War is the ultimate game because war is at last a forcing of the unity of existence. War is god . . .

I lay the open book across my chest. I'm over Egypt. Land of Pharaohs. In two hours we'll arm and test the weapons. In the colonel's jargon, a "function check." I yawn continually because (I forecast) I am spiraling into oxygen debt. It unnerves the colonel in the right seat because he imagines I am unserious about my duty. I rise and gaze out the portside windscreen, leaning forward from behind the seat.

Eastbound. Fifty miles ahead is the narrow-gauged Nile River valley—a shock of vegetation. The ground shadows highlight the Valley of the Kings just across the river from Luxor and Thebes. The Great Temple of Amun and Ramses III. The Temple of Isis. Necropolis. The pyramids at Giza are over the horizon to the northwest.

I grab a leatherbound journal from a helmet bag stained with hydraulic fluid and engine oil. Crossing the great river of Africa reminded me of a quote I copied into the journal a couple of years ago from an essay by Korean War fighter pilot and author James Salter. There it is, written in smeared blue ink backed by faded yellow highlights: "Literature is the river of civilization, its Tigris and Nile. Those who follow it, and I am inclined to say only those, pass by the glories." I will overfly both of these rivers—twice—within a matter of hours. Further down the page, Jim Harrison. "Great poems make good prayers."

Over the engine noise I hear the colonel order the trailing wingmen to stack up from our altitude in five-hundred-foot increments to compress our reserved air traffic block. The wingmen check their air-to-air radar as a precaution against the coming night. We are lit from below by a sand-blown, blood-orange sun that is waning below the horizon. The sun god Ra has already set for those in the valley beneath the plane. The late purples and reds of the desert contrast the underwhelming gray and black of the cockpit glare shield and switch consoles. The only colors stab out from eight computer cockpit displays. Through these we manage our mortal cargo.

The desert air cools rapidly, generating light turbulence. The plane pogos every few seconds. I return to the seat and buckle down until the sky darkens and the chop calms. The night is a quiet blessing. The world closes in as the sky opens with stars. The radios grow silent with the dark. Beryl Markham wrote that there is no twilight in Africa. Only night's sudden reclamation of the land. This reclamation is the haven of stealth. We own the black sky and the radar spectrum over distant countries.

The arid emptiness cleaved by the sudden green river valley over the left wing looks like a *National Geographic* photo. Glancing back to the darkening horizon, I imagine a Saharan nomad tending his camels and searching the sky for the low, quiet booming of three B-2s en route to a war that has not yet begun. In words and deeds, what of our humanity do we apportion? My flight coveralls are designed to protect me in a fire. For these long hours in the air my religion is fuel. My spirituality is speed. Every tanker who gives us gas is my muse, pushing me onward. I breathe supplemental oxygen at combat altitudes (sometimes switching to 100 percent oxygen in a rush to gather my thoughts). My great-grandparents, early in the last century on the unbroken plains of Nebraska, were the last of my American family to struggle hand-to-mouth for survival. I cruise at high subsonic speeds, 10 percent of the distance to the lower reaches of orbital space. What of the gazing nomad? Does he carry books with him in his travels or does the weight come at too high a cost? Would he fight an enemy with a sword? The curved scimitar of a mounted warrior? Yes? He would have to watch his adversary breathe his last. Watch his eyes glaze. *Feel his death rattle on the tip of his blade*, knowing that he must protect his family, his tribe, his very life. Rubbernecking up, would he recognize me as a man in this black machine 6 miles above the desert? Would he think me a bat-winged demon?

Pacing again, I center-up between the seats and look forward over the aircraft nose. The colonel is still banging on the data-entry computer and bumping the throttles periodically. I should try for another twenty-minute nap while he has the controls.

Back into the nest. I won't doze until well after the Baghdad firewalking stunt; a pretender to sleep and dreams.

Eyes closed. I cross into the territory of mind.

Clarity. Courage. Ambiguity. Context. These perceptions gain meaning and momentum through the processes of literature. The one thing, I believe, that burns through the veneer of civilization to gift us glimpses into the eternal truths of human nature. *The things we know but cannot name.* The books I pack in my flight gear: poetry, short stories, the world's classics, collected essays, glossy hunting journals with ads for $40,000 shotguns, and poetry. Poetry first and last. At the controls you can't disengage for more than about thirty seconds at a time. Darting attention and wandering thoughts; a prescription for lucid, brief, simple, and majestic words with the strength of memory. These words and their accompanying images provide thoughtful interruptions to the method and repetition of long-range flying. Life is given nuance between the lines. Between the soulless aircraft checklists designed to protect you from yourself.

Perched crossways on the half-zipped opening of my book bag is the frayed copy of *Heartsblood,* by David Petersen. On the cover is *The Hunter,* by N. C. Wyeth. My eyes still closed, the image focuses in my mind. The painting renders an idyllic Ojibwa hunter standing ankle-deep in water. He quarters right, toward the viewer. Naked but for skins wrapped around his waist and a red cloth tied close about his hair. Over his left shoulder is slung a Canada goose, wings askew, black-beaked head hanging limp by the hunter's knee. The hunter looks away, over this burdened shoulder, toward barren trees and a V-formation of geese flying south for the winter. He is wildness, simplicity, freedom, and hope. In his right hand a wood selfbow with a buckskin-wrapped handle.

I am that hunter. I build and hunt with primitive bows. I scrape wood with stone blades. It is experience stripped bare and it brings me, wrapped in stealth technology, closer to that hunter, closer to existence and the actual costs associated with living. It is the opposite of meaninglessness or absurdity. On the ground I am a living mixed metaphor of radar-absorbing material and the ancient woods of bows—hickory, ash, osage orange, yew. I fancy a bow in my mind.

A straight-grained limb with no twist cut to an arm-span's length. The face or "back" of the bow under tension, wider near the grip and tapering toward the nocks that hold and center the string. Width controls draw weight. In profile, thickness is uniform, excepting the buckskin-wrapped palm-swell at the handle. Thickness controls the bend throughout the length of the limbs. Unstrung, after the bow is finished and shot-in, there is a slight string-follow where the wood "remembers" the compression stress put upon it. When the bow is strung there is a gentle, even curve throughout, the string seven inches from the belly of the handle. At full draw the bow is a crescent—a new moon. If the wood is well-seasoned and I honor the craft, my bows pull forty-five to fifty pounds at a twenty-eight-inch draw. They will cast heavy wood arrows flat and fast.

Universally similar to the hunting bow just described, the selfbows of hunter-gatherers are simple and streamlined. The perfect weapon a stealthy woodsman might use to kill large prey animals reliably inside of twenty paces. With a dried stave, a passable hunting bow can be made in hours. These weapons of survival became more complicated when they evolved into the implements of warring pastoral and agricultural societies rather than tools of food procurement for nomadic peoples. The ancient Scythians did not perfect their high-performance sinew and horn horse-bows to hunt the steppes. The building process would have been inefficient for a man struggling to feed his family. These weapons were purpose-built for defense and brutal subjugation at range. Without hitting a major bone, these bows could be shot through two lightly armored footmen lined up in ranks. From the back of a rushing horse they were more accurate than a GPS weapon, with zero collateral damage. Warrior-nomads like the Scythians became specialized and wedded to the geography that bore them. Primitive rituals evolved. Organized warfare became a principal ritual over and above the struggle to survive and protect resources.

Centuries later the Athenian general Thucydides commented on war as a function of fear, honor, and interest. The agricultural and pastoral Greeks sought decisive battle in the open field as a cultural expression of strategy. They were known for their disciplined and courageous infantry. The Greeks favored spears and short swords in close-contact fighting. In contrast, the weapons of loosely organized cavalries were primarily bows. Archers control distance in a tactical engagement. The Scythians, and later the Huns and Mongols, were the peoples of stealth, deception, and hit-and-run, guerrilla-style warfare. Marauders on horseback, they treasured the bow in war and were deadly at range. They were undisciplined, individualistic, and tribal, but rarely were they lured to fight Western forces in a decisive, pitched battle.

The cultural effects of bows start early. At the age of seven Tatar boys were no longer provided food by their family. They only ate what they could steal or kill with a bow. If they lived to adulthood, they were vicious archers from horseback.

The Persians were bowyers. They were more culturally decadent than the nomad-warriors, but they knew the spiritual value of archery. During adolescence the sons of Persian nobles were sent to live with shepherds and farmers. They left the courts to learn horsemanship, to learn to tell the truth, and to learn to shoot straight.

The bow is complete, and I carry it now in my ritual. It is osage; the most difficult, most rewarding bow wood. Locating a tree straight enough and long enough is to find one in ten thousand. Snaky and twisted, the bow is orange-brown with a dark, closed grain. It pulls forty-eight pounds and has a rawhide string. The smooth-burnished wood is conditioned against weather with melted beeswax. This bow is a bridge to another world or at least to what is real in this world. It shoots true.

Once a week, during the lunch hour, I drive west out of the gate at Whiteman Air Force Base to the south parking lot in Knob Noster State Park. If any cars are parked in the lot, I leave. If no cars, I park my beater pickup in the shade of an old-growth shagbark hickory. In spite of any weather, I strip from my uniform and hop-step into a pair of black nylon running shorts that my wife thinks are unfashionably high-cut. I remove the smooth-worn truck key from the key-ring and place it, solo, under a rotting railroad tie in the dirt parking lot. No shoes. No watch. No thing. I cross the unnamed creek that borders the lot and join a trail that will draw me deep into the hardwood forest. If I plan on gathering river cane for homemade arrows, I pause on the creek bank to scrounge a good piece of flint. I rough-out a stone knife to cut bent cane close to the ground. I will carry it with me to where I know the cane grows straight and then toss it when I have six good stems. The spiritual rewards of inefficiency.

If it is hot and humid I linger in the relief of a light breeze on the ridge-tops. If the mosquitoes are swarming, a light coat of creek mud, a quickened pace, and an end-of-run dip in the flowing creek keep me bite-free. If it is snowing or raining the pace is faster, breath blowing through my nostrils like a horse. Steam rises off my shoulders. My stride changes without shoes blocking me from the earth; I glide low and smooth on the balls of my feet down a game trail. I see wild turkey, whitetail deer, red fox, possum, cottontail rabbits, and coyote. If the ground is quiet from a recent rain or the wind is blowing—if I measure my approach among the shadows—I get close to deer. Mere feet. I listen to the rippling alarms of songbirds and squirrels as I skim along the trail. My mind is quiet, movement purposeful and clean. Wood bow light in hand. The deer calmly survey, tails flicking. I am a hairless wolf. An unburdened predator. My kill comes clean and quick from one fire-hardened, stone-tipped arrow cast from full brace. I overcome distance with an arrow to compensate for the weakness of my instincts. It is *my* arrow that vaults from *my* bow and kills the deer whose eyes I look into as it breathes a final breath. I possess the deer and become the deer when I feed my body. My hands are dry. Feet cold. Armpits stinking. Owning the death I brought. Purging the toxins of a plastic-wrapped, military-industrial-complex life.

I am stealth. I am time and distance.

Scandalous shorts, mud camouflage, calloused feet, a bent stick, and lithic tools. My ritual.

The harmonic buzz of the turbofans prods me out of mind, to the dimmed Egyptian desert. Recurring questions about the task at hand: What have I forgotten? Do they know I'm coming? Are the surface-to-air missile operators trained and rested? Are their minders leaving them to a futile chore or are they pointing pistols at the back of menaced heads, ordering them to launch the surface-to-air missile or face an apostate's death? "Shoot down the Yankee Air Pirate and your family will be esteemed for seven generations."

Your feet are cold, your skin is dry, you eat and eat but you hunger still. You smell like coffee, sweat, beef jerky, and fouled shearling seat cushions.

Back on task.

The Kingdom of al-Saud.

The darkened Red Sea approaches. With it comes temporal dilation. Demarcation. A few hundred miles northeast lies a city that will soon spit fire and become fire. Swirling fighters will haunt the periphery of southern Baghdad while I ghost-in through the backdoor and bring hell from northwest to southeast. The city will hunt me down, but in the radar dark it will not find me. The city will not know I'm there until I'm gone, and gone's too late.

I twist into my chest holster and rack the slide on the old 1911. I thumb the safety up and slip the comforting heft into the tight holster that is now under my flight suit. The firearm will be covered and secure should I have to eject at upward of 80 percent of the speed of sound. At .80 Mach, the B-2 technical manual states, "moderate to severe injuries are likely." If I am shot to earth, my library will burn in a Heraclitean fire. If I am shot to earth, Iraqis will hunt me. If I am shot to earth, the smart thing is to bury the handguns because grounded pilots are most brutalized and likely to be killed with their own weapons by their initial captors. To the government and the military I am a political weapon. To the people living under a state-controlled press I am Satan's proxy. These men and women who have cowered with their families in ditches and alleys from Saddam's thugs and American bombs.

I am back in the seat, and the jet-stream winds are rapidly swinging between west and south and back again. The nose of the B-2 hunts left and right to maintain the planned track. I get a status report from my wingmen, Raccoon 32 and 33. The jets are in great shape with almost no oil consumption; weapons and aircraft systems tight. No target or route changes. All as briefed.

I can avoid the drudgery of the computers no longer. I reconfirm the latitudes, longitudes, and altitudes of targets to the third decimal point of minutes of degrees. Crossing into Saudi Arabia I will power all sixteen weapons with three switch actuations. The dedicated weapons computers will begin a deadly calculus of delivery. Within seconds of release, the latitudes and longitudes will be sent to the guidance units on the bombs. The most complicated drops involve the three "Bunker-Busters." In their parabolic flight, the eighteen-inch missiles will have accelerated to fifteen hundred feet per second when they strike within feet (often inches) of the objective. Upon sensing the deceleration associated with impact, the internal electric fuse will begin the countdown to detonation-charge ignition. No one will hear the bomb's supersonic approach to the target. Milliseconds later, the earth under Saddam's presidential palace will shake and fire will shoot from the domed roof. A "Special Issue" of *Time* will portray this on the magazine's cover, one week from now.

Written in yellow chalk on the dark-green steel bomb casings are words. Traditionally, weapons loaders and aircraft crew chiefs write sophomoric death taunts, love poems, and eulogies for friends lost to terrorists or combat in the Middle East:

"If the house is a-rockin, don't come a-knockin"

"Forgive us our trespasses and forgive them their sins . . ."

"For all you do, this bomb's for you"

"When it absolutely, positively has to be destroyed overnight—USAF"

"For A1C Brian McVeigh—Khobar Towers, 25 June 1996"

"All you need is love. Love is all you need."

"Saddam—Mess with the bull, get the horns! Johnny T.—Dumas TX"

"If you'd stop gassing Kurds and Shiites—stop torturing your own people—we wouldn't have to shove this candle up your ass and light it. Love—Tiffany S."

"May freedom follow chaos—Chief"

The colonel, earlier in the flight over Nova Scotia, told me that he inspected every weapon the day before we took off, now two days past. Every steel lanyard, bomb-fin configuration, power connection, and fuse setting. He told me he wrote a proverb on a bomb body and took digital pictures "for the squadron history books."

The Saudi coast passes right, then left, out of sight under the aircraft as we angle over the coastline.

Standing now, the colonel fiddles with an obviously non-functional piece of satellite communications equipment. He has spent at least five combined hours of this flight resetting and rewiring various components. There is no dead horse that he believes a proper beating won't revive.

From the right seat, I snap up the colonel's worn, leatherbound King James Bible. A silk bookmark in the Psalms of David. In Psalm 25, verses 19–21, the following:

> Consider mine enemies; for they are many; and they hate me with cruel hatred. O keep my soul, and deliver me: let me not be ashamed; for I put my trust in thee. Let integrity and uprightness preserve me; for I wait on thee.

I could have criminal charges brought against me by Al-Madina, "the Authority for the Promotion of Virtue and Prevention of Vices," if I were standing on Saudi sand caught in possession of this Bible. Interrogated and beaten as an infidel. A forced confession, but for the grace of altitude.

We have the fuel to complete the mission and hit the post-strike tanker. Our timing is spot-on, which means our bombs will hit on time, to the exact second. The British controller passes word to us that all support aircraft have checked in. There will be no timing slips. The war is to start on time.

Northbound now for our piece of it. We "push" far to the west, flanking our support aircraft. Serving deceptive ends, as we crossed the border into Iraq, our call sign changed from Raccoon 31 to Squeak 31. It doesn't much matter because we are radio-silent. A roving black hole of electronic emissions. We are over the moonscape Iraqi desert, southwest of Baghdad. Over the nothing. It's quiet from without and from within.

The winds have settled strong from the west. The weapons computers are grinding. We wait . . .

The books are stowed. My mind is still darting.

I read to rage against the constriction of my profession—the barbarity of all over-specialized professions. I look east to the kingdom of Uruk—the city of Gilgamesh—through the green haze of night-vision goggles. I know the first story written down, the oldest story in the world. A thousand years before the Old Testament. A thousand years before the *Iliad* and the *Odyssey*. *Gilgamesh*:

> As when one senses
> Violence gathering its force,
> Soon there is no sound apart from it,
> Not even one's own thoughts in terror.

In a long, slow right-hand turn to the southeast, I have arrived at my foregone conclusion. The possibilities of the day have all expired and action stands as the final test. I am in the Iraqis' space. They are not in mine. I am the sovereign nexus of ideology, weaponry, and a clash of civilizations.

Over Tharthar Lake, just upcountry from Fallujah. The Sunni triangle. *Don't punch out here.* The orange sodium lights of the city crystallize as they approach, sliding down from the far horizon. The power grid is not targeted this night. Five million people mark time with the lights lit. The Tigris a black velvet ribbon scoring the city. High cirrus clouds reflect the lights above our altitude. Wispy mare's tails. Maintain track right of course for winds or the auto-pilot won't hack the turns and the bombs won't release. I would *never* live that down.

A flood of words over the intercom, "Pattern management, weapons ranging, tapes running, target #7000, one GBU-37 on the Command and Control bunker, minute-forty to release." Right of course. Tracking.

"Checks. Switches up, clean and green, auto, station L-8 is a GO."

The small-caliber antiaircraft artillery is difficult to spot in the glaring brightness of Baghdad. Not that it matters. Only the largest rounds can reach us, and the one that could hit us we won't see. I force my gaze up to the darker horizon and the clusters of sparkling air defense rounds detonating closer to our altitude. Squeak 31, flight of three, is alone now. Above the air-raid horns and journalists and people and confusion. Our support aircraft are marshaled around the southern borders of the city. Antiradiation missiles and massive amounts of communications and radar jamming cloud the electromagnetic spectrum. We are a whisper in a very noisy, very dark room. The colonel is stooped over his situation displays tapping furiously.

The surface-to-air missile launches are starting. Three to our left on the east side of town and one off the nose. Unaimed. Undisciplined. We are—and remain—stealthy.

The colonel switches his focus to the weapons displays. I search my mental catalog for a Churchillian saying, something for the "squadron history books," a meager attempt at a redemptive appropriation of wisdom. Nothing. We have our own radio frequency. It's scary quiet above the melee.

"Sixty seconds." The number two wingman, Squeak 32, south of us, moving directly west to east, will have a weapon release in seventeen seconds.

I crank my lap belt tight and finger the grip of my pistol. Up to the horizon, look left, look right, left again out of habit. Another surface-to-air missile to the east—brighter—probably an SA-2. I watch it detonate above our altitude, guessing 10 miles away. Its final act, a steel rain on the Iraqis below—to be blamed on the Americans later, I'm sure.

"Thirty seconds, in the release corridor, stand by for doors on the left. Next release 7001, thirty-one seconds following, two 37s on the bunkers below Uday's palace." I am winding up. Breathe. Center. Work the routines. They can't find us. They'll know we're here when they see the explosions on Al Jazeera. "Doors in five, four, three, two, one . . . Weapon away, target

7000 at 1803:30 Zulu, doors closed. Impact at 1804:25. Shack timing, delta zero. In the corridor for 7001, L-6, R-8, clean and green, switches up, auto." Another SAM. More AA. The eastern edge of the city is passing under the nose of the aircraft, but we will be lit from below for another two minutes. We are not producing contrails. I crave complete darkness. I want Plato's Cave. I want these missiles to be the shadows of perfect missiles, our bombs to be the shadows of bombs.

Sometimes you must do a bad thing to stop something even worse? Make it so.

Two hundred eight seconds and out.

Tigris means "arrow" in Old Persian.

The air war was "victorious" in weeks. Fixed targets destroyed, statues toppled. Museums looted. Thus endeth the "major" fighting, but there are unclaimed dead throughout the buried bunkers and desert landscapes of Iraq . . . Babylon . . . Nineveh . . . Nippur . . . Ur . . . Uruk . . . Iraq. How many dead? In the aftermath of the air war, some now may be mine. Bodies disintegrated in holes below once lavish palaces, terrorist camps, command centers, and barracks. How to think on these things?

Three years later and I have not yet gathered the memories surrounding my three-week war. I tallied two missions—the first and the last for the B-2s flying from Missouri. These are the barest of facts.

My war memories start here; fifteen years ago I had a writing teacher who made—in my mind—a manifest and abiding link between great reading, writing, and a life lived well. A life that recognized and rewarded gentleness, empathy, artistry, and grace. After becoming an officer, and during the twelve years following as an aviator and student of aviation, I read when I was able and wrote little. I flew F-16s and B-2s all over the world with brief periods of combat action in both. In six months "on the ground" in the Middle East, I witnessed one terrorist bomb detonate and I came quickly upon the aftermath of two others. One—Khobar Towers in Saudi Arabia—was monstrous. Then 9/11. I was roused to fight.

As a pilot I have fallen into bed for years hoping that I know enough, that I'm skilled enough, to keep myself or my wingman alive through whatever imagined tragedy awaits us during the next day's flying: engine fire, midair collision, spatial disorientation, G-induced loss of consciousness, hypoxia . . . It can be easier to compartmentalize these morbid notions and train and train and train until you have acquired the expertise—even the art—of supersonic violence. But don't imagine that you might not compartmentalize your humanity in the process just because survival is paramount.

For years I worked desperately to not be the lieutenant in northern Japan who made a late decision to eject from a miserably executed takeoff abort due to a minor engine problem. A cascading series of errors and indecisions that ultimately had him parachute into the fireball of his own tumbling F-16. He died eight weeks later from a staph infection. His wife was twenty-three, and his picture now hangs in a fighter squadron bar. Six years later new lieutenants ask: "What's his story?"

The story daunts them. Daunts their sense of confidence in themselves, but they charge on. Later, at their homes, in bathroom mirrors, they lecture themselves: "That won't be me. I'm good. I'm better." At the bar they raise their glass and proclaim one of the most common axioms among pilots: "I'd rather be lucky than good." There is that, but that is not nearly all, and it's no comfort to those who loved, and love, the dead.

I've seen literature, faith, family, and friends equip those peripheral to a sudden loss as harrowing as this with the armaments necessary to defend their souls. Choice lies mainly in the first two. Faith and art for trials like death and war and what comes after. Conviction is personal and art is communal. Problem is, you must constantly strive for their possession *before* you need them.

Walking into the local market in my uniform, I avert my eyes from those I suspect will acknowledge me for service to the country. "Thank you for what you do" is difficult to hear. I am confounded by their innocence. I smile and nod—no words. I am embarrassed because troops are dying and I am here, buying fresh asparagus, wine, and apples. These people are kind and gracious, but I can't tell them what I have done because I don't know what's buried in the bunkers of an ex-tyrant's palace. I know I left over thirty-six tons of high explosive and weapons-grade steel in Iraq. Buildings destroyed, bunkers mangled beyond recognition, airfields once bombed into submission—now in use by our own forces. It is conceivable that I killed no one. It is, however, very unlikely.

I turn back to the *words*. Words I would like the people in local markets to read and own. Own and live. I read and write and read.

Hemingway wrote, "There are worse things than war and all of them come with defeat." I believe that—but just because one thing is worse than another, it doesn't make the lesser good. Just less bad.

Once more to Heraclitus, twenty-six hundred years ago:

War, as father
of all things, and king,
names few to serve as gods, and of the rest makes
these men slaves, those free.

Even the free, then, are subjects to war, and dying for freedom is easy, at least for the dead.

This is no boast. Killing's something apart.

I sit on an overturned canoe among budding wild rose bushes on the bank of a mountain lake that is named on no map. My son and daughter are fishing for trout and throwing pinecones at mallards. My wife is seven months pregnant. She sleeps on a couch in our small cabin with our youngest daughter. They are warmed by the late-morning sun piercing a picture window. I look up from Victor Davis Hanson's *Ripples of Battle*. My daughter beckons me to untangle a snag in her fishing line. I grab my fly rod and stride down the thorny bank to help her. The last paragraph I read before placing the opened book on the boat says:

> So battle is a great leveler of human aspiration when it most surely should not be. Stray bullets kill brave men and miss cowards. They tear open great doctors-to-be and yet merely nick soldiers who have a criminal past, pulverizing flesh when there is nothing to be gained and passing harmlessly by when the fate of whole nations is at stake. And that confusion, inexplicability, and deadliness have a tendency to rob us of the talented, inflate the mediocre, and ruin or improve the survivors—but always at least making young men who survive not forget what they have been through.

From a kneel in the cold water, I roll-cast to a rising trout from the shadows of an overhanging cottonwood. Stealthy even now. A slow retrieve and . . . nothing.

I have begun a new bow. Bamboo and cherry wood.

I will hunt elk in the fall.

I will make rosehip jam with my children.

Safety

REBECCA KANNER

When my brother has massed into a flesh-colored Incredible Hulk, it's time to starve. He doesn't eat carbohydrates and he restricts his water. I know how it works because this will be his second competition—he won the lightweight division at his first. He wants to win this next one as a middleweight.

His MySpace status reads: "Aaron plans to respectfully destroy all of his fellow competitors."

I'm not alarmed when I see him at Lifetime Fitness, where he works as a personal trainer, and he says it's nice to see me—all three of me that are shimmering in front of him. I'm not sure if he's hallucinating or he just doesn't have the energy to focus his gaze. He looks strong, invincible, but he can no longer do the planche push-ups he's put into his routine, and his backflip has been giving him trouble.

He's five feet six inches and 180 pounds, which makes him, technically, obese. He has to be under 176 to compete as a middleweight, and he'll have no trouble making it—he's not starving to make weight. He's starving so the veins bulge from his skin like little green rivers. He's starving so his muscles look like they might explode.

Later, when he comes home, he's so exhausted that he has to turn his routine song up as loud as it will go not only because he left a good deal of his hearing in Iraq, but to motivate himself to practice.

Let the bodies hit the floor
Let the bodies . . .

—Drowning Pool, "Bodies" *Sinner*

It's the song that PSYOPS (Psychological Operations) blasted over Fallujah when my brother's unit invaded on November 7, 2004, in what the American military named Operation Phantom Fury. The song was used not just to terrorize the insurgents who hadn't heeded the flyers dropped from the sky warning them to leave if they were to avoid a battle, but also to drown out the Marines' fear.

The insurgency had its own anesthetic. My brother said of the men he fought, "They were hopped up on something. They had no fear and they didn't die right away when you shot them."

This battle turned out to be the bloodiest in the Iraq War to date. A third of the men in my brother's unit were injured or killed, officially making his unit "Combat Ineffective." Nine of the 160 men in my brother's company lost their lives.

He finished his four years of active duty in October 2006. When he first returned to the home in St. Paul where he, my father, and I live, he warmly greeted all the people we'd invited to welcome him home—a mix of my father's friends, my friends, and my brother's friends—about twenty people. My father had the American and Marine flags flying outside, and the red, white, and blue streamers we'd decorated the living room with for his first visit home from the Marines three and a half years earlier were still hanging limply in the living room.

He ate the pies people had brought for him, and politely answered questions about how hot Iraq is (very, though it's cold at night in the winter), where he'd been on his three tours (Diwaniyah, Fallujah, Ramadi), what he missed most while he was gone (*Sleep!*").

As the guests left, my brother graciously thanked each of them for coming. Then he went down to the basement, turned the television on, and watched it, alone in the dark, for six weeks.

Not wanting to descend into our dank, dust-filled basement, and not yet realizing my brother couldn't hear well anymore, I'd yell down to him to ask how he was doing. When he didn't answer I assumed he wanted to be left alone, but sometimes that didn't stop me. I crept down the stairs without turning on a light—I didn't want to annoy him, and the television projected enough light to see by. Also, I didn't want to be reminded of the old bubbling floor tile and cobwebs full of dry, half-disappeared insects. I came to stand beside where he was lying on the couch and gently asked him what he was watching. Occasionally I'd pull up a folding chair and watch with him. We breathed the dust in together, watching colors flicker across the screen. I imagine the scene—with him lying down and me sitting beside him—looked like a hospital visitation, except that I was turned away, toward the television. We didn't talk about the war or, really, much of anything.

Then one day, as I stood at the top of the stairs deciding if I should go down or not, I heard the clanking of metal. A weight machine had been sitting in the basement since before my brother left for the Marines, and I realized he was using it. For a few moments I stood happily listening to the rhythmic squeaking and clanging of metal blocks being lifted and then falling gently down upon each other. I thought: *Maybe everything will be okay.*

My brother started to work out every day, and soon afterward he decided to get a membership at Lifetime.

He began to get bigger, and—seemingly in direct proportion—happier.

Though the money he lost in unemployment would be many times greater than what he made, I was relieved when he got a part-time job cleaning the fitness equipment at Lifetime, wandering around the gym dressed all in black, smelling of disinfectant and looking much more alive than he had in our basement. Half a year later he began studying to become a personal trainer. He stopped watching so much television and made friends with the people at the gym who shared his obsession with weight lifting.

I don't know if winning his upcoming middleweight competition will help him finally feel fearless and strong. But I'm hopeful. Being hopeful is the least I can do for him.

When he was a baby, I tried to make my brother safe the way my father had taught me.

As a bodybuilder he eats chicken, salmon, and protein shakes, but as a peaceful, runty baby he liked to eat plants. His fuzzy baby-gaze sharpened when he spotted a big shiny leaf poking out of one of the potted plants in our living room, and he rushed across the carpet in his walker, ecstatically waving his arms because he couldn't *believe* his luck!

I knew what I had to do when his tiny hand reached for the leaf.

My hands were twice as big as his. I was—am—five years older. I easily grabbed his little hand in one of my own, and hit it. If he'd been old enough to understand I'd have told him: *You shouldn't reach for things, you shouldn't tug, you shouldn't pull things apart, you shouldn't put strange things in your mouth.* Above all he shouldn't have messed with my father's plants.

How my father loved—and still loves—his plants! He also loves birds, trees, little bugs which we looked at and sometimes kept in jars. He and I once studied a broken egg under the microscope. We marveled at a tiny foot that seemed to be the only part of the chick that had had a chance to form before the egg fell from the nest. My father handled the egg like it still might come to life. He was careful not to damage it.

But us—my brother and me—he grabbed and twisted like he didn't remember being young and already having feeling in his arms and legs. I thought he knew everything and possessed the best solution to any problem. When I cut or bruised myself I felt I had no choice but to hold the problem out to him—my hand, my elbow, my ankle. He grabbed the limb, twisted it so he could examine it, and then painted it red with Mercurochrome. The Mercurochrome drew attention to the wound and therefore also to my klutziness. I wanted to wash it off but I was afraid of what might happen if I did, and how it might hurt. I knew I was wrong to hurt, and I would have been all the more wrong to show it.

My brother quickly came to feel this way too, and he does not seem to know—not anymore—when he's hurt.

At the end of 2002 my father and I went to Camp Pendleton, California, to see my brother graduate from Marine boot camp. It was a clear hot day—the temperature difference between St. Paul and San Diego was about seventy degrees—and I felt very pale among the other onlookers, at least a third of whom were Latino.

My brother had told us that he'd had some trouble with his left knee, but that everything was fine. He wasn't hard to spot. Hundreds of guys in uniform were in formation on the field, but he was the only one in uniform on the bleachers, his crutches leaning at a steep angle beside him. He'd confessed to me that he wouldn't mind not being in formation—that in fact he couldn't *stand* formation (ha ha!), and many others literally couldn't either: "Sometimes guys get dehydrated, or their knees lock, and they pass the fuck out." Still, he didn't look happy sitting on the sidelines all by himself. He'd been on crutches a couple of times before (due to rollerblading and gymnastics accidents), and afterward he hadn't wanted his crutches anywhere that he could see them.

After the formation ceremony and speeches, the graduates and their families were provided lunch, which we ate in a shelter on base. We mingled a little. Usually in mingling situations I will either babble at great length to avoid the risk of an awkward pause (while carefully scanning the people around me to make sure they aren't exchanging glances or rolling their eyes), or simply nod and smile. By this time I was a graduate student and anything free was of special interest to me, so I just chewed and smiled and thanked the many people who told me how tough and loyal my brother was.

When my brother went to get more food, one of his staff sergeants recounted for me how he'd tried to keep his injury hidden, even loaded down with a fifty-pound pack during a 9.7-mile hike that ended with a climb up The Reaper, a seven-hundred-foot-tall mountain. "It wasn't like him to be the last one. It finally became apparent that he was limping. His knee was swollen to the size of a cantaloupe," the staff sergeant laughed. "He almost lost it."

I tried not to look like I might regurgitate my free lunch. Later my brother would tell me that this same staff sergeant saw him heading back to his "rack" after breakfast one day, and my brother didn't say "Good morning," loud enough, so the staff sergeant made him do IT (Individual Training). My brother did mountain climbers for two minutes. He tells me this in the same tone as the staff sergeant told me about his knee—like it's hilarious, and I try not to show any emotion, though I'm thinking *Why the hell didn't you remind him your knee was about to explode?* With my brother it's best not to act like anything is a big deal.

But when the staff sergeant told me my brother almost lost his knee I refused to pretend it was nothing. "How is your knee?" I asked Aaron after lunch. I'd asked him earlier that day, when I first saw him, but this time I asked him without any pretense of casualness.

"It feels okay," he said dismissively. "I'm taking stuff and it's helping."

Later he showed me the knee—swollen unevenly, like our bubbling basement tile. Pink and red and white and angry. And also sad—something about its unevenness reminding me of a heart, and clearly, from the look of it, a bruised-until-broken heart, which has traveled down the length of the body, or has maybe even been dropped, and due to neglect is pressing outward, trying to escape. Unable to escape, it was rubbing hard against my brother's bones, as if to say, "I will bring myself to your attention. I will make a place for myself where you can't ignore me. I hurt and now you will hurt too."

I began to worry in earnest about his upcoming tour to Iraq. What if he got hurt—would he tell anybody? Would he even know that he was hurt? What had happened to his ability to cry out when he was in pain?

At one year of age, when I grabbed his hand he knew that it hurt. I spanked his smooth new skin like I could slap the urge to grab from it, and he did something he lost the ability to do in the Marines: he cried.

I'd felt sad that he was crying, and angry that he'd made me hit him, and, more than anything, angry that he'd been on the verge of eating the plant. *He had to learn the rules of the world so he wouldn't be hurt.* I wasn't always going to be there to protect him.

My father was, unofficially, a behaviorist. He had to take care of me the year after I was born, when my mother was hospitalized for psychiatric problems and chemical dependency. If he heard me crying in my crib he knew that he must not come to me, or I would learn that crying is a behavior that is rewarded. My mother told me that when she came home he wouldn't let her come to me either, and recently my father acknowledged it was true. His face looked heavy as he admitted this, as if he were remembering a terrible time. Now I think of the heaviness of his face whenever I feel too ready to blame him for everything.

By the time Aaron was born I'd become a behaviorist too. The slaps I gave him weren't always to his hands, and they weren't always physical. I used words like *stupid,* phrases like *how could you.* I wanted to make sure that he would *never again* do whatever it was that he'd done wrong. If he never did anything wrong, nothing bad would happen to him. My father had taught me, and his teaching method had made it true: one false move and the world will come down on you.

My father wasn't one to be argued with. And yet he and I yelled at each other across tables, through all the rooms of our house, inside the car, out on the lawn, until we were hoarse. I learned to stomp my foot, pound my fist on the table, yell so loudly I couldn't hear him yelling back. He told me to shut up, that he would slap me. Though I was scared—in fact because I was scared and knew I should hide it—I kept yelling.

Aaron rarely argued aloud with anyone.

Yet I suspect he was always striving to best my father—to be as strong, as fearless, as fearsome—and he finally did by joining the Marines. He told me, "I want to show the world that I can do anything."

By "world," did he mean "father"?

My father and brother have wrestled since my brother could walk. Even now they wrestle—one attacks the other and they bang into counters and chairs in their mock battle. Though it's not supposed to be a real fight, can't each feel the strength in the other's body, feel how easy or hard it is to lead the battle in the direction of his opponent—to make him step back, or to be unable to do anything but step back himself? Now, unlike in their wrestling matches before Aaron went into the Marines, my father is very careful not to lose control and escalate the mock battles. He wraps his arms protectively around himself and calls jestfully for me to come help him: "Help! Bec, help! He's beating me up!"

My father is such a loyal person that it's hard to find out anything that doesn't shine a good light on his mother and father, Jewish immigrants who came from Poland and Austria in 1919 and 1929 respectively. They lived in New York—first in Brownsville, and then in a little apartment on Coney Island from which you can see the ocean (and just as importantly to me years later when my father took me to visit my grandparents, the Sliding Ferris Wheel) and hear the screams of the kids on the Cyclone. My grandfather worked at a ladies' handbag factory and my grandmother worked at an umbrella factory and then as a subway token seller.

"They were liberal people," my father tells me, "until the ends of their lives." They'd worked hard in order to feed and clothe my father and his two sisters, and they resented people who expected the government to take care of them. By the time I came along they'd started listening to conservative radio programs and yelling at the guests on talk shows. Or at least I remember my grandma doing that. I also remember her doing everything for my grandfather. He didn't even pour the milk on his own cereal. My grandparents were like my father, and I suppose like me—a combination of very loving and very angry. My grandmother more loving than my grandfather, certainly, and not quite as angry.

I know my grandfather hit my father. My father doesn't want to talk about it, but when I see him getting frustrated with himself, a depth of sudden fear and anger triggered by something as small or smaller than spilled milk, I know there's an invisible person standing over him, yelling things only he can hear: *How could you pour too much milk? Look at all that's wasted!*

Except that I hear these things too.

My father has passed his ghosts onto my brother and me, and I have doubled Aaron's share. He doesn't blame me. Deep down he must think that my father and I slapped his hands and were critical of him because he deserved it.

During his second and third tours, when it had been too long since his last staticky 4 a.m. call and I'd started to imagine the worst, I asked myself: *Did my slaps send him to Iraq?*

The strain of the fourteen-week diet leading up to the competition is making my brother very intense—more intense than before the last competition. One of his trainers has noticed, and he's assured him that it's natural for the stress of training to bring him back to the last time he was under intense stress, which was when he was on his third tour in Iraq.

The stress has finally got my brother talking.

He tells me, one night when raccoons run back and forth across the roof and we think we hear them in the fireplace, of the huge mutant dogs at Camp Habbaniyah. They had strange bumps on their backs, and there was a rumor they'd killed a guy. Everyone had to carry their weapon with them at all times.

And then he confesses to me—as if he's confessing a horrible crime—that as a machine gunner in Iraq sometimes he'd been afraid. "Sometimes I felt like a scared dog running around with its tail between its legs."

"Of course you were scared, lots of men in your unit died. You had good reason to be scared."

"No, I wasn't scared then, during Operation Phantom Fury. Then—at the time—I was numb, and I didn't hardly even feel anything when those guys died. I wasn't scared until my third tour, when we convoyed back and forth through the Anbar Province on 'IED Alley.' We were told to go slow, that that would be the best way to avoid the IEDS. But we figured if we were going slow the insurgents watching with their fingers on the button could time the explosions better, so we drove erratically—sometimes fast, sometimes slow. The main thing was just to keep moving.

"Bullets hit my turret, and a few times we came within inches of a pressure plate (bomb), but nobody died. For a while nothing that bad happened, and *that's* when I was most afraid—I was sure something bad *had* to happen. I thought that at any second—sometimes at every second for days in a row—the road would explode. But then, the few times when I was actually sure I was about to die, I was completely calm."

He's sitting in his spot on the floor in my room, looking down at the weight-lifting calluses on his hands. He's been sitting there so often that there's a grey imprint of his back on the white wall. "That's what I'm always like now—numb. I'm not afraid anymore. I can't feel anything unless I'm angry."

He tells me, one night when he's sitting on my floor late at night, not wanting to go to bed, "I dream Iraqis have invaded our country."

I wonder if that is the dream he is having when I wake up later in the night and stumble across the hall, woozy from sleeping pills, into the bathroom. I hear him tossing with all his might from one side to the other and back. He is still tossing when I stumble back across the hall, into my bedroom, and close the door.

For a moment I think I should wake him—I want to rescue him.

Nineteen years ago, after we moved into the house we live in now, he developed a fear of the dark. He was seven, and absolutely sure that there were monsters in his closet and under the bed. "Don't worry," I told him, "I have just the thing." I knew he would believe in whatever magic I came up with. And as I walked a bowl of "Angel Water" into his room, holding it carefully out in front of me in both hands, I believed in my magic powers too. I placed the bowl of water on his dresser, then said a blessing in Hebrew which was identical to the one observant Jews say before eating, but with some gibberish tacked onto the end. Though perhaps "gibberish" isn't the right word for the sounds that left my mouth, which felt as if they were from the very core of my being, and were laced with a desire to keep him safe that was so incredibly strong and full of energy that surely it would protect him from whatever might come his way.

He left the bowl on his dresser, and whenever he got scared that it was losing its power I would bring him some new Angel Water.

But now, as he smashes around in the dark dreaming of an Iraqi invasion, he's not the only one who's afraid. I am afraid too. What can I say to rescue him? And if I touch him, how long will it take for him to realize it's only me?

My father and I are increasingly careful around him. We no longer suggest he go to the VA for an assessment and counseling; we don't talk about foods that aren't allowed on his bodybuilding diet; and we're vigilant about not mentioning the controversy surrounding the treatment of detainees ("What about *us*!?!?" my brother will ask. "We didn't get to sleep for days at a time, we didn't have the right armor until our *third* tour, five of our guys were killed because the army just up and left a secured area five hours before we arrived . . .").

The more he tells me, the more I understand why he usually only wants to talk about bodybuilding. He's quick to remind me and anyone else who cares to listen that it could be worse:

"Some people come back from Iraq and drink too much or beat their wives. I lift weights."

Then, displaying the hyperconfidence Arnold Schwarzenegger made famous in the movie "Pumping Iron" when he told a competitor before the show that he'd *already* called his mother to tell her he won, my brother adds, "And win titles!"

I help him prepare. I paint him dark, I clap when he poses in front of the bathroom mirror, I tell him he looks like he could uproot trees and toss them halfway down the block. I'm understanding when he gets Pro-Tan on the bathroom towels and toilet seat, and I don't say anything when he makes a mess cooking massive amounts of chicken and doesn't clean it up. He had to eat even more for this competition—he'll be twenty pounds heavier at this show than his first. I pretend not to notice that it smells like a barn full of chickens has bled, shit, and burned to death in our kitchen.

And then finally—June 7, 2008—he is on stage. He's been home for over a year and a half, and finally he's going to feel good. Finally he's going to be proud. I start screaming.

You're Perfect!

Beautiful!

It's yours—Go get it! All yours!

Bring it home!

Get Some!!!!!!!!!!!!!!!!!!!!!

No matter how loud I yell I can't get all the emotion out. I'm yelling at the top of my lungs not only because he doesn't hear well but because I feel like I might explode. Beneath what I'm screaming aloud is what I'm actually screaming: *You're damaged and brave and bleeding from the wounds we gave you which you've made beautiful, and everyone is cheering because they are large, and in perfect proportion to each other, and flexed so that they are shining through your skin like something godly.* His planche push-ups are perfect. His flip is perfect. His muscles pop and he can't help smiling when he hears me and his friends from Lifetime cheering for him. There are ten other middleweights but they don't stand a chance against all he has to prove.

"I want to be bigger next time," he tells me afterward.

He eats and eats. He has gained twenty-five pounds in the week since the competition. When we get home from The Grand Buffet he runs upstairs to weigh himself. He waits until my father and I gather around to step on the scale: 202 pounds.

"Do you need to get much bigger?" my father asks.

"Yes," my brother says.

Allawi

PATRICK MONDACA

Allawi, Allawi, Allawi . . . I hear it still, cutting across the din of the market. It is a place of employment, maybe. Or worship. Or school. I wonder what or where Allawi is. Or who. Allawi is lost perhaps. Or missing. I say a quick prayer for Allawi, whatever it may be. In Baghdad Allawi might be anything. I have no idea. Allawi might be my sanity.

It doesn't take much for me to be back there. Even now, fourteen years later. Every crowd or traffic jam, every shopping mall or bus stop, every queue at any place at any time, I am reminded of it, the market. When people talk about war, when I hear veterans talking about their wars, and I think about my war, I think about that market. I think about Allawi. It is the place I dream of. The place of nightmares.

The street through the market is so hot it scorches the soles of our cheap army-issued boots. So hot, the discarded innards from the sheep carcasses steam off the pavement and the stench hangs in the air, putrid and alkaline, clinging to our nostrils long into the night. The old men and boys tasked with the slaughtering draw their knives across the throats of doomed, wide-eyed beasts, glimpses of silver from flimsy blades glinting in the sun; slick red blood dripping raw from their hands and between their fingers, clotting and bubbling around their plastic Chinese sandals and fake Adidas trainers. The dull black of our machine guns and rifles and shotguns and pistols is a thin wall around us, its mortar our bristling ammunition belts and columns of green- and orange-tipped rounds pressed into gray magazines and olive-drab pods; shells of

Remington buckshot rattle loose in our pockets like handfuls of small stones. We pull the stocks tight into our shoulders, clinging to them like lovers: hard butts of rubber and plastic, grafted with dark steel and smelling of gun oil and cordite. Forged in America, and Germany, and Italy, comforting and horrifying, nylon slings wrapped around clenched fists like prayer beads, nerves and trigger springs together coiled tight, eyes unflinching for fear of blinking.

In the market outside Baghdad International Airport, I stared dully through the cracked, mud-streaked windshield of a banged-up Humvee. Weary but still alert, my eyes absorbed the empty, trash-strewn street. I was tired of it. Every goddamned day, patrolling this godforsaken market, sunup to sundown. Keep the convoys moving through. Push the crowds back. Back. Further back. Keep the roadway clear, at least two lanes worth of real estate. An endless and futile effort, like sweeping sand off a beach. I thought of the beaches back home. Low tide, high tide; but here the beach was just a dusty street and here the waves were human. Waves of people spilling and tumbling over each other; a demented desperate sea of people, the worst kind, the kind that would surely try to drown you in their wake given the chance, pulling you under, clawing at your straps and body armor and rigging. *Mister, mister, give me dollar.* Pushing and begging. *Chai, mister? You need chai?* Fighting and trampling and grasping over each other. I sipped tepid black coffee from an aluminum canteen cup.

I did not dislike this time of day. I had time enough to ponder but, not too much time, not enough to get all nostalgic. Early mornings were almost peaceful. Before the thud of the Blackhawks and Apaches would return overhead and the groans of the Bradley fighting vehicles and Abrams tanks would reverberate through the streets, the market slept. Before the sun would rise over the remnants of the date palm groves along the airport road, when the first rays of light would begin flickering through the charred leviathans, the sparse survivors with trunks scarred and blackened, all was quiet. While the dew still lingered on the aluminum skins of the parked Toyota minibuses, the multicolored taxis, and ancient Mercedes-Benz lorries, the market was at peace.

It never lasted long. The wailings of the muezzins' prayers would soon echo through the labyrinth of empty stalls, waking man and beast now asleep under flimsy metal card tables and wooden carts soon to be weighed down with the precarious livelihoods of so many. A robbery or a murder, a light till or an errant bomb—entire families could be ruined in an instant. How anyone could sleep in this city was beyond me. Though some could not and were already awake. A doctor, now compelled to sell parts stripped from a prized BMW. A widow, once whole, now compelled to sell parts of herself. They stood like statues of ancient lives long past, silent, hoping, and ashamed of what they had mustered up the courage to do. Between desperation and survival, there is a distinct absence of dignity. And I was ashamed to bear witness to this.

In moments like these I hated the market and wanted to not be there at all. I hated it with the same force that I loved the sheer defiance of my being there. I *had* to be there. So, I would be there. Because the army said I would be, mostly. It's too hot to care really. The mind wanders.

Allawi, Allawi, Allawi . . . I dream Allawi is in the turret, hunched over the stock of a short-barreled machine gun, eyes scanning the roofs of the sand colored buildings on our periphery. Sporadic shots fired at the patrol ahead of ours and the longer sustained bursts of return fire from the tanker scout ahead of us interrupt the relative afternoon calm.

Allawi kicks the back of the driver's seat and shouts down for the driver to step on the gas. *Move, move, move! Get this fucker moving! Don't get stuck in the kill zone!* And the driver floors it, the truck lurching forward toward the gunfire through the traffic. Smoke billows from a vehicle that has been hit by an explosive device and disabled in the intersection ahead, flames belching from its blackened underbelly as its fuel ignites and the thin fiberglass-and-canvas skin begins to melt and peel.

Covering fire, the only rounds we ever fired in Iraq were covering fire. Allawi fired them really. Allawi is my guardian angel maybe. Allawi is the angel of death.

Allawi says that the next morning you will wake as if that is the first day you have been on the earth—to savor the crisp cool morning air, the warmth of the sun on your face, the smell of the charcoal and meat from the kebab stands, the grit of dust in your teeth, the sounds of the bus drivers calling their fares, the voices and feet of little schoolchildren contrasting with the rumble of tanks and the vibration of helicopters above them, the taste of cordite and hot gun oil left on your lips after the firing of a machine gun—there is no greater feeling than the realization that one is still alive. Allawi sees this, he says. Allawi says I'm seeing things.

Mostly I see the market from the rear right seat of our unarmored fiberglass-skinned truck. As the day wears on, I blink the sleep out of my eyes and light another knockoff Marlboro, inhaling its dry chemical smoke. When I exhale, I aim the blue tinged cloud up at the turret hatch, partly out of boredom, mostly to annoy my gunner, partly to see if the kid is awake. He throws an empty Pepsi can back down at me in response, no words needed. And we listen for the sounds of the market stirring. The yelps of a startled dog, a restless donkey's bray, a rooster crowing, a small child crying on a distant rooftop, these are the earliest sounds, small reminders of humanity around us. We listen for the sound of the radio for the lieutenant to give the order, breathe in the smell of burning garbage, its acrid wafts drifting lazily upward in the early morning humidity, and of unwashed bodies and sweat-soaked gear, of days-on-end-worn uniforms, stale cigarettes, and half-eaten rations languishing in tattered plastic olive-drab packets.

Soon the smell of charcoal would be in the air from the small fires lit by the tea sellers to boil water in copper pots. The smell of lamb kebabs and chickens roasting on spits would hit the air only to be overwhelmed by the smells of mechanized transport, of petrol and diesel, of burning radiator coolant and hot engine oil and overheated rotors and brake pads. The smell of fear, too, would be in the air. And too soon, after another hot, restless night, it would be time for me to go back into the market, again to this strange waltz in the sun. Soon Baghdad would awake completely, its merchants and residents intermingling among the stalls and tables, among the decrepit plastic chairs and dusty piles of bricks, the rickety horse carts, shells of bombed-out cars, and bent frames of rusted bicycles and battered motorcycles. One step forward, two steps back; the market would expand like a tempest, intent on surging forward, on swallowing the roadway running through its center, swelling the sea onto a shallow beach, drowning, consuming, devouring, and killing us, erasing our very existence.

"Are you awake, Sergeant?" the private asks from above. We are waiting by the roundabout for the crackle of the radio, for the cursed transmission that sends us back in. We are in a nightmare, the one where the room grows smaller and smaller until we are crushed to death. We are at the bottom of a newly dug grave and wait for the earth to rain down on our faces. The market wants to swallow us alive; every cell and organism within it rebels against our presence there. The market wants only to consume and expel us. We are in its center, foreign, intrusive. We are a cancer, a gaping raw wound the market wants only to close. And beneath the noise of commerce, the market buzzes its hatred of us like a nest of provoked and angry wasps.

I check the lanyard on my pistol one last time, flick the safety off, black to red. I rack a slug into my shotgun. Then I step out of the truck and into the market. Toward the cries of *Allawi, Allawi, Allawi . . .* Always, always *Allawi.*

Scars

NOLAN PETERSON

The final night before the climb on Island Peak, I was in the dining room of the lodge in Chukhung, Nepal, eating a plate of Tibetan momos and enjoying an Everest beer. While talking to a Canadian climber about Afghanistan, I heard an American voice call out across the room: "Holy shit, dude, were you in the U.S. military?"

Through the haze of burning yak dung fueling the stove in the middle of the room, I saw a young bearded man. He had on a black beanie and his short sleeves revealed arms covered in tattoos. And there were scars beneath the ink. I'd seen arms like those before on brothers in Afghanistan and Iraq. Before he said another word I knew he was an American soldier, and I knew he was special ops.

His name was Kevin Law. Sitting next to him was his father. They were here to climb Island Peak with Adventure Consultants—the climbing company of ill-fated Everest guide Rob Hall (Hall was the New Zealand guide who famously telephoned his wife before his death on Everest to choose a name for their unborn daughter). I politely excused myself from the conversation with the Canadian and joined Kevin and his father at their table, where they introduced themselves.

I told them that I had been in the U.S. military and had also served in Iraq and Afghanistan. A light flicked on in Kevin's eyes, and conversation burst out of him like he had been filled to the breaking point for years with the words, waiting to tell his story to someone who might understand.

Kevin had served multiple tours in Iraq and Afghanistan as

46

an Army Ranger and was in the worst kind of fighting in both places. He told me about a friend who had been decapitated by an IED just yards outside the gates of a base in Afghanistan. "I had been talking to him just five minutes before that," Kevin said. "His body was completely fucked up, you couldn't tell it was him." And he told me about putting a tourniquet on the bloody stump of a friend's leg that had blown off in battle.

Kevin was in a tough time in his life. The army had recently medically discharged him against his will, due to injuries he suffered from an IED blast. During the time Kevin was being evacuated from combat following the IED, his mother committed suicide. And just months later, while recovering from his wounds back in the United States, his wife divorced him, taking his daughter with her. So he was here in Nepal to start over and reconnect with his father after spending his years as a young man fighting for his country.

In *Eiger Dreams* Jon Krakauer says, "Mountains make poor receptacles for dreams." I suppose he was right, since I never found any answers in the mountains to the questions in my life. But sometimes there just isn't anywhere else to go when everything falls apart. The mountains may not solve any problems, but the ones they create are simple and free from the complicated tragedies of the lives we leave behind. For Kevin the mountains were the only place where the world still made sense.

Kevin's dad said good night and went to get some much-needed rest before the big day. We were going to climb a 20,305-foot mountain the next night. Kevin and I kept drinking beer and sharing stories. I told him my old call sign, and he spit out his beer—"Are you fucking kidding me?" he yelled.

He was in a firefight in Afghanistan, a bad one, when a plane with my call sign had directed the air support that saved the lives of him and his men. He remembered hearing the call, just before death rained down on the Taliban insurgents assaulting his men.

It was probably one of my old squadron mates on the mission, since we all use the same call sign in combat. But it could have been me. He bought me another beer as a way of saying thanks—something he had wanted to do for a long time, he told me. My experience with war had been nothing like Kevin's. I mostly spent it in the relative security of a cockpit, with the ugliness of combat reduced to amorphous infrared images on my displays. But after a youth spent deploying and serving my country, I think I was there for the same reason as Kevin. I wanted to divorce myself as completely and cleanly from the life I had been living, with the hope that this experience could atone for what I thought I had lost, and inspire me to live in a way that was worthy of a second chance that not all of my friends would get.

So here we were. Two men, who unknowingly depended on each other in combat, meeting for the first time on the eve of climbing a remote Himalayan peak.

Together at the end of the earth, we were trying to make sense out of the senselessness of war and the unrecoverable currency of youths spent fighting for our country.

We drank Everest beer long into the night, and told stories like we were old friends. There was an instant connection based on our military experiences and the attraction we felt to the mountains. Soon we were the last two in the dining room, and the slightly exasperated lodge owner told us that it was time for bed. Kevin would be setting out in the morning with his group a few hours after I was scheduled to leave, and we would not see each other again before the climb. I said goodbye, and we exchanged contact information, and that was it.

I saw Kevin two days later as I was descending from the summit; he was still on the way up with his father, and they both looked tired. But they were determined to keep going. We stopped for a minute to shake hands, and I gave a brief account of my experience. Then we parted ways. I haven't seen Kevin since, and I've lost touch with him over the years. But meeting him on the eve of the climb was something I will never forget. The things I had so badly wanted to leave behind ended up being my greatest comfort.

War College

TERI CARTER

On June 4, 2009, nineteen Colonels, an ethics professor, and eight civilians sat sequestered in a windowless conference room in rural Pennsylvania, reading and marking the transcript. In the back corner a flat screen flashed a red FOX news logo as President Obama—speaking live from a flag-draped stage in Egypt—made his closing remarks. His voice radiated through the room. "Some suggest that it isn't worth the effort, that we are fated to disagree, and civilizations are doomed to clash. Many more are simply skeptical that real change can occur. There is so much fear, so much mistrust." While their commander-in-chief received polite applause from the students of Cairo University, his nineteen American officers, six thousand miles away, combed over the printed pages of his speech. They studied, parsed, drew circles, underlined, and made checkmarks while the eight of us civilians—their guests for the week—watched and waited.

This time last year I'd never even heard of the place. "What's a war college?"

"The U.S. Army War College is in Carlisle, Pennsylvania," Don said. "It's where high-ranking officers spend a year getting their Masters in Strategic Studies." When I didn't respond he added, "Think grad school for the military." I imagined saying, "But I'm in the English Department," which would only have led Don to say, "They speak English," so for once I just sat back and listened. The War College, he explained, trains officers from all branches of the military for strategic leadership. The 330 students spend one year divided into twenty smaller seminars. Right before graduation the school invites 160 civilians to embed with the class in order for students "to better understand the views of the society they serve." Don went last year. Now he was charged with nominating someone for the Class of 2009. "They mostly get a bunch of retired old Republicans like me," he said. "I think they have a hard time getting women to go, especially liberals . . . and from California, no less. You could add something. And you'd have fun."

"Me in a room with a bunch of conservatives like you?" I laughed. "Are you trying to punish me?"

Still, I was intrigued and he knew it. Don and I disagreed on everything from Iraq to gay marriage to President Bush, and we'd enjoyed some pretty impassioned debates over the last decade. This year, however, the ramp-up to President Obama's election had tapped me out. What used to be good philosophical banter too often morphed into venom-spewing attacks with normally sane folks shouting red-faced at friends and neighbors, even at their own spouses. Any dinner party could go rabid in a flash:

> The surge in Iraq is not working! The surge is a success!
> We shouldn't fucking be there in the first place!
> "Community-organizer" Obama has never been in charge of anything!
> W never had a real job and until he became President—for eight years!
> Go ahead, vote for your socialism!
> Michelle Obama is ashamed to be a citizen of this country! She said so herself!
> Sarah Palin doesn't read!
> Neither does Bush, unless it's My Pet Goat!

I wasn't much better. My last tangle had come over the phone with my aunt Mary from back home in Cape Girardeau, Missouri (also Rush Limbaugh's hometown): "Your Obama is a Muslim terrorist and he wasn't even born in the United

States," she said, matter-of-factly and not for the first time, after which I lost my mind and screamed—screamed and cursed—at my sixty-five year old diabetic, half-blind, cancer-surviving, favorite aunt until she hung up on me.

"Hey, it's just a nomination form," Don said. "They might not even pick you."

By the time the War College did, in fact, pick me to spend the first week of June at Carlisle Barracks, President Obama had been in office four months and I had backed off from discussing anything political with anyone. "Wish me luck," I said to my husband as he dropped me at the airport. "Maybe I should just wear a big Miss America banner that reads *Liberal Female from California Goes to Off to War College* and get it over with. God, I hope they don't hate me. What if I'm the only woman in a roomful of right-wing army brass, alpha males?"

"It's the military. Who do you think is going to be there?"

The Sunday night I arrived in Carlisle, thirty miles north of Gettysburg, my assigned escort offered to meet me in the hotel lobby. "So we won't have to find each other in the crowd tomorrow morning," Paul had said on the phone. "I'm tucking my daughter into bed and I'll be right over. Have you eaten yet?"

While I waited for Paul, I leafed through the welcome packet I'd picked up at check-in. I noted that the list of distinguished alumni read like a history of famous U.S. commanders: generals Dwight D. Eisenhower (Class of 1927), George S. Patton Jr. (1932), Omar Bradley (1934), and, more recently, Norman Schwarzkopf (1973) and Tommy Franks (1985). In the red-and-white course catalogue, I perused the list of class offerings.

CORE COURSES

NS2200—Theory of War and Strategy

NS2201—National Security Policy and Strategy

WF2200—Theater Strategy and Campaigning

LM2202—Joint Processes and Landpower Development

Economics of National Security

Law for Senior Commanders

Militant Islam

Dirty Politics: Drug Lords, Terrorists, and Non-state Security Threats

Terrorism in the 21st Century: Religious and Ideological Violence

Men in Battle: The Human Dimensions of Warfare

Military Leaders and the Media

Health & Fitness Challenges for Future Ops

Non-lethal Weapons

International Hotspots and the Military Implications

Ethics and Warfare

The War College staff had insisted there was no need to prepare, but the student in me couldn't help but do some secret, last-minute cramming, so I'd reread three months of Thomas Freidman's *New York Times* columns on Iraq and Afghanistan and I was twenty pages from finishing Dexter Filkins's *The Forever War*. It wasn't Dirty Politics: Drug Lords, Terrorists, and Non-state Security Threats, but it would have to do. Yes, I thought, my friend Don was most certainly having a big old laugh at having sold me on spending a week here.

Paul was six feet tall with a standard crew cut and round eyes the color of aged pennies that never seemed to blink. Dressed in a pressed polo shirt and khakis, he strolled through the lobby looking, I thought, like a man who grinds through a thousand sit-ups and runs a quick ten miles every morning without breaking a sweat. Maybe I was looking at the next General Schwarzkopf.

Paul led me to the hotel restaurant. We skipped any small talk—except noting that we were the same age, forty-three—

and he briefed me on his background while I wolfed down a giant Cobb salad. Before his year at the War College, Paul's most recent assignment had been three years as an attaché in Colombia. "I make $90,000 a year," he said after we'd known each other about seven minutes. I liked him instantly. "Ninety thousand dollars," he repeated. "It's public information. If you wanted to I'm sure you could find it on the internet. After graduation I'll get my promotion and start my new job in Washington DC."

"That should get you a nice pay increase."

"Oh, I won't see a raise until at least November."

"They'll pay you retroactively?"

Paul laughed. "Not quite. Too much red tape and paperwork."

I finished my salad and signed the check to my room, and Paul told me what he knew about the scheduled guest speakers for the week. It was an impressive list: a well-known general, the president of the ACLU, and a congressman who'd served as vice chair of the 9/11 Commission. He also rattled off a list of acronyms I would hear often during the week and emphasized the school's strictly enforced nonattribution policy. "Don't be afraid to speak your mind," he said. "We have a very opinionated group, and nothing is off the table." He stood up, shook my hand, and said he would pick me up first thing in the morning. "No need for you to wait around with a hundred people for the army's big blue bus when I can swing right by."

Carlisle Barracks looked like a cross between an army base and a college campus. There was a security checkpoint at the entrance gate and, once inside, I watched dozens of students toting books in under one arm, hurrying to class, as on any campus quad. Our seminar met Monday morning in a conference room in Root Hall. We shoehorned almost thirty of us around the inside *and* outside of a hole-punched table, a space surely intended for a group half our size, and I discovered I was not, as I'd feared I might be, the only female. The officers represented army, air force, Marines, National Guard, and coast guard, and included two women, two international officers (Australia and Mexico), and one special forces commander. Listening in from the back corners of the room were a military historian and an ethics professor. It would be their job, I learned as the week went on, to insert themselves like crowbars into our arguments when we (a) fell short on facts, (b) needed a firm yank to get us back on-topic, or (c) wandered too far across some invisible ethical line.

For a good two hours we went around the circle introducing ourselves. Listening to their truckload of accomplishments—and frankly I think they were giving us the short version—I realized that I'd never known a senior officer. Until today these guys—or rather the stereotypes of them—existed mostly as characters in books: Kurtz in *The Heart of Darkness*, Bull Meecham of *The Great Santini*, and even good old Pug Henry in *The Winds of War*. And though I now lived in California, the small-town Missouri boys I'd grown up with were my only real-life reference points. They had joined "the service"—as everyone back home called it—not as a career choice but as a means of last resort: they were not good in school; the factories in town weren't hiring; they had disciplinary problems and were forced into it by their parents. Both of my brothers had gone straight into the service out of high school for some—or all—of these reasons. Butch joined the air force and operated heavy equipment in the scorching Arizona desert; Chuck signed on with the Marines and came home an electrician. In all, regardless of their reasons for enlisting, everyone I knew served their four years like jail time and then got the hell out. This War College crowd was different.

My whole family is career military.
Mine too, but none of them ever worked in the Pentagon until me.
I knew I wanted to be a Ranger when I was a kid.
I was obsessed with the Eighty-second Airborne.
I always wanted to jump out of planes. I'm good at it.
I started in pharmacy school but ended up in law school—and the army.

Most had served multiple tours of duty and after their year here would be deployed yet again. The special forces commander, for one, would be heading straight back to Iraq after graduation for his fifth—or was it his sixth?—tour in the Middle East. They'd earned undergraduate degrees from top universities, as well as master's degrees and doctorates in subjects like applied math and physics and law. They were more educated, better educated, than most civilians I knew. Including me. I was impressed by our backgrounds, even amongst the civilians: a North Carolina cardiologist, a New York engineer, a retired Pennsylvania state police officer, a Green Bay Packers board member, an entrepreneurial Texan who built schools for kids with Down's Syndrome, a bank president from Iowa, a retired Utah news anchor turned humanitarian activist (also female), and me. If the people in this room were dropped on a desert island somewhere, I thought, we could start an entirely new and successful civilization. Easily. From scratch.

After lunch all five hundred students and civilians gathered in Bliss Hall Auditorium for the first speaker of the week, a retired four-star general from the Clinton administration turned pundit for television news. I watched Peggy Noonan from the *Wall Street Journal* (whom I'd just spotted in the cafeteria's sandwich line an hour earlier) take her seat down front. She smiled at the general. He smiled back. They talked. Then the lights dimmed and the room went quiet. Though I could barely see the notebook on my lap, I scribbled notes while the general presented a slide show titled "The Challenges Facing the Obama Administration" and threw around numbers: two million illegal aliens are living in the United States; we will largely draw down troops in Iraq in thirty-six months; violence in Iraq is down from 1,250 attacks per week in 2003 to 100 in 2009; Iraq, so far, has been a $700 billion war; we are spending $2.4 billion a month in Afghanistan; most of our special forces personnel have been on five to seven tours in a war zone; Afghanistan supplies 95 percent of the world's opium, with two million Afghanis employed by the opium trade and earning $4 billion in criminal funds.

When the lights came up the general took questions. I noticed our chairs had microphones attached—"to encourage participation," Paul said—and around the auditorium hands flew into the air above the sea of square shoulders and crew cuts, men and women hoping to be called upon by the general. After a half hour of Q&A, our group went back to our conference room and dissected his data.

His information is old. He must have recycled that presentation.

There are two camps regarding what retired generals should be allowed to do: Camp #1 says, "Free speech. Say what you want." Camp #2 says, "You shape policy and public opinion by speaking, and this is no longer your job."

You can really tell he's part of the old guard. Petraeus is part of the new generation, the first school of generals not shaped by the Cold War. This is not looked well upon by some of the older generals.

You don't hear much from Colin Powell anymore.

You mean the sacrificial lamb?

Let's talk about invasion. With Iraq we invaded a sovereign nation. We're a sovereign nation. Imagine if somebody had invaded us? We'd be pissed.

Well, we're in it now and we're stuck there for, what did he say, the next twenty-five years? And twenty-five thousand to forty thousand troops.

What about Mexico? He said that thing about the illegal aliens, but he didn't talk about the 2,000-mile wall we're going to have to build.

I thought he did.

Who's going to pay for that wall?

It doesn't matter. We need the wall.

I was not used to the lightning-round way these people said exactly—*exactly*—what they thought without any politically correct filtering, but also without coming across as defensive or self-righteous. It took me awhile to settle in. As the afternoon wore on we agreed and disagreed, agreed *to* disagree, raised our voices, threw our arms in the air, banged our hands on the table, and shoved our chairs back in protest. But unlike the personal attacks I'd grown so weary of recently, we did it all without the rolling eyes or the dismissive, offhanded smirk. We even laughed.

It was that first afternoon, in a roomful of strangers, when I remembered that arguing controversial topics could be civil. We listened. We made our points. We considered opposing ideals. It reminded me of being on a high school debate team where you've practiced how to clearly state your views and how to listen to your opposition without fuming over. This felt like that. And this was fun.

The few times Paul was unable to act as chauffeur, I meandered my way onto the big blue bus for the short ride between the hotel and Carlisle Barracks. One morning, as I made my way down the aisle, there sat Peggy Noonan. I plopped myself onto the seat in front of her and turned around, offering my hand to shake.

Hi Peggy. Nice to meet you. I admire your work.

Thank you. That's so nice of you to say.

I saw you at the general's talk the other day. You're here as press?

No, I'm in a seminar. You?

I'm in seminar B.

Sure. I'm right down the hall in C. Are you enjoying it?

We're having a great time. It's a lively and enlightening bunch. Ours too.

They're not afraid to talk, in your group, with you being a member of the press?

Not that I can tell! (she laughed) They're pretty open, I think.

Well, I didn't want to bother you. I just wanted to say hello.

It was a bit of a white lie to say I admired Peggy's work. It was more like I admired Peggy. I disagreed with her on a number of issues, but as a professional woman I respected her long, successful career in the male-dominated universe of news and Washington politics. I remembered that I'd loved her book, *What I Saw at the Revolution,* about working in the Reagan White House. I couldn't wait to call my friend Don and tell him tell him I'd met his girl Peggy. He would be jealous.

For the next few days we followed a rigorous schedule. We listened to speakers in the auditorium, and then our smaller seminar crammed ourselves back into the windowless conference room and debated every subject, from every angle, for hours. True to what Paul had promised that first night, nothing was off the table.

On the Media

We don't have news in this country. We have infotainment.

Yeah, I remember driving a tank down the street in Baghdad right after the invasion and throwing candy to the children. When I saw the news clip the next day they were saying, "Look at how happy they are to see the Americans!" I felt like screaming at the TV, "They aren't happy to see us! They're hungry!" The news spins everything to what they want it to be.

I read all of my news, but in a pinch I like the BBC. And Al Jazeera. I figure AJZ has to work the hardest to sound fair and balanced.

So what's with the TV in here being tuned to FOX?

We keep it on mute so we can see the ticker, to see if some "breaking news" happens that we need to be talking about.

I avoid all U.S. stations. Too many talking heads telling me what to think. I want to say, "How about you just give me the information and I'll think for myself, thanks."

They're not all bad. I remember the first time Lara Logan from CBS interviewed me. I wasn't through my first answer before she said, off camera, "Stop giving me the fucking company line and answer my question." I respected her for that. And when I'm in my command center in Iraq, running a dozen or more high-value target missions a night, I have embedded media sitting on one side and my lawyer on the other. I wouldn't have it any other way.

Next time you watch some general being grilled by a congressman on C-Span, remember this: all questions and answers have been negotiated and prearranged. There are no surprises. No matter how surprised or put-out they might look, it's all for show

On Torture and Guantanamo Bay

I don't believe in waterboarding.

Name somebody who does. It's a ridiculous statement.

I've had this conversation with my mother-in-law. She's against it, of course. But my training includes *me* being waterboarded, which I'm not going to tell her, so how am I supposed to answer that?

Forget torture. What I need are female interrogators. These guys lose it when confronted by a woman in a power position. It's so far beyond their reality.

What about the speaker today . . . She said all the prisoners at Gitmo don't really need to be there.

Is that what she said? I thought she said 10 percent of them were probably not guilty.

Is that her expert legal opinion?

Actually, I think she said that if even one prisoner in ten wasn't a terrorist, it would be worth it—from a humane standpoint—to release ten to save the one.

Like I said, her "expert opinion"? Let me just say this: if they've made it all the way to Gitmo, they've made it through an awful lot of other checkpoints. You don't get to Gitmo by accident; you get there because you're damned dangerous.

I get why it has to close, but it's a shame. Gitmo is a state-of-the-art facility, and we're going to have to put them somewhere.

On Religion

It's not all about religion.

The hell it isn't. How can you do anything without bringing God or religion into it?

What if someone doesn't believe in God?

Are we talking about God or religion? They're not the same thing.

If you believe in God but you're not "religious" does that automatically make you immoral?

I'm not saying that. Religion is fine, but it's personal. Private. You can believe what you want. I just don't think I need to see it bleeding through your sleeve.

On the Office of the President

President Bush came here last fall on his farewell tour. He gave a pretty standard speech at first, and then he had the press leave the room, closed the doors, and he talked to us from his heart for over an hour.

And what did you think?

I wished that second guy, the one with the doors closed, could have been our president.

Social media is scary. Kids post every stupid thing online. Who's going to be able to run for president—or any office—with all that baggage?

They'll all be doing it so it won't matter.

I don't know about that.

You're missing the point. Nobody will care.

That depends.

Think about it this way: forty years ago who would have thought we'd have a Black president? Forty years from now we'll have a gay president and nobody will blink an eye. Times change. All the stuff we're fighting about now will be irrelevant.

I had to admit, the idea of a gay president had never once crossed my mind. Last week, if someone had told me that a colonel in the United States Air Force would beat me to that kind of open-minded speculation, I would have called them all kinds of crazy.

I pictured my Miss America banner with an addendum: *Liberal Female from California Goes Off to War College . . . and Gets Out-Liberalled.*

On June 4 President Obama wrapped up his much-anticipated Cairo speech to thunderous applause. The TV in the corner of the room was still tuned to FOX, but the screen was now split into four boxes of talking heads and the president's big international speech was being spliced into snippets. "All of us share this world for but a brief moment in time," he was saying. "The question is whether we spend that time focused on what pushes us apart, or whether we commit ourselves to an effort—a sustained effort—to find common ground, to focus on the future we seek for our children, and to respect the dignity of all human beings." When the talking heads started ripping apart the speech and each other, we hit the mute button, and the men and women who served the president scanned their notes and opened the discussion.

Who was he talking to?

Better yet, who wasn't he talking to?

Right, who's going to feel left out?

He said the word "Muslim" more than forty times.

I counted forty-five.

He only mentioned the Koran a few times, but that's more than anyone else ever has.

He pronounced all the words properly. That's huge.

He said there's a mosque in every state of the United States. I didn't know that. Who knew that?

He never mentioned terror or terrorism.

The speech focused a lot on Islam being equal to all religions, about all people being equal, that kind of thing. And he said here, "Just as Muslims do not fit a crude stereotype, America is not the crude stereotype of a self-interested empire."

Did he accomplish what he set out to?

Sure. It sounded to me like he was just trying to let the air out of the balloon. I certainly felt the big "let's all take a deep breath."

He didn't shy away from any topic. He mentioned them all: Iraq, Afghanistan, Israeli settlements, the Palestinians, tension with Iran, women's rights. I can't see that he missed anything.

And he certainly didn't hurt anything. It was a high-gloss speech.

He's only been in office four months. It was pretty good for four months.

He's a young president being lobbied by the most powerful egos he's ever dealt with. So we'll see.

Exactly. We'll see.

The War College commandant hosted his civilian guests for dinner. We filed through the receiving line for a quick shake of the hand and a *Thank you for coming,* but when the commandant saw my nametag he gripped my hand a little tighter, held it a little longer.

All the way from California! I'm so glad you took the time.

Thank you, sir. It's been great.

I'm going to ask you to do me a big favor. Nominate someone next year. We need more people like you—more citizens from the West Coast—to come here and spend the week with us. We want to hear your point of view. Can you help me?

Of course, sir.

I'm counting on you, California.

I returned home feeling both exhausted and reenergized, like I'd been through some kind of political detox. My core beliefs remained, but the edges had softened and blurred.

"They brainwashed you," a friend insisted.

"No," I said. "I just feel like a rational human again." When the rhetoric at a dinner party sailed into the stratosphere, I stated my views without raising my voice. If I felt like I was being baited, I backed off or changed the subject. Even when

Aunt Mary quoted Rush Limbaugh I kept my cool and, eventually, I think, convinced her that President Obama is not a terrorist. I even started reading Peggy Noonan's opinion column in the *Wall Street Journal* to keep up with what "the other side" was talking about. I was proud of myself.

Six months later I hit my first snag.

When the time came for me to nominate someone for the War College class of 2010, I thought carefully about whom to recommend. It had to be a woman, and it had to be someone who could add some real meat to the debate. I chose a politically active California liberal, well-informed on the issues, and who—let's be honest—could hold her own in a room full of strong-minded, charming, quick-witted colonels. I made contact:

This is going to sound a bit out of left field, but I have something I'm hoping will interest you. (I then gave her a list of the details.)

I'm a little intrigued. How much does it cost?

You pay for airfare. They cover everything else including hotel, transportation, meals, everything. I didn't spend a dime. Honestly, I couldn't even buy a beer.

I'm trying to decide what would be the point.

It's an honest and open discussion about every topic you can imagine. We debated everything you could think of: Iraq, Afghanistan, torture, religion, Bush and Obama, border control. You'll also have a chance to go on a guided tour of Gettysburg with the resident scholar on the Civil War.

I'm sure it would be interesting, but I'm not sure I want to spend any of my own money on this. What's the point again?

They say they want the officers to better understand the civilian population they serve. You can tell them exactly what you think about the state of things and hear what they have to say.

I guess I'm just feeling particularly cynical and jaded, given how much I'm seeing education decimated in California. I'm not sure I need to see how good the military has it with their education, and how our money is being spent on these stupid occupations in Iraq and Afghanistan.

I understand.

No. You know what. This all sounds to me like some kind of "agenda" and I'm not sure I feel comfortable with that. I'm afraid I might find myself being the person who says, "Why the hell are you spending good money to get me here to convince me we're in good hands?!" These wars are nothing but an attempt to make a few people rich while destruction is really the motive.

I don't disagree.

You know, I'm going to pass. I appreciate your thinking of me, but I don't think this is the best use of my time. I'd rather go on a real vacation and channel my money and my energy into something more meaningful.

I thought back to last year when Don had convinced me to go. Why had I said yes? And why could I not convince this woman, this fellow liberal, that a week at the War College would be the *best* possible use of her time?

When I couldn't quite put my finger on it, I shared her feedback with the officers in seminar group via email. Within minutes, two colonels—one who is now on the ground in Iraq, the other serving at the Pentagon—responded as follows:

(1) You may want to point out that liberal folks advertise we should all have open minds and that we should not draw stereotypical conclusions about groups of people. Based on her attitude, is she not sounding stereotypically conservative? It is unfortunate that there are people in the best nation in the history of mankind (I said best, not perfect) who are unwilling to become informed through experience instead of through anecdotal evidence. Personally, I would welcome meeting her to hear that point of view and to discuss the issues as intelligent, civilized people.

(2) She is exactly the right person for the seminar. Tell her I'll cover her airfare and see what she says. I'll do it if she agrees. Coach only, of course, for a liberal.

I thanked them for making me laugh, took a breath, and tried again.

The Colonel's Bicycle

JORDAN HAYES

A chocolate brown horse with wide eyes and nostrils fluttered its tail in flaccid resistance as a child beat its brains in with a hammer. Next door a man quarreled over the price of shoes. Behind him the first M-ATV in our convoy barreled over a pothole deeper than most men's knees at forty miles an hour. Dust blew over the man, filled the shop where he was haggling, covered every shoe in the store. It blew onto the child, into his hair, his clothes, and his dead horse. It stuck to the hammer.

We followed the road around a bend onto what we called Sunset Boulevard. To our right, as we lumbered by, was a steep hillside peppered with mud huts that shone the color of sangria when the setting sunlight made its way through the dust, exhaust, salt, shit, and gunpowder in the air. I wrapped a balaclava around my face. I tried stuffing it in my mouth. I tried holding it over my nose. Everything tasted dirty. Ahead of us, in the distance, was a hill called 500 Families. It was a tightly settled village on the slope of a mountain, one of the many that surround Kabul. It was a squatter town, packed full of refugees from Helmand and Kandahar, and was a fertile recruiting town for the Taliban, home to disgruntled people prone to fighting, especially the children. They were also prone to painting their huts bright colors like pink, green, orange, and white. From Sunset Boulevard, it looked like San Francisco.

An M-ATV is an MRAP made for Afghanistan. Made by Oshkosh. Just like OshKosh B'gosh. As in overalls. It's a toy. We could talk to each other over the radio. I would relay suspicious things I could see from my position in the turret to the nine other airmen on my team. New pavement, men with cell phones, broken-down cars, piles of trash. Because we could talk to each other, we would also joke. We would joke because Spider-3 was driving too slowly. We would joke because an IED was going to take my head off. It was going to fly across the road and land somewhere funny. It was going to land among the construction workers who were building a warehouse we passed. When finished, that warehouse was going to be the largest building in Afghanistan. It was the centerpiece of the Afghan base where we worked. We slowed down as we approached the main gate. Weaving through concrete barriers, I turned my turret around and scouted behind us. I saw trucks with murals painted on the sides and tassels hanging from the mirrors. The murals were scenes of Arcadian green pastures, blue ponds, and homes with Doric columns. I saw children kicking soccer balls into the windows of empty businesses. A man rode his bicycle along the road with a hundred red, black, and green balloons tied to his seat. When we got through the gate, we parked in a gravel lot.

The three trucks in our convoy parked next to thirty identical sand-colored Ford pickup trucks with ANA spray painted on the side. Afghan National Army. Our Oshkosh trucks stood head and shoulders above an F-150. When we dismounted we shed headsets, body armor, magazines, multitools, flashlights, glow sticks, zip ties, zip-tie handcuffs, bullets, bandanas, and helmets at the trucks and locked them. We kept our weapons. Across the gravel parking lot was a low-lying two-story building. It was the American advisors' building, where we worked. It had a four-foot brick wall around three sides, for protection, and there were steps up to a tall, unadorned steel door. Near the front door were meticulously kept flower beds, and along the wall were trees and rose bushes. The bushes' branches were tied together in some places with IV tubes, crimping them into different shapes. Shapes like *Hope, Grief, Want, Flattery, Fear, Regret,* and *Dancing*.

Afghans call Thursday *gol shambay*, or "flower day." At least our Afghans did. This was because Thursdays were half days and historically the least active days for the ANA. Thursdays were only meant for drinking tea and smoking cigarettes. It was the day that the soldiers relaxed, the officers closed their doors, and no serious work was accomplished. Unless, of course, you were a gardener.

I was a second lieutenant, the lowest-ranking American on our training team. We were embedded on this Afghan base. It was my job to mentor and advise the Afghan education and training officer for logistics. His name was Colonel Shirazod. He was a commando who had fought the *mujahedeen* in the eighties. He was a full colonel. At least, he wore a colonel's uniform. He had been promoted to colonel under the Russians. He became a farmer under the Taliban, and when he was reinstated under the new regime he was placed in a major's position. This technically made him a major; however, he would not wear a major's uniform even if it was against regulation. If his wife found out that he had been demoted, even administratively, she would *kill him.*

I passed the door guard, Aziz, on my way into the advisors' building, where Colonel Shirazod's office also was. Aziz slouched under the weight of his AK-47. He wore tattered woodland camouflage and a faded blue beret. He had a gray beard and deep wrinkles like the folds of a gown. When I passed Aziz I nodded to him, and he nodded in return. The rest of the team and I went into our office, which was a long room with many broad desks, like a classroom for secretaries. I grabbed a prepackaged blueberry muffin from our supply cabinet and put the coffee on. We had more than fifty pounds of coffee that we had convoyed in, courtesy of my mother and all her friends. And all their friends. Being the lowest ranking, I was also the coffee boy. I didn't mind. I skipped the Folgers pile and pulled coffee from the Dunkin' pile. The good stuff. I filled a thermos labeled "Air Force Retired" and went to find Mahmoud, my interpreter.

Mahmoud was tall with curly black hair like a pop star. For that reason the Marines in Helmand had nicknamed him Julio Iglesias. Mahmoud was proud of that nickname, without really knowing why. He had stitched it into the back of his jean jacket. He stitched it in English and Dari, his native tongue, so that everyone could read it. Mahmoud taught me Dari every Thursday. We would sit on the wall around our building and go over flash cards. He taught me to read and pronounce Arabic letters. I wrote like a child: large, clearly distinguishable letters, no calligraphy. Mahmoud could write calligraphy. Mahmoud could dance the Charleston. He always smiled.

"Good morning, Jordan."

"Good morning, Mahmoud."

"Today we will study?"

"Sure," I said, "Later. Is Colonel Shirazod here?"

"Yes, he asked if you brought him medicine," he said.

"I sure did," I said, "one pack of mentor-approved headache pills."

There was no carpet inside the advisors' building. No tile either, but the concrete floor shone. White-painted plaster arches trimmed the ceiling. The walls were a faint peach color. There were posters on the walls with pictures of Afghan soldiers holding M-14s, RPGs, or AK-47s that had slogans in Dari written on them like "Jihad is on the side of the ANA" and "Glory to God and the government." One poster showed a soldier on a mountainside throwing a grenade with the slogan "Do not smoke indoors."

We walked up the stairs and down a hallway that was empty but for a fire extinguisher box, and that was empty too. There was a glass door at the end of the hall that led to a balcony. On either side was a door. On the door to the right hung a paper sign with the words "Education and Training" enclosed in a thick black-dashed border. At the bottom it read, "Colonel Mohamed Shirazod <Chakaree>." It was Scotch-taped to the wall. At the end of one of the pieces of tape was the plastic green tab that starts a new roll.

Mahmoud and I went into the office, passing a woman asleep at her desk wearing combat boots and a burka. She was a soldier, but she sold her uniform at the bazaar because she didn't think it was pretty. Inside was an old man in woodland camouflage with dyed black hair, a dyed-black hair-comb moustache, and bright-red felt pads on his lapels. This was Colonel Shirazod. He was watering his plants with his back to us. He had several plants around the office, and they grew very well. There were ivies of all sorts: some with long, flowing stems, others with short, dense bursts of leaves, and still others with broad leaves that looked as though they had been dipped in Merlot. I took off my M-4 and placed it between the couch and the far wall, as I was accustomed to doing. There was a coffee table in the room with an ashtray on it. Colonel Shirazod brought nuts and raisins in a dish and placed them on the coffee table. He took some candy from his pocket and added that to the dish. I lit a cigarette, sat down on the couch with Mahmoud, and said, "Happy *gol shambay*, Colonel."

"*Salaam*, Lieutenant Jordan. *Walaikum Salaam. Fameelat chetor ast? Khoob asti? Jour asti? Tamom khoob ast?*"

"He says, 'Hello, Jordan! How is your family,' and also some other things like 'How are you?'" Mahmoud translated. The three of us had worked together for three months and knew each other so well that I understood most of what Colonel Shirazod said without Mahmoud translating. He also understood most of my English, though he had no formal training.

"My family is good, sir." I said. "*Koobis.*"

"*Khoob ast*," he said.

"*Khoob ast*," I said.

"How is your girlfriend?" he asked through Mahmoud.

"She's good too, man," I said as I passed him a cigarette. They were Gauloises Blondes. Five bucks a carton.

"How's *your* girlfriend?" I asked.

He laughed and pointed a finger to the woman in the next room.

"Sleep," he said in English. Then, "Mustafa!" Colonel Shirazod shouted.

Mustafa was Colonel Shirazod's only sergeant. He was an E-8 and had ascended very quickly though the enlisted ranks. He was yet to be twenty. As the lowest ranking, he was also the *chai* boy. He didn't mind. The colonel gave him orders to bring in tea. Mustafa had already prepared, as was his routine, by heating the water in a mop bucket with a copper heating coil that he plugged into the wall and submerged into the bucket. He took some hot water into a tarnished brass kettle, and threw a handful of green sticks, leaves, twigs, nettles, shell, and dirt that they enigmatically called *chai*. Mustafa poured hot *chai* into a dirty glass, transferred it into another glass, and so on until he had swished water in all the glasses, cleaning them. He poured the leftover *chai* onto the floor in the corner of the room, cleaning that too. I was staring out the window, watching an officer chase gardeners. His name was Lieutenant Colonel Gol.

"Colonel Flower busy," I said.

Colonel Shirazod roared with laughter.

"Colonel Flower yah beesy!" He said and then, through Mahmoud, "Colonel Flower is only busy on Flower Day. Lieutenant Colonel Gol. He is the only officer with no job. He monitors the gardeners out of boredom."

This he knew I knew and he was happy to retell as he dipped his cigarette butt into his tea and blew through the open end for increased smoothness.

"Lieutenant Colonel Gol wasn't always the Flower Commander," he said through Mahmoud. "Once he was a very powerful supply officer. But that was because his brother, a full colonel, was well connected in the government. His brother had a bicycle. It was red with whitewall tires. It had a little bell on it. He cleaned it every day with paper towels that he got from American supply depots. He oiled the chains, checked the air in the tires, touched up the paint, reupholstered the seat, checked the brakes, the shocks, the gears. He would never let his children ride his bicycle. He would only let mechanics do the work when he could not do it himself, and even then it was jealously so. Colonel Gol was proud of his bicycle. He was a stupid man . . . a coward. The colonel rode his bicycle to work.

"He had been in the army with me when the Russians took over and we fought the *mujahideen*. We were commandos together. Commandos are the bravest of all Afghan fighters. After the Russian war, when the Taliban came in to control the chaos, we hid from them by pretending to go along with it. We grew beards. We buried our uniforms and our pictures. If the old *mujahideen* knew we had fought with the Russian mentors, they would have killed us. Many years we hid from the Taliban, farming fields, feeding our families, and only singing under our breath when we felt bold and bulletproof. As he grew older, however, Colonel Gol was very afraid to die. So he did not ride the ANA bus."

Colonel Shirazod pronounced ANA "UNA." Mahmoud corrected him.

"He rode his bicycle to work," he continued. "He was convinced that one day the Taliban would blow up the bus, because they know we work with the American mentors, and he would be a damned fool to ride it. Last year there was a Taliban attack on an ANA bus, just as he predicted.

"It was a Thursday, *gol shambay*, and historically the least active day for the Taliban. No soldier expected an attack that day. The bus driver wasn't even worried. It was a sunny day and the bus driver was whistling to himself from the minute he awoke. He drove his bus around tight turns with finesse and gusto. He pulled his bus over at a stop near 500 Families, and a group of soldiers got on. Behind them a boy broke away from a soccer game, chasing after a loose ball. Colonel Gol was passing by and stopped to pick up the ball and then held it, arms outstretched. The boy ran up, out of breath, reached into his jacket stuffed with plastic explosives and nails, and blew himself to pieces like a porcelain doll so that his clothes were tattered and singed and crumpled around his little bloody chunks of ankles in cleats, which was all that was left of him. Except cleanup crews did find his head the next day. Usually, the bombers don't kill anyone but themselves, but that day Colonel Gol and his red bicycle were found mangled together under the seat of a bench, as if placed there. None of the soldiers on the bus were hurt."

Colonel Shirazod laughed heartily and drank off his *chai*. Then he rose, took the kettle, and poured the leftovers into his flower pots.

"And now Lieutenant Colonel Gol is in charge of the gardeners!" He snorted.

I rose, thanked Colonel Shirazod, and promised to come see him later. When I stood I patted myself down, and dust flew from my clothes into the morning sunlight that filtered through his office window. Outside a forklift drove in circles, carrying empty pallets. I grabbed my M-4 from behind the couch and slung it over my shoulder, checking the safety as I did. I put out my cigarette in Colonel Shirazod's ashtray and took a few raisins. They were pale raisins, dried in the shade instead of in the sun. Almost forgetting, I handed him a Ziploc bag with multivitamins.

"For your headaches," I said.

Mahmoud translated.

Outside Aziz was sitting in his chair, asleep. A few ANA soldiers were walking back from their dining hall with bread tucked under their arms and apples in their pockets. They waved to us as Mahmoud and I stood by the front door, smoking. They shouted something to Mahmoud. He laughed. They were holding up their pants. Mahmoud and I hoisted ourselves up and sat on the perimeter wall. I took a stack of three-by-five note cards wrapped in a rubber band out of the chest pocket of my desert uniform.

"*Een chee ast?*" he said, holding up a card with Arabic letters. His cigarette dangled between his ring and pinky fingers.

"*Een chee ast?*" I said. "What is this?"

"Very good," he said and held up another. "*Ketob.*"

"*Ketob,*" I said. "Book."

"*Brietman,*" he said.

"*Brietman*," I said. "Soldier; also, lieutenant."

"*Urdu.*"

"*Urdu.*" I said. "Army."

"*Man shamora doost doram.*"

"*Man shamora doost doram,*" I said. "I love you."

"*Jordan bagel ast,*" he said.

"Screw you, dude," I said, and laughed.

There was an old man tending to bushes nearby. He wore a thin corduroy jacket with a matted felt collar. He stood bent over like he was shoveling snow, and he was sweating. He had IV tubes sticking out of the pocket of his ANA-issued camouflage trousers. The needles were still attached. From either side of a bush the old man took a handful of branches, bent them to the middle, and tied them with an IV tube so that they met. He stood back, wiped his brow, and looked at the bush. He might have called it *Applause*. The old man noticed us practicing and stopped to watch. I showed him a flashcard.

"Look," I said, holding a card out to him. "See? I'm learning Dari. Mahmoud is my teacher. Mahmoud *malem-e man ast.*"

The old man looked at the card, and then looked at me quizzically. Mahmoud didn't translate. I looked at Mahmoud quizzically.

"He doesn't read," Mahmoud said. "He doesn't read, so he's a gardener."

We heard shouting and the old man scurried back to work. It was Lieutenant Colonel Gol. He shouted at the old man, gave direction. The old man was still slouched, so that he looked inattentive, but he nodded in understanding. When the colonel was through, he walked proudly to where Mahmoud and I were sitting on the wall.

"Hey, Colonel Flower!" I said.

"*Salaam-a-laikum, Dagar-man Gol,*" said Mahmoud, covering my tracks.

"How are you, sir?" I asked.

"Very well!" He said through Mahmoud. "We will have very good plants this year. We will also have grapes. The commander was gracious enough to buy seedlings. We will be the only base in the ANA with a grape crop. Eventually we will have more fruit trees and vegetables. Someday we will be the only self-sustaining Afghan base. You know, when I was a supply officer I was going to be promoted to major for designing the base warehouse. When it's finished it will be the largest building in Afghanistan. Perhaps they will make me a full colonel when the grape crop is harvested. They may yet."

"Very good," I said. "*Koobis.*"

"*Khoob ast,*" he corrected me.

"*Khoob ast,*" I said.

The colonel returned to his work, issuing orders to his gardeners and ensuring they were all kept busy. Ensuring good order and discipline. He weeded his gardens every day with tools that he got from American supply depots. He tilled the earth, repotted plants, trimmed trees, crimped bushes into shapes like *Love*, picked fruit fresh from the vine or the branch, pushed seeds into the soil with his forefinger, watered roses from his cupped hands. He would only let his gardeners do the work when he could not do it himself, and even then it was jealously so. Lieutenant Colonel Gol was proud of his gardens. I watched him hustle as Mahmoud held up another card.

"*Atfal,*" he said.

"*Atfal,*" I said. "Children."

Phalanx

GERARDO MENA

They say he ran.

He had a first name once. It is now buried with his honor. He is only a rank and a last name. Staff Sergeant Harris. They say he ran when he saw the blast.

An action, an impulse. Seduced by lady fear, wearing her gown of tangibility, speaking materialisms into his ear, as she traced a finger down the slope of his neck and drew a line of succulent life down to his navel. He looked upon her, lying on the foreign earth, and draped himself over her. She whispered into his skin as he covered his *Death Before Dishonor* tattoo in Arab mud.

He stretched the night over his face and wept as a child that realizes that acts have consequences and punishments are real. Death is not a dream here. There are no monologues, only a violent instant where our limbs are torn from trunks and we fade as our bodies struggle to breathe. Our bodies struggle to blink. For those of us that remain unlucky, we must react. We must close the phalanx. There is still work to be done. There is still death to gift.

They say he ran when he saw the blast that killed Gary.

And to all those who see Staff Sergeant Harris sitting behind his little wooden desk, pretending to be a Marine, I beg you to ask him, "Do you remember Gary Johnston?" And when he smirks and replies, "Yes, I was there the night he died." I want you to look him in his beady coward eyes and say "Alpha Company, Third Platoon says go fuck yourself. It should've been you."

They say he ran.

A Promise to Keep

J. MALCOLM GARCIA

—*Dedicated to Olga Contreras*

In March 2004, as a reporter for Knight Ridder newspapers, I returned to Afghanistan for the fourth time to cover the war. My Afghan colleague, translator Khalid Saraway, picked me up at Kabul International Airport.

A boy stood outside my hotel, the Mustafa, when Khalid and I pulled up. I recognized him instantly. Jawad. His white shirt and pants were blotched with dark, wet stains. He wrung out a mop. He looked at me and cocked his head to one side as I stepped out of the car. Slowly a look crossed his face.

"You're late," he said after a long pause. He smiled but I heard no humor in his voice.

Four other boys joined him but they were as subdued as Jawad. We shook hands stiffly.

"I'd hoped to come back sooner," I said.

An onslaught of beggars interrupted the awkwardness of the moment by offering—demanding—to carry my duffel bag into the hotel. Khalid shooed them away and we went inside. Jawad and the other boys did not follow us.

I registered at the front desk, dropped my duffel in my room, and returned to the lobby. I joined Khalid in the hotel restaurant. He ordered us tea.

"The boys have changed," he said.

"I see."

"They have all dropped out of school."

In 2003 Khalid and I took on Jawad and the other boys, all

of them war orphans, as our personal project. It was my idea. We fed them, made sure they had a daily change of clothes, and enrolled them in school. The boys, I told Khalid, fell under the category of "other duties as assigned." They didn't know their birthdays. I guessed them all to be about thirteen.

Each evening Khalid and I reviewed their homework in the back room of a pharmacy owned by his brother and near the Mustafa. We also taught them English. When I left Kabul five months later, I promised, based on what my editor had told me, to return in two weeks. Khalid assured me he would go over their homework in my absence, and the boys vowed not to skip school.

We all believed the commitments we had made to one another, but we had not anticipated how the demands on our lives would influence and in the end shatter those commitments. I suspect I was the first to break my promise. I did not return in two weeks. A year would pass before my editor offered me another assignment in Kabul.

"It was very hard to keep helping them," Khalid said of the boys. "You did not come back. I had to find work. There are no jobs in Afghanistan. No future. I needed to work, if not with you then someone else."

"What are they doing now? The boys? If they're not in school."

"Jawad and Jamshid work here at the Mustafa cleaning and running errands," Khalid said. "The other three work for shop owners. They make about seventy U.S. a month."

I nodded. Seventy bucks a month. Good money in a country where the average monthly income was fifty bucks. How could school compete with success like that? When I left, I knew Khalid wouldn't have the money to feed and clothe the boys and keep them in school. Who would? Me. But I returned twelve months later than I promised. What had I expected Khalid to do in the meantime? I was in no position to scold.

"I found a job with the United Nations," Khalid said. "I was a data entry supervisor for a voter registration drive. I didn't have time to come by the pharmacy and meet with the boys."

"That's okay. No need to explain."

I looked out a window at the street. I saw two of the boys, Sohail and Noor. Sohail was sweeping the floor of a photocopy shop; Noor was hawking magazines. I watched them work. I had been selfish. I had not considered the obligation I'd taken on by helping them. What I did for them I did for my benefit, not theirs.

My days in Kabul had been filled with despair. Daily I heard the desperate pleas of war widows and amputees and the angry shouts of Afghan soldiers and police. I saw shop owners whip beggars with metal cables to clear them from sidewalks. I watched freaked-out Westerners flee from hungry children shouting, "One dollar, mister!" I saw legless men in doorways pleading for money. For the sake of my sanity, I needed more going on inside my head than the stories I was writing and the lingering cries and the screams of people being beaten. I can feed, clothe, and help educate the five homeless boys I see every day polishing shoes outside my hotel, I thought. I can do that much.

At night, as I tried to sleep, the shrieks of "Money, mister!" grew louder in my head. The snarling images of people fighting for food tossed at them from UN trucks filled my room, hovered over my bed with suffocating intensity. Thoughts of the boys reciting their lessons just hours before, however, eased my mind.

"I am thinking of going to Iraq," Khalid said. "The UN said it needs staff there. It will be good money, I think. What do you think?"

"I think you're silly," I said, using one of his favorite English words. He smiled. He remembered as I did the time when he told an Afghan bureaucrat who was putting us through needless hoops of red tape that he was a "silly man." I wanted to talk about that day, the moments that made us laugh. Instead I grappled with my conscience.

"I have to support my family," Khalid said. "There's no future here."

We finished our tea and agreed to start work in the morning. Attend a press conference, find a daily news story. A full, long day. I walked to my room past the open door of another room where flies were tormenting an American—perhaps a journalist, perhaps someone with an NGO. I didn't know or care.

"You can run but you can't hide," he screamed, swatting the flies.

I closed my door and sat on my bed. I stared at the walls, the light outside turning to gray. A turmoil of dusty air seeped through the cracks of my windows. A fan stood in one corner. It didn't work. Someone knocked. I opened the door. Jawad.

"What does this mean?" he said. He showed me a slip of paper, the word *pizza* scrawled across it. He handed me the tattered Dari-English dictionary I had given him the previous year.

"I can't find this word. A guest asked for it."

I knew pizza would not be in the dictionary, but I thumbed through it anyway, reeling off words in Dari for him to repeat in English, an exercise I used to do with him and the other boys.

"Tarafik."

"Traffic."

"Kuchi."

"Nomad."

"Sasej."

"Sausage."

After a few more words Jawad stopped me. He needed to get back to work.

"What is this word?" he insisted.

I explained what a pizza was and he nodded. Then he asked me to buy him a bicycle.

"A bicycle? Where'd that come from? What's that got to do with pizza?"

He shrugged.

"Where have you been?"

"I was in the States."

"A long time."

"I'm sorry. I'll see about getting you a bike."

He left. I presumed he would forget about the bicycle. I presumed he would wake up the next morning as I would to the demands of our jobs, our lives.

I shut the door. I listened to dogs barking and the wailing of cats, the screech of tires, and the shouts of beggars until I heard nothing more, leaving only my thoughts to intrude on the long, deep night ahead.

I remained in Afghanistan for three months. A few days before I returned to the States I caught a bus bound for Khost, a city near the Pakistan border on Jalalabad Road, for a feature story. When the bus stopped in Gardez, about an hour outside of Khost, I was advised by local villagers to go no farther. Security along the road was very bad, they told me. Bandits and Taliban fighters hid in the mountains and attacked passing vehicles.

One man offered me tea. Then he took me by the hand and led me to an empty lot in a wheat field not far from the bus station where he was building a house on land, I gathered by the way he gestured toward a cemetery and then back at the house, that had been in his family a long time. By his gestures I understood he had carried buckets of water to the lot so he could turn the dirt to mud and build the walls of his house. One side was almost finished, thick and drying in the sun. Shattered walls riddled with mortar holes stood not far from where we were. He handed me a shovel. I held it, not sure what to do. In my four trips to Afghanistan, I realized, I had never given anything back to the people who had told me their stories, offered their hospitality, shared their lives and often tears. I took what they had given to me and left for the next story. I thought about that. Then I pushed the shovel into the mud.

As I worked beside him, I thought about Khalid and his father, Aziz. Just twenty-four hours earlier we'd spent the afternoon together in Aziz's hardware store. The three of us stood behind the front counter and drank orange Fanta, escaping the oven-heat of Kabul. Khalid should have been home celebrating his four-year wedding anniversary with his wife. But she was pregnant and grumpy, and he was tired from work and avoiding her. So we drank our Fanta and took a break from the day and our lives.

Khalid's marriage had been arranged by his parents just as their marriage had been arranged by their families. Khalid ran away to Pakistan to get out of it, but his father tracked him down and brought him back.

One evening I dropped by Khalid's house and saw him with his wife in their garden. They were laughing. They had two daughters. I wanted to believe Khalid had found a way to love his wife.

"The Taliban was in power when I was married so my wedding was very quiet," Khalid recalled as we stood in his father's shop slouched against the front counter. "No music. If the Taliban hears music, they will take the husband to jail for ten days. After ten days the husband can go on his honeymoon."

He stopped talking, his mouth sagging into a pout like that of a child. He was thirty years old but retained the face of a boy. However, he was as stocky as a bear with hands that could swallow mine. Aziz, on the other hand, had a lean build and a well-trimmed black beard, and when he was angry his blue eyes stared down whoever had crossed him.

I looked at them both, surprised how Khalid had lapsed into the present tense. I assumed it was more difficult than I could imagine for him to believe the Taliban were gone. He had served six days in jail for trimming his beard.

"It was a very quiet time under the Taliban," Khalid said. "You forgot how to talk to people because you never went out. If the mullahs saw people on the street, they beat them for not being in the mosque."

A customer walked in, greeted the three of us, and began sorting through spark plugs. After a few minutes he left without buying anything. I listened to the slap of his sandals on the sidewalk, and then I heard nothing more.

Khalid began talking again about the Taliban, but Aziz interrupted him. He had his own arrest story to tell. During the Taliban years Aziz and his brother worked for a Japanese aid organization that cleared mines. One day a member of the Taliban came by their office. He said he wanted one of the radio antennas they used on their cars. Aziz said the antennas were not his to give away. Four minutes later he was arrested. He spent eight hours in jail. He asked what he had done. He was told nothing other than he would be killed.

The Taliban official in charge of the jail allowed him to call his employer. Aziz told his employer he had a problem. His employer spoke to the Taliban official and agreed to give him an antenna. After he hung up the phone, the official told Aziz he had killed a hundred people. You will be number 101, he said. Aziz told him he had a family to support. He worried all day that he might die until the antenna was delivered and the Taliban released him.

When his father stopped speaking, Khalid reached over and squeezed his shoulder. I did not know how to react and just stood there and looked away to give them both a moment together. Sometimes I wish I had come to Kabul when the Taliban ruled so I could put in perspective the stories I heard about the regime. I have tried and tried, but I can't comprehend what it must have been like.

"It was a very bad time," Khalid said. "We were always afraid of the knock on the door."

In Gardez the man with the house had no stories to tell. Or, I should say, he most likely did but I could not speak Dari, the language of northern Afghanistan, and he had only a few words of English.

We worked in silence, smiling at each other from time to time, slopping mud on the wall and patting it flat with our shovels. After a while we took off our shoes and worked barefoot. When we needed a break, we sat in the shade offered by trees near a creek and drank with our hands the water spilling over stones. We looked at each other and rolled our eyes at the heat and laughed. Then we got up and started again.

Khalid and Aziz had opposed my traveling to Khost. Khalid said because I had never lived in fear inside my own country, had not felt threatened by my own people, I did not appreciate the risk I was taking leaving the relative safety of Kabul. I had the self-confidence of my inexperience.

"Times are still bad here," he said. "You should know that. People don't like this government because they say the Americans control it. The south is very violent. The east is very violent. No one in my office wants to go there. There is no security. The women are like prisoners. They still wear the burka. I take my two little girls to the zoo. I get them out of the house to see the city. They are not locked inside. When they are older, I will let them choose their life. I will let them choose a love marriage, not an arranged marriage."

Aziz rolled his eyes. He did not like the Taliban, but he gave them credit for upholding traditions of faith and marriage and roles of men and women. He had three daughters and he allowed none of them outside without a burka.

Khalid ignored his father.

"I want to show you something," he said to me.

He reached into his pocket for a Thuraya phone. His office had ordered six thousand Thurayas at $2,500 apiece, but they could not use them because too many UN personnel were afraid to work in the villages outside of Kabul. They refused to leave their offices and therefore had no need for the Thurayas.

When he finished talking, Khalid cursed and tossed his phone on the counter.

"This is very expensive," Aziz said, picking up the phone.

"I don't care," Khalid said.

Aziz frowned. He did not want Khalid to create trouble. He should be happy to have a job. He should be happy to be alive.

"At least the UN pays you better than I did," I said.

Khalid looked at me and then leaned back and laughed.

"That's true."

"Go to your wife," I told him.

"Yes, I should go. You know *National Geographic*?"

"Of course."

"I was watching it on satellite television. A man lived with a lion for twelve months. Twelve months. Imagine. By the time he left he had tamed the lion. I used to think Afghanistan was like the lion. It would be tamed. I don't think that anymore."

Khalid stood up, and we shook hands and hugged. Aziz offered me a ride to my hotel. I sat in his car and looked at the pale mountains rising above the outskirts of the city, the same mountains I'd drive through to Gardez.

I worked on the wall until late afternoon. Then I had to leave, find a place to stay overnight, and return to Kabul in the morning. I explained this even though I knew the man would not understand. However, I felt compelled to tell him anyway because I did not want to just walk away. I had enjoyed his company despite the absence of conversation. Giving him my shovel, I pointed toward the city and made walking motions with my fingers to indicate I was leaving. He nodded and we smiled and shook hands. I didn't look back to see if he had resumed working.

On the bus the next morning, I thought of Khalid and Aziz and how they had withstood the Taliban, damaged in one way or another but still here, and I thought of the man and his incomplete house and the remains of blasted walls around it. The ruined homes, what remained upright but beyond repair, had survived bullets and bombs. I stared out my window and wondered how long my section of wall would last, my small mark upon the land.

Service with a Smile

BOBBY BRIGGS

"I've got a story," I said. "It's a war story." It was late October 2014, and except for my friends Josh-Wade and Lizzie, I'd just met everybody at the restaurant either that Sunday morning for brunch or earlier that weekend in Baton Rouge for the Ole Miss game. Jared, Sydnie, Maggie, Chad, and I had ordered the bottomless mimosas and Bloody Marys. I was two, maybe three, mimosas deep, and I cannot remember if I had mentioned before now that I was in the army.

I rarely tell war stories, but sometimes, when the moment feels right, or the liquor loosens my gums, one slips out. I usually keep the stories light, like the time a baby goat ran onto my helicopter during an exfil, or my first night in Afghanistan when I drew my gun on a Taliban mouse, or the time I pulled off an elaborate prank advertising a Justin Bieber concert with opening acts from Rascal Flatts and Sean Kingston. I'd even told Josh-Wade a couple war stories while we were running at Ole Miss as a method of distracting him from the discomfort. I'd never told this particular story before, and, looking back, Sunday brunch with strangers might not have been the most opportune moment.

Even though Ole Miss had suffered their first loss of the season the night before, this had been a great weekend. Sydnie, Lizzie's sorority sister when they were undergrads at LSU, and her husband, Jared, hosted us. Back home in Oxford my wife, Jaime, was up all night with three-year-old twin boys in the throes of ear infection season. While she was tending to coughing fits and low-grade fevers three days after her birthday, I was enjoying one of Jared's chocolate margaritas, complete with chocolate straw, concocted in his lime-green Jimmy Buffett Margarita Machine.

When Josh-Wade had told me we would be staying with Lizzie's sorority sister, I had pictured a weekend full of the same fake smiles and wealthy sense of entitlement that permeates Ole Miss's sorority row. Josh-Wade, a native of Saskatoon, Saskatchewan, embodies everything one desires in a Canadian: bearded, thick, overly friendly; one could easily imagine him standing in the middle of a river, shirtless and hairy, taking a bite out of a salmon he had just pulled from the water with his bare hands. He and Lizzie started dating at Ole Miss. Lizzie, an olive-skinned Vietnamese American with a perfectly round face, soft brown eyes, and a disarming smile, has the tendency to zone out of a conversation and think about, literally, nothing.

Sydnie was refreshingly down to earth, and Jared had a sharp wit and a way of making you feel like you were always in on the joke. I knew Jared was a keeper when he joined Josh-Wade and me in our rendition of Taylor Swift's "Shake It Off" while walking across LSU's campus. In fact, he had to carry us through the parts where the lyrics get tricky. In addition to taking us out for the best pulled-pork sandwich I've ever eaten, Sydnie and Jared introduced us to their guilty pleasure: *Baggage,* a dating show hosted by Jerry Springer that reveals each potential suitor's "baggage" in painfully awkward rounds of self-admission. Only later would I realize the irony behind the story I was about to tell and the TV show *Baggage.*

On the far end of the brunch table that Sunday were Chad and Maggie. Maggie was tall and pretty in the traditional sense with straight brown hair and high cheekbones. She, like Lizzie and Sydnie, was funny, grounded, and easy to talk to. Chad was not. Chad, as Maggie hinted the night before, had a bit of a gambling/drinking problem. Instead of meeting Maggie at our tailgate as planned, Chad joined his old buddies for an all-night bender. Chad was still drunk at brunch, and his blood-shot eyes, three-day stubble, and slurred speech reminded me of the guy my mom almost married, Earl, who lived with us when I was in elementary school and made over $3,000 a month at an office supply store, a fact Earl brought up many times while giving his inebriated *Work hard in school* speech.

Brunch was the perfect way to end the weekend before getting back on the road with Josh-Wade and Lizzie. It was a clear, sunny day, perfect flying weather. We sat on the patio at two metal tables of unequal height. I was the seventh wheel. I sat on the corner.

I could see myself becoming good friends with everyone at the table except Chad. I felt like I had known them since high school. The conversation was such that I felt comfortable and in an element I had not experienced since I was in Afghanistan the year before. Maybe that, too, fostered a false sense of camaraderie with my brunchmates as the girls were sharing funny sorority memories, and all of us were enjoying making fun of our waiter's bowl cut and dark sunken eyes as he struggled to remember drink and food orders.

"My guess is he's on Molly," Josh-Wade said.

"No way. Have you looked at his eyes? Definitely meth," Sydnie said.

"Either way, he's not going to last long at this job," Lizzie said. She was right. Portico would be closed down within a year, and if he wasn't fired, I'm pretty sure our waiter contributed to its demise.

My chair was the only one without shade from the sun, which may have assisted the alcohol in loosening my inhibitions and ability to gauge the mood of the table. I had just housed a four-story brunch burger stacked with a sausage patty, Black Angus beef, two fried eggs, bacon, three kinds of cheese, and dressed with a special sauce that I'm convinced was made from unicorn blood.

Our mathematically challenged waiter had finally delivered another round of mimosas, Bloody Marys, and a second incorrectly totaled check for Josh-Wade and Lizzie. Bringing the checks, we guessed, was a hint that we were probably on our last round of not-really-bottomless drinks. Nobody, except Chad, looked ready to leave. Josh-Wade was trying to explain simple addition and subtraction to the waiter, so with everyone's attention partially divided I offered the story.

"As far as I know, I've had four RPGs fired at me. Well, not me, as a person, but at my helicopter. But it should have been five, maybe six. This is about one of those times that it should have been me." I put my unused silverware on my plate and pushed it away. "I flew the Chinook helicopter, which is the big one with two rotor blades" (I spun my pointer fingers in the air about shoulder-width apart) "that looks like a giant green penis." Maggie chuckled.

I heard Josh-Wade tell the waiter that he'd overcharged them ten dollars as Josh-Wade pointed to the total on the receipt with a pen. The waiter bent at the waist and squinted at the numbers that befuddled him. Maggie was on the other end of the table and leaned forward to hear me better. Sydnie and Jared were on my right and turned in their chairs to face me. Chad stared at a wooden post, or the sky, or a future with multiple DUIs, broken relationships, and cirrhosis of the liver. I reached for a napkin and one of the pens the waiter left with our checks.

"Okay, so I'm a picture person," I said. I drew for them a rudimentary map of Afghanistan. On this map I scribbled some triangles diagonally across the country to represent the Hindu Kush Mountains. I pointed to the western border with Iran, the eastern border with Pakistan, and the northern border with various other -stans: Turkmenistan, Uzbekistan, Tajikistan, Kazakhstan, Kyrgyzstan, and maybe some other -stans. I flipped the napkin over and drew the border between Afghanistan and Pakistan. "This is where I worked."

I drew some more triangle mountains to show the Kunar River Valley, the gateway to the Hindu Kush, that runs north-south along the Pakistan border. I drew a dot at the southern end of the valley. "This is Jalalabad Airfield, or JBAD. This is where I lived. Twenty-five miles north is a city called Asad-abad, or ABAD. We normally refuel here before and after we go into the Pech River Valley." I drew a line perpendicular to the Kunar River Valley from ABAD to the edge of the napkin to represent the Pech. "This is a bad, bad place. Have any of you seen the movie *Restrepo*?"

"No, but I've heard of it," Jared said as Sydnie and Maggie shook their heads slowly. Chad pulled on his face.

"It's a super-powerful movie and really emotional," I said.

Sydnie shook her head rapidly. "Sydnie can't watch movies like that," Jared said. Sydnie shook her head faster.

"Well, the four RPGs launched at me, and the other one that should have hit me, came from somewhere in the Pech. Also, this story starts after we had just finished a resupply mission in the Pech."

I pointed to a spot on the Pakistan border east of ABAD. "This is Ghaki Pass, and it's a known Taliban border crossing point."

"Okay." I put the pen on the napkin and pushed it a little closer to the center of the table. I took another drink of my mimosa. "Like I said, we had just left the Pech, and we landed at ABAD to refuel. We had one last mission before heading home. We were supposed to take approximately thirty Afghan National Army (ANA) soldiers and a pallet of water up to Ghaki Pass."

I told them that a Chinook has thirty-three seats, but in an emergency can carry more. The average Chinook, combat loaded, weighs just over 30,000 pounds, and a pallet of water weighs 8,000 pounds. A Chinook can carry a max load of 50,000 pounds, including the weight of the helicopter. An average American soldier, fully loaded, weighs about 250 pounds, but when they are Afghani, we change that to 175 pounds for planning. One Chinook could easily carry a pallet of water and thirty Afghanis unless we are operating at high altitudes.

I was flying with Rob. He was the air mission commander that night, and I liked flying with him because he was one of our best pilots. Our call sign was Lift One.

"Looks like only half the PAX are here," Rob announced over the radio to Lift Two, the other Chinook helicopter on the mission. "It doesn't make sense for both of us go to up to Ghaki. Since I planned it, I'll take it." Lift Two had already hooked up to the fuel hoses so they didn't respond. Rob was a muscular country boy from Nebraska with a thick Midwest accent. He had a sharp wit, bic-shaved head, legs, and chest, and, as the company's safety officer, was averse to taking part in anything he hadn't planned himself.

Rob switched frequencies and called the Apache helicopters to let them know our plan. "We're just gonna grab a splash of gas and hook up this load of water," Rob said. The Apaches, who were our escorts/bodyguards, didn't need to refuel, so they were circling above Asadabad City, probably looking for someone to kill. "Which one of you gunships will be joining us?" Rob asked.

"Lift One, this is Gun One, it'll be us," the voice said over the internal frequency.

"Great, Gun Two can't see shit anyway," Rob said. He tapped my right shoulder with the back of his left hand and grinned.

"Fuck you, Rob, I can *see* that you need to go to the gym more often," Gun Two said.

"Shit, I'm heading to the gym after this mission if you ain't a bitch."

"Oh, I'll be there, watching you tear the shit out of that elliptical."

"Oh, yeah, I forgot, you only lift lats. You know, friends don't let friends skip leg day," Rob said.

"Shit, Rob. We ain't friends."

I was smiling at the exchange and monitoring the gauges in our cockpit when an infrared illumination round lit up the sky above Ghaki. I leaned forward to look at the bright light, which hung in the air like a star for 120 seconds before fading into the darkness. Ghaki was more than a mile away, and a smaller mountain obstructed my view of the pass itself. The moon wasn't out, so when another illumination round lit up over Ghaki, it revealed the dark mountains that rose all around us, casting long shadows along the valley floor. Rob didn't have his night-vision goggles down, so he couldn't see the infrared illum rounds.

"Hey, Rob, someone's shooting illum rounds over Ghaki," I said.

Rob flipped his goggles down and looked out my window. He got on the radio and called ABAD control to find out what was happening. After a few moments, ABAD control got on the radio to tell us that both rounds sent over Ghaki came from the howitzers at a nearby U.S. base, FOB JOYCE, because they'd heard reports of movement in the area.

I noticed that Jared cocked his head a little when I mentioned the report of movement in the area and figured I needed to explain. I told everyone at the brunch table that Ghaki Pass, until three days earlier, had been manned by a three-letter agency and a small contingent of Afghan special forces. As part of the long-term plan to transfer ownership of Afghanistan's security to Afghanistan's forces, Ghaki had been handed over to Afghan control. A fifteen-man squad of ANA soldiers was left to guard the pass until we could drop reinforcements the next night. Weather had kept us down, and tonight would be the first time we could attempt the resupply.

Jared gave an understanding nod.

"Hey, Guns, you guys see anything up there?" Rob asked.

"It's hard to tell from here, and FOB JOYCE isn't announcing their rounds, so I don't feel like getting much closer," Gun One said.

"Well, I'm not goin' up there to get an illum round shot up my ass," Rob said. "Let me make some calls."

Rob called ABAD control for an update, to which ABAD responded, "Wait One." Rob cursed to himself and pulled out the Blue Force Tracker, a moving map that allows us to send text messages to friendlies (blue forces) all over the country, and sent a message to our Tactical Operations Center (TOC). After approximately fifteen minutes of sending messages back and forth, our boss, Lieutenant Colonel Von Wonderbach (which we shortened to Lieutenant Colonel V), made the call to cancel the mission and ordered us to head home.

"Hell, yeah," Rob said. "Let's get out of here before they change their minds."

ABAD and JOYCE were pissed when we told them that our boss ordered us home. They tried to play the guilt card and told us that the ANA troops up there were black on water and weather looked bad for tomorrow.

"Sorry, ABAD control, I want to help them out, but our squadron commander ordered us to head home, and I'm not in the business of ignoring orders from superior officers," Rob said.

"Roger, but our brigade commander is telling us to make this mission happen," ABAD said.

"Well, this sounds like a discussion that needs to take place above our pay grade," Rob said. "We'll see you guys tomorrow."

ABAD didn't respond.

Rob turned to me. "Take us home, Captain."

"Roger." I grabbed the controls, called for departure, and eased the bird off the ground, being careful not to overfly the artillery. JOYCE sent another illum round over Ghaki. "I wonder what's going on up there?"

"Hell if I know, but I'm not on the schedule tomorrow, so it's not my problem."

Sydnie looked shocked by Rob's reaction, and I felt the need to defend Rob's statement. "Rob did care," I said. "He was all talk. If he had known what was going to happen, we never would have left."

I told them that I wasn't on the schedule the next night either, but something about Lieutenant Colonel V's decision to cancel the mission didn't sit right. He rarely, if ever, took the decision out of the hands of the pilots. I remember feeling like we didn't get the full story behind the decision, and when we got back to the TOC, Lieutenant Colonel V pulled Rob and me to the side and asked if we had received any pressure to ignore his orders.

"Just the normal bitchin'," Rob said. "Nothing unusual, sir." I nodded in agreement. The whole exchange at ABAD did seem odd, but ground units were always trying to convince us to do one or two more things while they had us on hand. "Good," Lieutenant Colonel V said, rubbing his right fist into his left palm. "Just so we're clear, you're my guys, and I have full authority of the aircraft under my command." I had never seen Lieutenant Colonel V so spun up. I could tell he wanted to say something about what had set him off, but he was too professional to talk about anyone behind his or her back.

The battle captain didn't share this virtue. As soon as Lieutenant Colonel V walked out of the TOC toward his office, the battle captain told us that the ground force commander, Colonel Pompas, had ripped into Lieutenant Colonel V because his pilots (Rob and I) were a bunch of pussies who were scared to fly. Colonel Pompas was one rank higher than Lieutenant Colonel V, and his bullying tactic backfired when Lieutenant Colonel V referred to the standard operating procedure (SOP) that grants the aviation commander full authority over the aircraft in his fleet.

"That's why Lieutenant Colonel V is the best boss I've ever had," Rob said.

I nodded in agreement. Lieutenant Colonel V was also the kind of boss who encourages every soldier to have something, besides work, that they can escape into to keep their sanity. This escape could take many forms: video games, Skype with family, reading. For me it was running.

After we finished the flight debrief with the battle captain, turned in our gear, and made our way to the B-Huts to change, Rob went to the gym and I hit the road, alone. While I was in Afghanistan, I ran, a lot. It was my release. I ran because I could be alone with my thoughts. It was how I processed my day, my experiences, my emotions. It's how I forgot.

The next afternoon I woke up earlier than normal. We were at the end of summer, and even though I had lofted my plywood bed to sit right next to the air conditioner, I still woke up every day encased in sweat and a light coat of dust. I showered, changed, and made my way across the runway to the company CP.

I have fond memories of JBAD, but the landscape was ugly. Besides the freshly paved runway, JBAD was all dirt and rock. JBAD was hot. Even the wind was hot. One of my guys said it was "like sitting in an oven while someone pointed a blowdryer at you." That's probably why I always ran at night—that, and an irrational fear of snipers.

We only kept one crew on day shift, which always included our maintenance test pilot, Steve. Steve was our most experienced pilot with over twenty years in the army, and this was probably his fifth or sixth deployment. Steve had made a deal with our company commander that he would keep the birds in the air as long as he didn't have to go out on any missions. Steve used to be an infantryman, and he was looking forward to submitting his retirement packet when we redeployed around Thanksgiving. Steve was tall, thin, and always smiling. He could talk to anyone, and he had been known to start a conversation at lunch and still be in the same seat, in the same conversation, at dinner. He had even befriended the locals. They were building us a new Chinook parking ramp when he brought them ice-cold Gatorades on a scorching day. Steve was often invited into their work tents for tea, and I had the pleasure of joining him a few times when I was on day shift. Nobody questioned Steve's new friendships until the time that Hussein, the engineer, brought Steve a traditional Afghani outfit that Steve wore to work the next day. That ruffled a few feathers, mainly Rob's.

I started every day by finding Steve and getting an update on maintenance. I also really enjoyed talking to him. But that day Steve was not in the CP or the maintenance office. On my way back across the runway to our ramp to look for someone on the day crew, I popped into the TOC.

"Hey, Beau, you seen Steve or any of the day hookers?"

I asked. *Hookers* is a term used when referring to Chinook crews, mainly because of the large hooks under our helicopters used to carry heavy loads.

"Day crew's on the ramp, and Steve's on his way back from Ghaki," Beau said.

"Ghaki?"

"Oh shit, you haven't heard?"

"Heard what?"

"Pull up a chair."

Beau told me that after Rob and I went to bed last night, Colonel Pompas went nuts. He went over the head of the aviation brigade commander to the general and demanded that Ghaki get resupplied immediately. The general ordered Bravo Company (one of the other Chinook companies in our brigade) to complete the resupply, a leg they added to another mission they were already flying to Paruns.

"They went to Ghaki last night?" I asked. "No, during the day," Beau said.

"The day? Did anybody tell Bravo what was going on last night?" I tried to remember if I mentioned the illum rounds and the reported movement around Ghaki to the battle captain last night during the post-mission debrief. I must have. Why wouldn't I?

"Just wait, it gets better." Beau clicked on his computer a few times and brought up the mission card and map for the Bravo Company mission. "Notice anything unusual?"

I examined the mission card. "They don't have any Apaches," I said.

"Yep, and their sister ship was a Blackhawk." Beau often criticized Blackhawks for their weaker engines and insufficient firepower. Not that Chinooks have significant firepower either, but our engines did make us useful in Afghanistan's higher terrain.

"So what happened?" I asked.

"You know that cement bunker that sits behind Ghaki's LZ?" Beau asked.

"Yeah."

"Some Haji was sitting in there with an RPG and sent one into the back of the Chinook."

I sat back in my chair and put my hands over my head. "Is everybody okay?"

"The computer added the bill incorrectly, so I had to manually override it to make it right," the waiter said.

"No, the computer was right. You still overcharged us ten dollars," Josh-Wade said. Lizzie put her hand on Josh-Wade's arm. He took a deep breath and exhaled slowly.

"Me and the manager both looked at it. The only way to fix it was to manually override it."

"So you're telling me that you *and* the manager looked at this, and it's still wrong?" Josh-Wade asked. "Look . . ."

Josh-Wade continued to explain the error. I noticed Sydnie was staring at her empty plate. I have no idea what Chad was doing.

I told them that I would later learn that the fifteen ANA soldiers guarding the pass until reinforcements arrived had run out of bottled water within the first twenty-four hours. As a result, a few of them went to a nearby town to get water from the well. Someone tipped off the local Taliban leader, who took the opportunity to capture Ghaki Pass and set up an ambush.

"I have spent many late-night runs reflecting on Bravo's mission and my mission the night before," I said. "If Lieutenant Colonel V hadn't ordered us to come home, that would have been us on Ghaki. I couldn't understand why Bravo Company took the mission without asking us why we turned it down." I told the table that I called my best friend Will, who was the battle captain when Bravo Company took off, and asked him what he knew. Will was beating himself up because he thought it was his fault for not looking into the mission more fully when he came on shift, and I tried to tell him it wasn't his fault.

We learned a lot more when Steve got back from Ghaki. He gave us his account and showed us the video he took as part of the Downed Aircraft Recovery Team (DART).

The next night Rob and our most experienced crewmembers had to slingload the downed Chinook back to JBAD, and before the Aircraft Accident Investigation Team could secure the bird Steve and I snuck on to look at the damage. The first thing I noticed was the blood.

"It looks like melted crimson crayons," I said. Blood had adhered to the ramp and the seats. Small pools had collected around rivets and d-rings, giving the impression the blood wasn't fully dry.

"I figured they would have washed it out by now," Steve said.

"There's more than I expected."

Steve stood on the ramp, faced outward, and looked up. He moved his arm in a large arc to show me where the shrapnel had sprayed into the hydraulic and fuel lines directly above the ramp. "It's a perfect circle," he said, still amazed. "I figure Sam was standing right here when it hit him." He showed me the path of the charge that tumbled toward the front of the helicopter seeking out another victim. I still had questions.

I kept seeking out information because I needed to know if anyone blamed Rob and me for not taking the mission. I know I did. It should have been our bird up there. It was supposed to be our mission. Could we have done anything to change what happened? Did I tell the battle captain about the illum rounds? I'm certain I did, I think.

The waiter hadn't been back for a while. I remember Josh-Wade was staring at me intently, and I think everyone at the table, Chad included, was waiting for me to continue. I prefaced my next statement by saying that since I wasn't there, some of the events are speculation. However, I have done my best to gather the most complete and accurate record possible.

I glimpsed our waiter walking onto the patio with another receipt.

"The next time I was in Bagram, I found the pilots and got their version of the story. Spotts didn't really want to talk about it, but Astorga, who we called Astro and sported the sickest moustache in the Brigade, indulged me.

"Spotts and Astro arrived at Ghaki in the morning. They had about twenty passengers onboard, and they had just dropped the water. Nobody had told the flight crew anything about what happened the night before, so the pilots and crew were treating it like any routine drop-off. When Spotts set his aircraft down on the LZ, the ramp gunner lowered the ramp to let the passengers off. There was no sense of urgency as the passengers walked off the ramp. In fact, one of the interpreters walked back onto the helicopter to grab a bottle of water. As he turned to walk back off the ramp, a Taliban fighter raised from the cement bunker just off the south end of the LZ and launched an RPG into the back of the Chinook.

"The RPG hit the interpreter in the stomach, splitting him in half. I don't know if I ever learned the interpreter's real name, but Steve named him Sam. The rocket exploded when it hit Sam, and the shrapnel of the rocket sprayed in an arc at the ramp, disabling the aircraft. The concussion of the blast blew the doors off the helicopter. The cabin was instantly filled with smoke and fire. The charge from the RPG continued through Sam's body and found its next target, the left door-gunner, Sergeant Patterson, and took his legs.

"Spotts tried to take off. He pulled an armpit full of power" (I made the motion of grabbing the collective at my left side and yanking it up the side of my body), "but because the hydraulic lines were gone, the bird only screamed in place. Almost instantly they began to take small arms fire from the opposite ridge.

"What happened next, probably due to the chaos of battle, is unclear. Eventually, the Blackhawk was able to land and carry the flight crew to an aid station while the ground forces pulled security over the fallen angel.

"A short time later Steve led the DART team to the site to evaluate the damage and assess whether or not the aircraft was recoverable. He told us that they started taking fire from another ridgeline as soon as they landed on the LZ. By this time some air force and navy bombers were overhead, and they dropped a 250-pound bomb on the bad guys. The blast and con-cussion was so great, though, that Steve thought the bombers were accidentally aiming at them. The small-arms fire contin-ued and the bombers dropped a bigger bomb, a 500-pounder, on the same ridge. This silenced the enemy for a while.

"Steve turned on his video camera to begin the assessment. When Steve got to the ramp he saw Sam. Nobody had taken the time to cover Sam up, and his legs were still lying on the ramp. His torso had been thrown onto the seats to the left, and his head was hanging off the edge. 'I tried to cover him,' Steve said. 'It seemed more respectful.' The blanket didn't cover all of the body, and when Steve showed us the video of his assessment he didn't warn us that half of Sam's torso and his feet were still visible. It looked like a magic trick."

I started to notice everybody at the brunch table becoming uneasy with the story after this statement. But it was too late now.

"When it was all over, the damage, with the exception of Sam and Sergeant Patterson, wasn't really all that bad. Both pilots had concussions; the ramp gunner, Sergeant Allen, had burns on his face and shrapnel wounds; Specialist Huber took shrap-nel in his thigh that the doctors left in place because they said removing it would cause more damage; Sergeant Patterson lost both of his legs; and two infantry escorts, a captain and a staff sergeant, I think, were wounded. Sam was the only per-son that died, but if he hadn't walked back onto the bird for a bottle of water the RPG would have travelled all the way to the cockpit, killing both pilots and both door-gunners. He actu-ally saved their lives. He was an involuntary hero."

"I'm not really sure how to end this story. I guess that's it," I said.

Sydnie was still staring at her plate.

Maggie gave an uneasy smile.

Jared filled the silence by saying something funny about being glad he was done eating.

Josh-Wade had finally fixed the issue with his receipt.

"Sorry," I said. And I was, actually, sorry.

I could tell the story didn't go over well. The mimosas were wearing off, and I felt like I was on an island. Lizzie looked at me with eyes that said, "What did you just do?"

"Cool," Chad said.

We said our goodbyes, and Josh-Wade, Lizzie, and I walked with Sydnie and Jared out to the parking lot. I apologized to Sydnie and Jared again for bringing down the brunch. Sydnie tried to assure me that it was fine. "It was a good story," she said. "A little gory." She shrugged her shoulders and tilted her head. "But I enjoyed it."

I think Jared said something about how it is good to be reminded that a world like that exists. I wanted to change the subject. I wanted to run to the car and leave Baton Rouge. I think I said something about the Saints' game.

When I got home to Savannah, Georgia, in 2010, shortly after missing Thanksgiving, I didn't want to be around anyone except Jaime and our two-and-a-half-year-old daughter, Meredith. But even that was a difficult adjustment.

I dreaded weekends because it meant I had to wait two whole days before I could get back to work and be around my guys again. Don't get me wrong, I was happy to be home, but I felt more comfortable around these guys. I didn't have post-traumatic stress disorder, but I couldn't cope with people, their questions, or the way they placed importance on trivial topics like the *American Idol* controversy behind Scotty defeating Lauren. *It doesn't matter.*

I remember, vividly, the moment that I realized I was home, when I could finally relax. It happened more than a week after I had returned, and it came the day after a balloon popping on the neighbor's mailbox caused me to duck and spin violently in my driveway.

"Is everything okay?" Jaime had asked.

"Yeah, I just dropped something," I'd lied.

I woke up early the next morning, about four o'clock, and snuck out of the house to go for a run. I was still fond of running in the dark. It was an unusually warm and humid December morning, and I remember a fog had settled in the trees that lined the jogging trail in our neighborhood. I was about two miles into my run when I felt my shoulders relax. Before then, I wasn't even aware that I had been pinching my shoulders in a raised position. How long had they been like that? I was finally able to run without fear. I was overcome with a sense of relief and tears filled my eyes, blurring my vision. I could feel the warm lines streaming down my face when I blinked. I started to laugh. I laughed and cried. I ran.

I've been in Oxford almost two years now, and I still don't feel welcome in my church. I don't like to stay at a Grove tent for too long at football games because I'm afraid of what I might say if caught in conversation. At English Department functions, I try to find a seat that faces no more than one or two people. I get nervous around poets. They make me feel naked and transparent, like they know my secrets. I'm always looking for ways out of conversations with women, and with most men.

For a person who uses stories as a way to connect with people, being unable to share my experiences with those closest to me prevents me from fully integrating. I feel, at times, like I'm living a double life: there's the face I show in public and the one that wants to remain detached, filtering life through the lenses of apathy and cynicism. I think that's why I'm constantly reading people's reactions, making sure I'm not exposing too much. It's exhausting. Even Jaime has said that sometimes she doesn't feel like she knows the real me anymore.

Looking back at brunch in Baton Rouge, I misread the moment. I thought I had an opportunity to connect with these people by bringing them into my world. I was wrong. If our lives are a collection of the stories we carry, what does it mean to exist in a world where you cannot share them?

I don't know what compelled me to tell that story in Baton Rouge. I am not sure what reaction I was expecting. Maybe I was just confirming my suspicion that I will never be able to fully articulate what war was like for me.

And yet I wonder: do these experiences need to be shared? Maybe Jared's wrong; maybe people don't need to be reminded of that world's existence. I'm beginning to believe that war is like Vegas—*what happens here . . .*

So, I'll stick to the stories about goats and mice and everything nice; at least I won't ruin brunch.

The Man I Killed

BRIAN DUCHANEY

I woke up at 4:45 a.m. to take a shower and dress into my uniform, an old one from a couple of days ago that was hanging off the chair by my bookcase. All the starch was out of it and there were small grease stains visible on the pants. Sitting on my bed, I flipped through the TV to absent-mindedly watch the news while lacing up my boots, not bothering to polish them. I reached into my fridge and pulled out a half-full Gatorade from Monday night's basketball game, grimacing against the awkward tang of citrus and toothpaste. Groaning my way to my feet, I picked up and attached my pistol belt, shoving my sunglasses into one of the ammo pouches. The sun wasn't up yet, but it would be by the time I got back.

The side door clicked open as I made my way out to the parking lot toward the soft top Humvee that we kept in the lot for such missions. Opening the door, I threw my helmet on the passenger seat and sat down on the cool canvas seat, which was a bit soggy from the morning dew. The truck shuddered as the diesel engine whined, then finally turned over to a soft rumble. Once I shifted into drive, the truck rolled out of the barracks parking lot and lurched toward the mess hall.

I was early. I had enough time to walk through the kitchen, where soldiers in starched white cook's uniforms were preparing meals fifty servings at a time and transferring them into insulated olive-green plastic containers. Since the cooks weren't done getting everything ready, I walked across the waxed, burnt-orange-colored floor, past a row of ovens and stainless steel prep tables.

The double doors swung open wide as I entered the service line. Making my way over to the fifty-gallon coffee urn, I grabbed a white Styrofoam cup, filled it up (no sugar), and snapped on a lid. It was still only 5:30, so no one was in having breakfast yet. Looking around at the empty tables, I walked over to one of the mounted TVS to see some of the baseball highlights that were playing on ESPN. After seeing that the Red Sox had won a close game against the Blue Jays, I walked back through the serving line to the kitchen to wait for my soldier's breakfast.

After all seven food containers had been loaded into the back of my Humvee, I drove out of the mess hall onto Riva Ridge Loop and turned right onto Second Street. The sun was beginning to come up over the long hill in front of me, and I fumbled in my ammo pouch for my sunglasses. In my lane further up to the right, a platoon of soldiers was running down the street. All were in uniform: gray army T-shirts, black army shorts, fluorescent yellow safety belts. I couldn't hear what they were saying, but the familiar sounds of cadences were clearly recognizable. Passing the formation and the few stragglers, who were being motivated by higher ranking sergeants screaming for them to "get their ass up to the front," I took a sip from my coffee, being careful to avoid any bumps in the road, and continued down the street on my way toward the firing ranges.

After passing through the post gates, I crossed over Route 26 and made my way through the back entrance of the airfield. Beyond the chain-link fence that ran next to the road, the old water tower with its white-and-red checkerboard paint job could be seen rising above the trees. The red was rusty and looked more like a dark maroon, and I wondered how often they kept up with the painting. Continuing forward, past the large vehicle wash racks, I came to the end of the pavement. Crossing the bump in the road, I tilted my cup to avoid spilling coffee in my lap and passed a familiar sign. It was a white sign with red letters. It read simply: "DANGER—Live Fire Area."

Even though the trees cast long shadows on the road, I drove forty miles per hour instead of the posted ten, zigzagging around the corners and kicking up dirt, singing to myself, trying to stay entertained in lieu of any music. Back where the pavement began again on Range Road, I turned right, following the fence around the back of the airfield and behind the control tower, about a half mile from the main terminal. I crested a small hill and turned left to the mock-up that our unit built as a training simulator in place of a real Iraqi/U.S. base.

After the bright red gates (which I had previously bought at a tractor supply company in town) the road made right-angled paths preventing anyone from driving with too much speed. Entering the compound, I could see the dozen tents arranged two by six on plywood platforms that were in my inventory of supplies. They were supplies to me, but soon they would be home to another batch of soldiers who were preparing for war.

The setup of the field never ceased to amaze me. For the two weeks that soldiers spent out here, our unit maintained a realistic setting. Soldiers alternated pulling security at the perimeter of the compound twenty-four hours a day, even though we were still in New York. The soldiers didn't salute officers. The members of my unit and our sister unit, who were in charge of training, even played Muslim prayers over loud speakers five times a day. Every aspect of the field was meant to simulate the real thing. Soldiers were walking around, rifles slung over shoulders, muzzle down, readying themselves for the day by washing under portable showers and utilizing field latrines. Passing the water buffaloes, five-hundred-gallon capacity water coolers mounted on trailers, I turned right, passing the tents on my left, and up a hill toward the designated mess tent. I drove over the bumpy terrain of sand and roots and pulled up next to a skinny pine tree. I opened up my door and yelled over the noise of the Humvee to a young private: "Hey, can you guide me in close?" Because of the lack of a rear-view mirror, and the dim light of the morning, I wanted to make sure I could get close to the tent without any damage. Plus, it would make moving the meal a lot easier. I shifted into park, put on my soft cap, and stepped out into the sand.

"Good morning, Sergeant Adams. Breakfast is here."

Smiling, he said, "Aren't you supposed to have a helmet?"

"I do," I said, returning his smile. "It's on the front seat. Where do you want this stuff?"

"You can just leave it there. We'll have a couple of these guys move it."

I left the troops in the field eating their breakfast of eggs, bacon, oatmeal, and bread and made the twenty-minute ride back to post. I arrived near our company headquarters just in time to see the rest of my unit finishing up their stretching from the morning's scheduled run. I beeped the feeble horn of the Humvee, waving at everyone who was stuck doing PT. I turned left and drove the half-mile past the scattered rows of other barracks. They were two-story buildings with open floor plans that were shabbily converted and used as individual housing. Though the stairs and patios had been fixed, with either new pressure treated wood or dark stained pine, the buildings retained their aluminum siding. The buildings alternated powder blue, green, tan, and cream and included little carved signs out front that had names such as "Pine Ridge" or "Glen View." After securing the steering wheel with the long cable-and-steel padlock that was tucked under the seat, I walked across the parking lot and looked left at the horseshoe pits and putting green that lay inside the loop of the road. I thought to myself how bad the putting green was. It was rocky, and instead of the plush turf found at the golf course, it was just regular grass. The only difference was that there was a cup with a tilted flag sticking out of it. Seeing this, I made a mental note to try and get out of work early so I could go into town and play nine holes before dinner. I walked toward the side door, skipping up the steps. Once I got inside, I went back to my room and changed into one of my clean uniforms. I brushed off my boots, but I didn't bother to put any polish on them. I knew they'd only get dirty again. Before putting on my coat I went down the hall to shave and rinse the fine dust out of my hair that had blown into it while I was in the field.

I left my barracks again, this time feeling a little more professional and put-together. I got in my truck and drove over to the breakfast lodge. It was usually quieter than the larger mess halls on post, and, though the food was a little worse, it was easier to take something and leave. I toasted myself a bagel, wrapped it up in a paper towel, and walked back outside to my truck. My unit was just coming back from PT. I said hello to those who were close by. I got into my truck, rolled the windows down, and turned up the CD player. It was still before actual working hours. I decided I'd drive out to Dunkin' Donuts and pick up coffee for my office.

I got into the office at about 9:30 with coffee for Sergeant Major Harper and Lieutenant Colonel Donnelly. They insisted on giving me money, but I wouldn't take it. LTC Donnelly asked, "What are your plans for the day? We need to sit down and go over the unit list for the 208th. Will you be around?"

"I should be, ma'am," I replied. "I have to run into Watertown and pick up some lumber at Home Depot, then I have to pick up some paperwork. I should be back by twelve."

SGM Harper added, "Well, if you're coming back at twelve, would you pick me up a salad at Wendy's? I'll give you money when you get back."

It was moments like this that made me think of my service as a joke, probably because I knew I was safe. My role was support. Even though I had my bosses, I really didn't answer to anybody. If I were back later than expected, I wouldn't get in trouble if I told them I had gone to the mall to pick up a DVD. As long as I could be found when they needed me, I was okay. "No problem," I said. "Just call my cell phone and remind me, would you?"

It was about one in the afternoon when I got back to my office. SGM Harper was gone, so I put her salad in the refrigerator. I turned around and walked outside and across the gravel parking lot from my office to Matt's to beg some DVDS off him. I was tired from getting up early and I knew I'd feel guilty about leaving work early, so I decided to just waste some time at the office. I could clean out my desk. I could finally take care of the inventory of body armor that had been piled up on the conference table in my office. I turned the corner of the building and saw Corey's truck parked on the lawn outside. The grass still smelled sweet from when I had cut it the afternoon before. Cutting the grass was a nice escape from the office. It got me outside and I could listen to my iPod and still call it work.

I walked up the steps and pushed the door open, hearing the door scrape across the floor. I called out into the empty room, "Sergeant Ricci? Parker?"

"Yeah, we're out here."

I removed my beret and threw it on a table in Matt's office. It was cluttered with computer parts, wire snips, and cables. Grabbing a Styrofoam cup, I poured myself a cup of black coffee and walked out the side door to find them taking a cigarette break.

Matt was standing with one hand in his pocket, flicking his cigarette. Corey stood on the other side of the back steps with his beret in his hand, slowly rocking back and forth on his heels. Without interrupting their conversation, I grabbed a cigarette from Matt's pack on the railing and lit it, listening to them talk. I was standing on the wooden platform outside the door, looking down on Matt and Corey. Corey looked up at me and shook his head, noticing my puzzled look. Squinting from the sun that was coming over the roof of the building, he asked me, "Did Ricci tell you yet?"

"Tell me what? I just walked over here?"

"One of our guys got hit."

"What do you mean hit?"

Corey exhaled and said, "We lost one of the guys we sent over."

Matt continued, "One of the dudes we just sent over got fuckin' killed." His southern accent didn't have a trace of emotion. He was just stating a fact. Mark peppered his speech with swears the way a girl in high school says the word "like." Though he was thirty-eight, he still had chipmunk cheeks. These were emphasized by sunburn. Matt lit another cigarette using the remnant of the one he was finishing. He kept the new one in his mouth while he ground the ash off the old one, putting the butt into his pocket. Exhaling a fog of smoke, Matt said, "The guy didn't even get a chance to get his boots dirty." We talked for another twenty minutes or so. Corey's ringing cell phone interrupted our talk of what we guessed the possible consequences might be. I left Matt and walked back over to my building, completely forgetting why I went over there in the first place.

I spent most of the afternoon at my desk, surfing the internet for items to buy and following the email traffic that the unit was spreading about, confirming what we knew and speculating about what we didn't. There were emails about praying for CPT Alvarez's family. There was one from our commander about the loss of one of our soldiers, of reaffirming the mission of the unit, that we needed to carry on with business as usual. Every time the desktop flashed a new email reminder on the screen, it always continued to show the subject line as "CPT Alvarez." I sat at my desk, with my boots up on the mahogany and my hand moving the mouse about the screen, from websites back to the emails. For each new email that I read, the content shifted from everyone's personal opinion or insights, yet the subject line remained the same.

As I sat at my computer I thought back to last week, at all of the times I made a run for Corey when he couldn't get to something. We had roughly the same jobs. We dealt with the same people. The only difference was that he handled individual soldiers that would be lumped together, while I handled larger units, either coming from or going overseas. Lately it had been a lot of units coming home. I would get an email a few days in advance and usually meet a unit representative a few days before the unit arrived in order to coordinate transportation, appointment times, specific supplies, and sometimes awards. All I had to do was authorize what they needed, and that was it. For the most part I only dealt with people who were happy to be coming home. I heard about what soldiers planned to do. Where they were going. Stories they shared in the desert (we had one soldier who "lost" a uniform because of an "accident." He smiled when he simply said, "I had to go.") Most of all, I heard stories of the first thing they'd do when they got home. Drinking. Screwing. Sleeping. Just hanging out. I heard about futures after the war. Corey, on the other hand, dealt with soldiers who were heading out. He heard what people were leaving behind. He heard the sacrifices. I didn't realize the difference until I saw how hard he took the loss personally.

I began to feel guilty. I thought about one time when I helped out during issue procedures at the Central Issue Facility. I recalled a time when they were shorthanded, and, against regulations, I offered to go behind the counter to help speed up the process. It was Saturday and I knew the staff was working overtime to help us. Lisa, the manager of CIF, said it was no problem as long as her boss didn't see anything. I made my way around the long counter toward the stainless steel bins of uniforms. Facing the long rows of chairs filled with soldiers, I checked their equipment inventory, looked for the size uniforms they needed, and handed over the appropriately sized desert uniform: four tops and four bottoms. I usually didn't make eye contact. I remember, over the noise of soldiers talking and gear being thrown around, that I'd take the sheet, glance at the rank, address the soldier, and hand over his gear. "Hi, sir. Four Medium Regular tops. Four Medium Regular bottoms. One helmet cover, desert. Okay," I'd say, as I signed off on the issue sheet. "Try those on. If they fit, pack it up and slide down." It was like all the other processing I did. It was repetitive. I'd see the name, but never bother to connect it with a face.

I looked up toward the row of skinny gray lockers beside my desk, the type that resemble gym lockers at a YMCA. They were full of dents, scratched up, and mostly off balance. I had pictures of my nieces on the side facing me. While I looked up, I realized that I could pick up my phone and call them any time I wanted. I wasn't worried about a seven-hour time difference or, worse, the remaining months that I would have to wait to see them. I could take the time and drive home the five hours whenever I felt like going home. Looking back at my desk blotter, I saw a list I had made that afternoon of things I wanted to get done that day. None of it got done. All I'd really accomplished was picking up some packing boxes, getting myself coffee, and picking up some uniforms for Corey. I looked over my list, but I wasn't focused on it. Instead, I was trying to remember who CPT Alvarez was.

I couldn't remember him. The more I tried to picture him, the more the faces of others blurred together. He was just another person that blended into the other faceless soldiers that I ended up sending into harm's way. I thought about some of the people I got a chance to talk to. They were real, but they were all faceless. There was the one guy in his early thirties, slightly graying and bulging a little in the middle. He told me he got reprimanded for carrying around a "medic pack." It was nothing more than bandages and general first aid supplies, yet he got in trouble because he was handing out aspirin. He told me the only reason he had it was to help out the people around him. There was the young private who was too skinny and wore ugly brown military issue glasses. He was concerned about where he'd find cigarettes. There was another who told us of his eight kids, even though he wasn't much older than thirty-five. I spoke with taxi drivers, businessmen, teachers, lawyers, college students, stay-at-home moms, and people in all other walks of life. All of them had sacrifices to make. And all of them are a faceless blur.

I was snapped out of my daze around four when Lieutenant Colonel Donnelly called me into her office. She was sitting at her desk, leaning back in her desk chair with her hands buried in her red hair. I sat on the corner of the sergeant major's desk on the other side of hers. "What's up?"

"By now, I'm sure you've heard." She let out a soft sigh and raised her eyebrows, a sign I recognized as her trying to shake off fatigue. "I just came from a meeting with Colonel Wood, and first thing is we're not supposed to mention this to anybody. I don't know too much of what happened, but I'll fill you in when I do find out. I've got to go pick up my daughter from day care, so you can take off for the day. If you want, come in late tomorrow since you had chow duty this morning."

"Okay, ma'am. Thanks. Have a great night." I walked back to my desk and picked up my belongings before walking out to my truck for the evening. I looked at my computer and noticed I was still receiving emails about what happened. By now everyone knew what happened. Word gets around quickly when you have front-line communication.

We knew three days before the press got the word and the television stations started reporting about a "fragging" incident. "Fragging" is another piece of military slang. It's when a soldier kills a superior in the unit because of hate, jealousy, ill-will, or whatever reason someone could have for taking the life of someone on his own side. In this case the sergeant that killed CPT Alvarez wasn't even after him. CPT Alvarez, new to the country, had been getting briefed by his new CO in their billets. While the captain and the commander were talking, this sergeant decided to drop a grenade in the window. CPT Alvarez was killed his third day in Iraq. And I'm partly responsible for him getting there.

After leaving the office I drove back to the barracks. I walked inside, tired and worn out. The TV was on but it was silent, the volume turned down. Matt sat sideways in an armchair, still in uniform with a beer in his hand. Another person had his boots and coat off, but was lying on the couch, flipping aimlessly through the stations. I walked past them and went straight into my room. I changed out of my uniform and put on a pair of shorts and a T-shirt. Sandals. Keys. Wallet. After I changed I decided that I needed to go out. I didn't want to see a uniform, a pair of boots, or our dilapidated World War

II barracks. I put on my beat up Red Sox hat just so I wouldn't have to look at my close-cropped hair. I walked out of my room, pulled my door shut without locking it, turned right, and headed for the back door. Matt looked back over his shoulder toward me. He asked, "Hey, where ya headed?"

I paused to look over at the TV and then at Matt. "I just need to go out for a bit. I'll be back in a little while."

Matt was looking back toward the TV. "Alright, man. I'll be here. Smitty and I are probably gonna grill if you're gonna be around."

"Oh, okay. I'll be back by six." I walked across the floor toward the back door. I pushed the metal door open harder than I had anticipated, so that the handle swung into the metal railing outside, making a loud, echoing "ping."

Free-Falling Soldier

ALYSSA MARTINO

Ben slips out the sliding door to my balcony. His calloused hands grip two glasses filled with equal parts Newcastle beer and Woodchuck cider. I balance a plate of Brie and butterfly crackers on my right palm and follow him outside.

Across from my fifteenth-floor apartment is an office building. Its dark tinted windows reflect and warp us into different shapes: Ben, short and stout like a coffee mug, and me, curvy and complicated like a candlestick.

I set the plate down on a small black end table, glancing at Ben. The pale skin on his face is now freckled. A fresh buzz cut seems to push his ears forward. His feet inhabit clunky but durable brown boots that look as if they could use a good scrub in the sink. Ben hands me my drink, then takes a few large gulps of his own. I watch his Adam's apple bob in and out like a buoy at sea.

We sit down on two tiny lime green patio seats. Our silence is obvious as we sip and spread cheese, but whether there's nothing to say, or far too much, I do not know. Ben has been like an older brother to me since his mom dated my uncle, and we unofficially adopted him into our family. He is someone I could only ever love platonically, a very dear friend, yet today I find myself wanting to please him like a husband, to prove I've matured in the two years since we last saw one another.

Ben doesn't mention Afghanistan, the country he returned from last week. The previous night my uncle looked our soldier directly in the eye and asked, "What's it like over there?" Ben choked out one word: "Tribal." He is nothing like I remember him: comforting, wholesome, and wise. The brotherly figure who advised my sixteen-year-old self to be cautious around horny teenage boys; who delivered the news my aunt was dying of breast cancer; who, giddy and grinning, used to pile my younger cousins into a big minivan for ice cream runs. Now Ben's voice is monotone as he recounts tearing his ACL in Haiti playing football with some buddies. When he pours another drink his movements are robotic, as if someone had fused a flagpole to his spine. But I am careful not to judge; I know nothing of what Ben has experienced since enlisting.

Ben stands up and tips his nose over the balcony ledge, balancing on his combat toes.

"Don't freak out at this question," he says, ankles stretched, rising out of his shoes. "But do you ever wonder what it'd be like to just"—his voice slows—"jump?"

I cock my head and stare at him.

"Or not to jump, but to fall all that way?"

I, too, am now perched on my toes, peering down to the pavement, to the sea foam pool, to the inertia of the world below.

What about his next tour? Ben may return with far worse injuries than a torn ligament. Like our high-school class clown, he may not come home at all. I think about what I'd do: hang a yellow ribbon on my balcony—right near the plant Mom sent when I graduated college and moved 400 miles from home. I suddenly have the urge to toss it over the edge, to let those roots feel no weight but their own as they tumble to the earth below.

I don't really think Ben's going to jump. Not now. Not here. Probably not ever. But his question leaves me unsettled. I think of the newspaper headlines, the rising soldier suicide rate, what horrific things he might have witnessed abroad. My fingers fidget together, antsy, anxious bones on a loom.

And so I'll lie, reassuring him it's fine, it's normal, if only to curb his plan to free-fall straight back to Kandahar or Kabul.

"Sure," I tell Ben, faking a smile. "I've thought about falling. We all have."

A Sliver of Blue

PAUL VAN DYKE

The iPod in the lead Humvee played nothing but Irish music that morning. The playlist was organized by my lieutenant, Dan Kingsley. He sat in the passenger seat. Kingsley was a goofball with a spot-on Jerry Lee Lewis impersonation. He was built like a single solid muscle, and when he wore his glasses we called him Clark Kent. He was full-blooded Irish and had a shamrock tattooed between his shoulder blades. On his shoulder he wore a Ranger Tab, so he knew his shit backward and forward.

What I liked most about Kingsley was that he had no interest in becoming a career officer, so his decisions were never based on a need to cover his ass or rack up promotion points.

And the morning the Irish music played, Dan Kingsley saved my life.

With the sun still low on the eastern horizon of a cloudless late-summer sky, our Humvee led a file of four gun trucks off the pavement of Supply Route Uranium and onto the sands of Iraq. It was just over a kilometer from the road to a railroad bridge where we were going to search for signs of a sniper.

I drove the Humvee into a dried riverbed which led to the bridge, and I had to maneuver a shallow ditch about two feet deep and two feet across in order to reach it.

I wasn't buying the story about the sniper, and I knew I wasn't the only one on the patrol who felt that way. I'd been traveling Uranium for five months without seeing so much as a rodent stir on that bridge. There were convoys though, that claimed to take small-arms fire as they drove past.

The bridge was a perfect place to pretend to be attacked from; it was far enough from any real civilization that nobody could contest the claims, and because the desert around Uranium was a minefield in the Saddam era, it was considered too dangerous to safely react to an attack. I figured all these claims of small-arms fire were other units inflating their statistics and making sure all their people got their combat awards. It wasn't my job to decide if the sniper was real or not. My job was to search the bridge.

Having crossed the shallow ditch, I drove to the western end of the bridge where Kingsley and I dismounted and searched on foot. In the shadow of the bridge was a small village, just a cluster of hovels. Nobody was out, and the people were probably still sleeping. We looked around for a few minutes, checking the tracks for any shell casings, loose rounds, or other signs a sniper might have been there, but we didn't find anything. We mounted back up.

I drove underneath the bridge and grapevined the support pillars from east to west. Private First Class Gerry Perkins was my gunner that day. He was a nineteen-year-old aspiring cage fighter who managed to get himself in trouble every chance he got, and always had about a pound of Skoal chewing tobacco stuffed in his lower lip. Perkins didn't know much, but he knew his Mark II Browning .50-caliber machine gun—the Ma Deuce—as intimately as a lover.

Perkins stood tall in the turret as we searched, which negated the protection provided by the turret shield, but afforded him a better view as he scanned the pillars and trusses above. While he searched high, Kingsley and I searched low. We looked for triggers, suspicious dirt mounds, wires, debris; basically anything that might go boom.

We didn't find anything.

Kingsley called in our findings—or lack thereof—and told me to find a path back to Uranium.

An Irish folk song titled "Whiskey in the Jar" played in our headsets as we approached the ditch. I had heard a cover of the song by Metallica on the *Garage Days, Inc.* album, but was touched by the sincerity and simplicity of such a bare-bones rendition.

Now some men like the fishin'
And some men like the fowlin'
And some men like ta hear
Ta hear the cannonball a roarin'

I found a spot to enter the ditch that looked like it would be relatively smooth. The front end of the Humvee dipped into the trench, then launched skyward in a single violent, chaotic heartbeat. I slammed chest-first into the steering wheel with enough force to bend the steering shaft. The steady rumble of the engine was gone. My ears rang and it felt like I was swimming too deep underwater. The windshield was black and warped, in some places melting. Everything happened so quickly that I couldn't put anything together.

Then I heard screams.

They sounded distant with the din in my ears, but I knew Perkins's voice and could tell they were coming from the turret. Smoke was pouring into the cab through the radio mount and dashboard vents, so I couldn't see my gunner. I had to allow my ears to paint the picture in the fog. Judging by the pain and fear I heard in his cries—the cries which haunted me for years—the scene was painted crimson.

In my mind's eye a red haze surrounded him, but I could still see his face. Skin flayed. Blood everywhere. He appeared more monster than man, like Freddy

Krueger without the wide-brimmed hat.

Without my realizing it, my hand instinctively went to the ignition switch. The engine was dead and we needed to be moving, to be anywhere but right there. I quit hitting the switch when I realized what had happened.

IED. Our truck blew up.

Kingsley reached across and put a hand on my shoulder. He was alive. Gerry was screaming in the turret. He was alive. I was alive. That made all three of us. Thank God.

"Van Dyke! You okay?" Kingsley screamed.

There was enough adrenalin coursing through me at that moment to animate a corpse, so I didn't feel even a hint of pain, only fear.

"Yeah!" I shouted back, half deaf and probably equally tone-deaf.

"We need to get the fuck out of here!" For an officer, Kingsley had some good ideas.

I tried my door handle, but the heavily armored door wouldn't budge. I started ramming my shoulder into it, but I was just hitting a wall. I could see flames rising between our seats.

I've done my best to piece together all that happened that morning, and I can remember quite a few details, but coherent war stories are a myth. Explaining what happened after that bomb went off is like describing getting my ass kicked in a dark alley. Too many shadows. Too much movement. Too much fear. All I can hope for is truth.

Here's a truth: the moment I realized my door wasn't opening and that I wasn't in the clear yet, the number of people in that truck went from three to one. It may not be valorous, but survival rarely is.

I don't know why I chose the back door as my escape route. Maybe with Perkins screaming, I knew I wouldn't be able to get out the gunner's hatch. Whatever my reasoning, I swung around my seat to climb out the back door.

What I saw when I turned around was a mess. First aid bags, gas masks, ammo cans, rifles, all these things which had been so neatly organized just a minute before were scattered wildly throughout the cab. There was also something that hadn't been in the truck before.

The Ma Deuce weighed 140 pounds and the hundred-round belt loaded in the feed tray weighed another 25. Somehow it had broken free of its mount on top of the Humvee and ended up on the floor with only a spent shell casing wedged beneath the butterfly trigger to act as a safety.

If that makeshift safety hadn't held, there probably would have been four-ounce bullets ricocheting off the inside of the armored chassis at 2,700 feet per second. We would've been fucking hamburger.

I was unfazed by the chaotic scene, or maybe just too stunned to react, because I climbed over the M2 with no respect for its killing power. All that mattered was getting out of that truck. There was a red beverage cooler in the backseat I had to climb over, and as I did, I felt myself get snagged.

My body armor had a strap on the back just below the collar, which made it easier to drag me if the need arose, and the strap was hooked on one of the latches used to lock the turret hatch.

I tried unsuccessfully to wiggle free, then I made the knee-jerk decision to jettison the armor. I ripped the vest open by the Velcro strip in front, and then it suddenly felt as if somebody had snuck up behind me and clamped on a full-nelson.

In my panicked state I gave no thought to a silly pair of shoulder pads I had recently been issued that wrapped around my bicep and connected to the cuirass of my armor. The fifty pounds of Kevlar and ballistic plates fell to the floor behind me, and my arms went straight up to be pinned over my head.

I was trapped.

I tried to reach one shoulder pad or the other, but it was like trying to itch the sweet spot in the middle of my back. The black smoke and dancing flames were ever present. I was choking and half-blinded, but I could still see the door handle on the other side of the cooler.

My forward reach was less hindered than my side-to-side, and with some strain I could just barely reach my fingertips to the handle. I could put enough weight on it to click it open, but with the armor weighing the door down, I could only open it a few inches.

I saw that sliver of blue sky for just a moment, but the sight will stay with me until the day I die. It was more beautiful than any sunrise or sunset, because it was thousands of sunrises and sunsets rolled into one. It was a flash of hope, a glimpse of survival. It was life.

Then the door swung shut again.

I don't know how many times I tried the door. I just know that every time I did, I had to watch it close. I can remember being scared and thinking I was going to die. I remember choking on smoke and the bitter acrid taste in my mouth. I remember seeing blue sky. Seeing life. I remember being angry. Really fucking angry. Twenty-one is too young to die, especially by smoke or fire while I'm strung up like a goddamn marionette!

Fear. Hope. Anger. I used them all. I pushed the door open, and started kicking the cooler in a desperate fury. The cooler pushed the door open and spilled its contents in the sand as I watched the sliver of blue grow wider and wider until the whole sky opened up before me.

I was stuck, but I could breathe.

I don't know how long I hung there. It felt like forever, and sometimes it feels like I am still hanging there. If this were Hollywood, this would be the time I reached into my boot sheath and cut myself free with a K-bar. But this wasn't Tinseltown; it was a railroad bridge in western Iraq. I just hung there, struggling futilely to free myself until Kingsley appeared in the doorway.

It took a simple flick of the wrist for him to unstrap one of my shoulder pads, and I was able to slip free of the other and crawl out of the Humvee.

I've been told that in a life-or-death situation the brain goes into a hyperconscious state, basically kicking into overdrive to stay alive. Afterward it can shut down to recover from the exhaustion and to protect itself from immediately processing everything that just happened. It sounded pretty sensible when it was explained to me, but I could've been fed a line of bullshit and I wouldn't know better.

A clinical term for what happened is fugue, but I'd describe it like this: I wandered, yet I didn't.

A body wandered the desert. No mind. No soul. Just an empty shell. It wore no armor. It carried no rifle. It saw nothing. It heard nothing. It was oblivious to the lessons I'd been taught concerning insurgent tactics. It walked unprotected, ignorant of the likelihood of a secondary explosive within twenty meters. It felt nothing. No anger. No relief. No pain. No fear. Nothing.

I was ripped from the bliss of unawareness when my squad leader grabbed me by my shoulders. It felt like being born again and remembering it. Everything washed over me in a single terrible, overwhelming moment. It was too much to bear with my soldierly stoicism still intact.

I reached out and hugged Sergeant Strouth. That's when the tears came. Strouth was anything *but* an affectionate guy. He wasn't uncaring; it was plain to his men that we meant a lot to him. I think a better word would be callous. He's the kind of guy who would tell you to fuck off on your birthday. That being said, Strouth didn't hesitate to hug me right back.

After purging the eyes, the stomach came next. Black chunks tainted with smoke and explosive residue came out. It tasted like a mouthful of charcoal.

Strouth took off to fetch me some water. Smith was his driver, and Strouth *screamed* at him when he couldn't figure out what he wanted.

"Get him some fucking water!"

I smiled for the first time in what felt like years.

I met back up with Kingsley, and he and I helped Perkins away from the truck. Kingsley had a hard limp, and Gerry wasn't using his legs at all. There were no bloody wounds though, which was a pleasant surprise—if anything about that day could be called *pleasant*. Having escaped without injury, I felt most fortunate of all; I also felt guilty.

Once we reached a safer spot, the other two were laid down to receive medical attention. I wanted to take off and assist my platoon in the aftermath of the blast, but Doc Ackerson forced me to sit down and get checked out. My protests that I was fine and that I knew my own body fell on ears even deafer than my own. I sat down and told him to tend to the others first.

Kingsley was just as determined to be of use. "Call in a nine-line!" He barked, "We need a security cordon. Where's Sergeant Price?"

We weren't very good at surrender.

Ackerson was taking care of Kingsley's leg when he stopped and looked at my arm.

"Hey, Van Dyke, you have some blood on your sleeve."

Doc was right. I hadn't felt anything, but my right sleeve was torn and there was a bloodstain about the size of my hand. It's strange, but my immediate reaction was relief. I wasn't the only person to in the truck to walk away without an injury. I also had a physical wound to match the emotional wounds I felt; the ones that never really heal. It was only two small pieces of shrapnel, but it was easier to say I was hurt than to admit I was scared.

On the morning of 29 August 2006, vehicle w306 ran over a doorbell in a ditch, initiating the simultaneous detonation of three 130-millimeter mortar rounds, each with a seventy-five-meter kill radius. The rounds were wrapped in homemade c-4. The detonation occurred directly beneath the right front tire of w306. PFC Perkins sustained minor wounds when the Mark II Browning .50-caliber machine gun struck him in the legs, and was given one week off missions. SPC Van Dyke had two pieces of shrapnel removed from his right forearm and was given two weeks off missions. 2LT Kingsley broke his left leg and was given six weeks off missions. All three received the Purple Heart for their injuries, as well as the Combat Infantryman's Badge. 2LT Kingsley was also awarded the Bronze Star with Valor for rescuing the other two members of his crew after crawling out his window. No secondary explosive was found. No sign of a sniper was found.

A few facts that didn't make the official report: Pieces of shrapnel more than ten inches long were lodged into the ceiling above mine and Kingsley's heads; it took our platoon more than ten minutes to pry the front doors of w306 open; engine debris was found more than a hundred meters from the blast site.

This was one of those nexus moments in which my life was changed so drastically that I can't help but consider the possible outcomes and be left wondering how different things would be if the slightest details were altered. The ten-inch piece of shrapnel strikes my arm. Perkins is standing at the moment of detonation. The .50 cal fires inside the vehicle. I step on a secondary. Kingsley dies and doesn't rescue the rest of the crew. I pass the doorbell and Strouth runs it over. I spot the doorbell.

If is the longest and most dangerous word I have ever heard.

The morning the Irish music played left me with too many questions and the realization that I'll never have answers. The IED was terrible, but, unfortunately, not every nightmare teaches a lesson. It is hard to draw meaning from hitting a blind bomb under a railroad bridge where no trains run while looking for a sniper that doesn't exist.

Lucky

NICHOLAS MERCURIO

"I can't feel my body," he said, his voice rising faint over the sound of the helicopter rotors pulsing in the darkness as our litter team carried him down a path illuminated on either side by Chem-Lites. We moved slowly, careful not to lose our footing on the loose gravel that covered the hill leading down to the clinic.

Once through the flight-line gate we were met by doctors from the Forward Surgical Team, backlit like shadow puppets by light rushing from the open clinic doors. They leaned over the patient, tracing his body with a flashlight while I watched. The light fell on the neck brace he wore, and the blood trickling from his ears and bubbling from his mouth, and the alarming whiteness of his skull, out of place amidst the blood, matted hair, and sand. "Urgent," a doctor said, and moved past us to the litter team emerging from the night behind.

We carried our patient into the aid station and laid him on the second of three beds. The distinct hospital smell, one of unapologetic sterility, reminded me of my mother and the times I would visit her in the basement pharmacy of Our Lady of Fatima. "He said he can't feel his body," I told the medic.

"How you doing, buddy? Can you hear me? We are going to take care of you, okay?" As Doc Johnson spoke, he removed the straps and heat blankets that wrapped the patient.

"I want you to know I swallowed a lot of blood."

"That's alright, buddy; we will get that fixed. Try to relax for me." He began to cut off the patient's uniform. "What's your name?"

"Jeremy."

"Okay, Jeremy, you're doing really well."

"I can't feel . . . I can't feel my body."

The beds on either side had patients now. Clear tubes ran from pale arms to IV bags. Heart-rate monitors displayed sinus rhythms and elevated pulses. Discarded needle caps and opened dressings collected on the floor beside bright spatters of blood which looked like dollops of strawberry syrup in a glass of milk on the clean white tile. I exited through the side door with the rest of my litter team and we circled back to the flight-line gate to await more patients.

"Okay," I said. "Where are my guys . . . one, two, where's the third guy?"

"Constanza went to get another guy off the bird."

"The big guy?"

"Yeah."

"I need another guy for my team," I said.

"I think the other bird landed already."

"Lieutenant Goble said we would get the second bird in six mikes," I said.

"There are two birds up there, sir. I think we got everybody."

"Okay, let's just stand by."

"Heads up." We moved to the side as two more soldiers came through, buddy-carrying a third between them, his arms draped over their shoulders.

"Lieutenant Goble said we are done; head to the PRT building." I clicked on my red light and followed the group down the gravel road. We huddled in a quiet circle, waiting in the dark and dust and heat seeping up from the ground.

"Alright guys, can everyone hear me?" Goble said as he approached. "Y'all did an exceptional job tonight. It went much more smoothly than last time and we are going to continue to improve. Next time we are going to number the guys on the litter teams—odd will go left and even will go right so we can avoid some of the confusion." As he spoke he rotated slowly, looking at everyone while they searched the ground at their feet. I knew they were thinking that their bodies were just as fragile, that any number of times it could have easily been them all fucked up on a litter, staring up into strange faces and wondering if they were dying.

"Guys, we need to kill the red lights up there. I know it's dark and it sucks, but they are flying with IR so we can't have any lights. Litter teams three and four, y'all almost lost your lives tonight." They looked up. "Never, ever approach from the rear. If I hadn't grabbed this kid he would have taken it in the face, alright? However, excellent job overall, I thank y'all, have a good night."

"Scottie," I called after Goble.

"Yeah, Merc, you're with me, I gotta take some X-rays."

I followed him back up to the clinic. "This is for you," he said, passing me a full-length lead apron. "Okay, we need to get a lateral c-spine of this guy," he said as we walked to the patient I had carried in. He handed me a black X-ray cassette and I moved to the far side of the bed while he wheeled up the X-ray machine. He punched in the correct exposure settings and positioned the machine level with the patient's neck. "Hey buddy, we have to take a picture of your neck, okay? The doc is gonna pull on your arms and I need you to relax and lie real still for me. Merc, when I tell you, I need you to push the cassette down into the bed and make sure your fingers aren't in the way. Okay, here we go."

I pushed down as hard as I could on the sides of the cassette, stiffening against the tremors of adrenaline rolling through my forearms. There was a soft beep. "Okay, got it."

I followed Scottie to the X-ray kiosk and he snapped the cassette down into the reader. The image slowly formed on the screen, cascading down from the top like a sheet sliding off a statue. Skull then vertebrae; one, two, three, four, five, six, "Fuck." The sixth and seventh vertebrae were not neatly in line like the rest; one had slid past the other, a car overtaking a slower vehicle on the highway. White, displaced bone fragments formed an archipelago floating in a black sea on the screen. Scottie called the doctor over.

"Shit, okay, we've got c6 and c7 displaced, and c7 appears to be crushed. Yeah, he has to go to Bagram." He moved back to the bed. "Okay, people, we need to stabilize him, he needs to get out of here. Cynthia, I need you to tube him now, please, he's going into spinal shock. Let's get a chest X-ray, then prep him."

I watched as Scottie X-rayed the patient's chest and then he hurried past me to the kiosk, attempting to shield the cassette from me. He wiped off a streak of something deep red that stained the cloth with a ring around it, like cranberry sauce mixed with olive oil. "Is that what I think it is?"

"Yeah, man, that's that kid's brains. I didn't want you to see it."

"From the head wound? I saw his head was split open."

"His ears. His brain is swole up, hemorrhaging out his ears."

"Fuck, dude."

We X-rayed the remaining patients, each time hoping the screen would tell a different story than it did. Shattered ribs, a humerus snapped cleanly and suspended in the upper arm like the packages of broken candy canes we had distributed at the Christmas party a week ago. The last patient was awake and talking. "How's he doing, sergeant major?" I asked as I came around the bed.

"Well he's doing okay, aren't you, Robert? We are just trying to figure some things out—looks like he whacked his head pretty good. We found a ring on him, just trying to figure out if he's married."

"Wait, am I married?"

"Well you've got a ring, Robert, but it's okay if you can't remember."

"How are my guys?"

"Everyone is being taken care of, don't worry."

There was a long pause as he tried to blink away the confusion.

"I'm married?"

"It's gonna be okay."

I took off the lead apron and stood in the hallway that connected the aid station to the Forward Surgical Team facility, looking past the medics as they treated the wounded, the scene unfolding before me fueling a burgeoning existential crisis. The blood was too red, impossibly red, not the comfortable deep crimson hue I had come to know through years of television and movie violence. It looked fake, a high-fructose fraud cooked up for some low-budget production, which, in turn, explained the bad acting. The A-listers whom I was accustomed to watching had to delve deep into the well of their memories to tap into the faint echo of past trauma. Their pain was deep and searching and delivered confidently. The war-wounded in this scene portrayed pain that was too immediate, their delivery too diffident, to be believed. I started worrying that I might be fucked up. Then I started hating myself for selfishly wondering if I was fucked up while people around me were legitimately fucked up.

I was rescued from my self-hating spiral as my roommate came into the clinic. He had been in the Tactical Operations Center and started speaking as he came up alongside me.

"It was a rollover. The truck commander said they were turning onto a bridge and hit something, a pothole, maybe a rock, and fell like sixty feet down into the water. Luckily it was only three feet deep. How are the guys in there?" He leaned in. "Careful by the way, that's the driver behind you."

"That's the driver?" A muscular kid, maybe twenty, sat in a black waiting-room chair, holding an ice pack to the back of his neck and staring straight ahead while the chaplain spoke to him.

"Yeah, he walked away."

"Holy shit. Lucky."

"I don't know man. He's gotta live with this."

I looked at the driver again. Tears had started to form in the corners of his eyes. He would probably have hidden them if he'd noticed.

31 North 64 East

MATTHEW KOMATSU

APRIL 2012

Third in a stack of six men lined up on the shoothouse entry door. Two PJs in front of me, three behind, rifles at the ready. I awaited the squeeze from the man behind; a squeeze I'll pass to the shoulder in front. A squeeze to release us into a room with an unknown number of hostiles and friendlies. Arkansas humidity bore down; sweat beaded under my helmet and ran down my cheek. Right index finger on the trigger guard. Thumb on the selector switch. Dead calm. Live. Fire. Shoothouse. Sweet Jesus. Don't fuck this up, Komatsu.

2200 hours, 14 September 2012

Through my office door into the Rescue Operations Center, or "ROC," I see the TV screen in the corner, hear the laughter of the guys. My computer screen blurs—in two months we've generated nearly a hundred award packages already. I review every one. The ritual: Check the name on the form. Check the name on the continuation page. Check the name on the citation. Now, check the social security number on the form. Check the continuation. Check the citation. The guys have learned efficiency, the administrative art of cut-and-paste. But when the Control-C/Control-V dance spirals out of control, a mismatched name or incorrect social input can cost months of coordination. Attention to detail, gents.

I'm the commander of the Forty-sixth Expeditionary Rescue Squadron, Camp Bastion, Afghanistan. My squadron of

Air Force Pararescuemen, or "PJs" and Combat Rescue Offi-cers, "CROs," fly casualty evacuation missions into the heart of the Helmand Province several times a day, plucking the battlefield wounded through the doors of "Pedro," as the HH-60G helicopters are affectionately known. Each mission counts toward the twenty total required for one Air Medal; some of my men sport twenty Air Medals. Then there are the special missions, the ones that went a little sideways, worth a bit more.

It's 14 September 2012, and we are, in theory, a few weeks from going home. I've flown a handful of missions, none of them special. I've put six of my men in for Bronze Stars with Valor; my award for this tour will be seeing them pin on those medals. But it won't happen without the paperwork. Tonight I'm off alert. Reserve for anything else. Anything else doesn't happen much, so it's a good night to catch up on awards packages.

I shuffle electrons dutifully. I click. I drag. I type. I cut. I paste. By 2200 I need a break. In the team tent next door the guys will be up to the usual: email, movies, cleaning weapons, busting each other's balls. I grab a soda, dip spit bottle, and head over.

JULY 2012

When I first ran the loop around the Bastion runway during a 2009 trip through Afghanistan as a staff officer, it was about seven miles. Bastion was still a new UK/Marine outpost back then, Dodge City to Afghanistan's wild southwest.

Three years later Bastion was swollen, the loop now over ten miles. I set out from the compound at two in the morning, running by feel. But everything had shifted over time. A few miles in, I hung a right and dead-ended into a cluster of airfield lights.

I stopped my watch. I couldn't see much—my headlamp illuminated as much dust in the air as it did the ground below. But I could tell the perimeter was nowhere near. I turned around and eventually found the perimeter road. Running along the fence, I had a weird feeling, like I shouldn't be there. I took my headphones out. I thought about my headlamp bobbing along in the night. One well aimed shot—that's all it would take. I considered turning it off. Then I thought of the armed guards in the towers seeing a shadow run down the road at midnight. I left the headlamp on, and ran on, past the Harrier, attack helicopter, and Osprey areas, to the other end of the runway.

Shortly after 2200 hours, 14 September

It begins with a call over the personal radios used to notify alert crews of a mission tasking. A "tasking" that means someone on the battlefield might be dying:

"We are bunkered down and taking fire, over." The call comes from our HC-130 sister squadron, located down the runway and tasked with flying patients to and from hospitals across Afghanistan. I look at the PJs. No fucking way. That's what our faces say. But as I grab my radio and head back to the ROC, my stomach tightens. Something is up. The ops center is quiet, TVs muted. Everyone huddles around the radio.

"I say again. All personnel accounted for. We are bunkered down, taking RPG and small-arms fire."

I look at Intel. Intel shrugs back. Someone says there are fires on the other side of base. Outside an orange glow lights the horizon, silhouetting the scads of containers, tents, and buildings between me and the other side of the airstrip. Camp Bastion is a small city; Anytown, USA, or Wherever-ford-shire, UK, depending on your point of view. On the other side of town something is going down.

It's not a drill. The base enters lockdown: find a bunker or shelter in place. We send the guys into security positions out along the compound perimeter. The Marine HQ calls. There's been an attack, and there are casualties somewhere near the Osprey hangars. NFI—No Further Information. We're to cross the runway and find the casualties.

Three volunteers to go: Paul, Kyle, and Dan. They ready a vehicle while I kit up and hope for better intel. My stomach is knotted—we're about to step purposefully into something.

I scroll through radio channels—the frequency you need is often the one you don't have.

I meet the guys at the truck, a little white Isuzu. Kyle will drive, I'll ride shotgun. Paul and Dan in the back. Before we head out I brief the guys on the little I know. For now, there are casualties at an unknown location on the other side of the runway. Our arrival is expected but our destination unclear.

APRIL 2012

"Find work, guys. That's the fuckin' deal. Bro bird-dogging a door, you peel off and stack on him. Squeeze and go." The instructor was at the front of the classroom. The air was artificially dry, tangy with air-conditioning and weapons lube.

A prior Marine, he was skinny, short, a boiling undercurrent of lethality. Like most of the instructors, he did his time, got blooded, then got the fuck out to make some real money. Trigger time on the contract side. And there was plenty of it. "Don't just take your corner, and then stand there like a dumbass, right? The job ain't over, right?"

Modern mercs, these guys, but no need to overthrow governments abroad when their own needs them so badly and will pay top dollar. Over the past decade, security-related contract groups have sprung up to offer everything from tactical training to overseas personal security contracts. Dozens of companies have grown fat off the government dime.

Now it's 2012, and even here in Tactical Disneyland there is a sense that the good times are over. The lights are out in Iraq, a no-man's-land save for the guys lucky enough to work for the State Department. Afghanistan, on the downhill slope to "mission complete." Our instructors talked about offering more for less, teaching fewer kinetic skills, moving into other areas. Find work.

2215 hours, 14 September

Crossing the runway is no joke. The flames across the base bloom out our night-vision goggles and make it impossible to see the ubiquitous ditches. Driving off the pavement will park us in a four-foot trench. Kyle pulls it off and we make it to the Harrier area, on the northern end of the runway. We park and take a look. Shit burns, has burned. Lights flash near the hangars, but we can't see any friendlies. We see no movement at all. It's quiet, unsettling.

We drive south toward the Ospreys. There's a fire engine on the runway near a wall of fire; could be casualties there. We don't make it too far. We hear sporadic gunfire and park behind some cover. Dan comes over with a Marine. He says bad guys are inside the wire; grunts are securing their areas. He knows nothing about casualties. As we speak, the gunfire turns into a gunfight. We drive to the fire engine.

APRIL 2012

How fast can you run a mile in full kit with your weapon? Full kit: Ballistic helmet, headset, body armor, three full magazines, hip belt and harness, two radios, first aid kit, infrared marking kit, M-4 and suppressor with a full magazine. Seven minutes is flat-out for me. At the end, my hips feel like warm rubber, my legs strands of limp spaghetti, and my breath a freight train.

2230 hours, 14 September

The fuel farm blazes. Flames boil up hundreds of feet from an artificial pond holding 1.6 million gallons of aviation gas, baking and illuminating our faces. We park next to the fire engine expecting to find casualties. Attack helicopters hover overhead, unleashing fire a couple hundred yards away *inside the wire*.

A Brit runs up to Paul and Dan and exclaims, "Thank God you're here." No casualties here, he says, firefight over there. That's all he knows. A small armored vehicle skids to a stop. The driver jumps out, talks to Paul. There are casualties up a hill past the fuel farm and he'll give us a ride.

Space is tight—we leave behind everything but medical gear. I'm next to the driver. The noise from the gunfight outside intensifies. We drive maybe 100 yards, then halt next to a large vehicle behind a tall concrete barrier. I exit to the drumbeat of multiple .50 cals through my headset. Tracers arc through the sky in both directions. The enemy is somewhere north of us. Paul's silhouette appears. "KU, they've got casualties on the hill. They're going to provide covering fire while we run up."

I look ahead. It's a dash across open terrain to some Brit vehicles. "Where are the bad guys?"

"Couple shooters 50 yards north of us, other side of the road."

"All right. Let's do it."

As we stack up behind the barrier, the volume of fire is suddenly deafening. Paul dashes off into the night.

"I guess we're going. Dan, then Kyle. I've got rear." I slap Dan on the ass, and he's off. Then Kyle. Then me.

I run. As hard as I can. There is gunfire above and around me. Look to my right 25 yards in. Spot the insurgent position. Consider squeezing off some rounds at them. Think better of it. Keep running. One foot in front of the other. Don't think our silhouettes in front of the fireball to the left.

I arrive, last to duck behind the cover of the first Brit vehicle.

- -

APRIL 2012

Our rifle "silencers" were anything but silent. The correct terminology: "suppressor," as in "muzzle flash suppressor." I was the only guy sporting one on my rifle, and I figured I'd run a whole day of shooting with it.

It was now lunchtime. I needed to clean my weapon, and the damn suppressor wasn't coming off. I loosened the ratchet and gorilla-gripped it. Nothing. An instructor saw me wrestling with my rifle.

"Hey, sir, what's going on?"

"My suppressor isn't coming off." He grabbed it, gave it a twist. Same results. A large man, he glared at me through his sunglasses.

"How many rounds did you put through it?"

I shrugged. "I dunno, at least a couple hundred." He grimaced and sent a look right through me.

"Seriously?"

"Yes."

"Sir, these suppressors are meant for a few rounds. You put it on when you need it, then take it off."

"Oh."

"Yep, chances are good you've fused this thing right on to the barrel."

Shit.

"I'll take it to the armory and see what the boys can do." He walked away with my weapon. Fortunately, my PJs had already left for the chow hall and missed this embarrassing exchange.

After lunch the instructor returned with my rifle in one hand and the suppressor in another. He pointed out the layers of carbon on the muzzle. Relieved, I asked how he got it off.

He smiled. "We hit it with a fucking mallet until it came off."

2245 hours, 14 September

Dan and Kyle treat the wounded. The helo gun runs are done, the firefight over. Through my NVGs I see no movement at the enemy position. My position, however, bustles. Three large Brit vehicles grumble a diesel idle. Then, there are the Brits. In and out they run, shouting at the tops of their Scottish lungs. I can't understand a damn word and it's fucking loud. A sergeant rips into their asses.

"Ef you thenk them cunts over the road canna hear ya, yer fekkin' wrong. Quiet the fuck doon!" Of course he's shouting—he's as deafened by the gunfire and explosions as the rest of them.

Dan and Kyle treat five casualties—mostly shrapnel wounds from an insurgent RPG. All serious, but nothing life threatening. The Brits will assault the cryogenics complex across the road and ask for our help. Paul and I agree: embed with the Brits. Find work, we smile. With a little luck we might even find the casualties we originally set out to find.

I sliced my rifle's infrared pointer though the night. Invisible without night vision goggles, I positioned the green line on a steel target 300 meters away. I sighed into the ground, felt the rifle buttstock become one with my cheek and shoulder. At the end of the sigh, I squeezed my index finger against the trigger. The rifle erupted, followed by the ping of the round hitting steel.

"Hit," announced my spotter.

Ping after ping. Until I expended my ammo, satisfied with my accuracy.

2330 hours, 14 September

We're in a trench watching the cryo complex, but I focus on a small bunker the helicopters shot up during their last gun run. That bunker, meant for friendlies, now shelters enemy, or what I hope is left of them. The small slits of black—gaps between slabs of concrete—I see through my NVGS unnerve me. Ten years at war: this is the closest to the enemy I've come.

The cryo complex looks like serious bullshit. A standard barrier-hemmed conglomerate of containers, tents, and work areas, save one big difference: this one houses liquid oxygen generation equipment and storage. The liquid oxygen, used for aircrew breathing at high altitudes, is a pyro's dream down here on the ground. One container erupting in the complex would level the place. I hear Kyle from down the trench:

"Hey, I've got movement."

"Where?"

"See those small barriers?" I see them. "I saw something move behind them."

"I don't see anything, man." Then I look at Kyle. "Dude, where are your NVGS?"

"I left them in the fucking truck. Can you believe that? I took them off my helmet because they kept snagging while I drove. Forgot to grab them in the excitement."

The Brits are taking too long. Suddenly Dan calls out two movers. I see two shapes headed our way. Rifles in hand. Are they wearing pajamas?

"Hands up! Get your fucking hands up!"

They respond in perfect English: "Marines! Marines!"

Calls of "Friendly" echo up the line; the two figures jump into the trench. Kyle and Dan dress some wounds and debrief the Marines. They were sleeping when the attack commenced and don't know how many insurgents are left. They hid outside the complex as long they could, then saw us and made a break for it. One of them wears boxer shorts and a tee.

We send the Marines down the line and pass the intel to the Brits. I watch the bunker and wait to assault.

APRIL 2012

Clearing rooms and buildings. On TV it's always dramatic. Option one: explosive breaching. Option two: battering ram. Option three: kick that damn door down. Our approach: If it's unlocked, open the door. Make entry and shoot targets as we see them in our assigned sectors of the room. Flow through other doors until there's nowhere else to go.

The other half of the team watched from the gangways above and the instructors recorded video as we entered. I entered the room third in the stack. First and second man shot on entry, telling me to do the same. I had time for two quick shots, then turned right. Scanned. Looked for work.

Second man stopped at a door. Hinges visible on the left. He moved to the left side of the door, reached across for the handle. I paused on the right edge. Someone pulled in behind me. I awaited the squeeze. I got it, nodded and the door opened. I stepped through. Target down the hall. I put two rounds into the target silhouette and kept moving.

After clearing the house, we debriefed while walking from target to target. When we got to the target I shot down the hall, the instructor looked at the paper target and pointed at a hole. "Who's got the suppressor?" That would be me.

"What happened here?" The hole should have been somewhere midmass inside the printed image of the obvious criminal. Where it was: in the body of the hostage he held as a shield in front of him.

I explained. When I took the shots, I never saw a hostage.

"Well, the good news is, you were accurate. The bad news is, you shot the hostage." He turned to address the rest of the team. "Take a sec before you engage and ensure you know your target."

I felt bad. But our job was to save lives, not take them. We weren't SEALS. We got into a shoothouse maybe once every couple of years. But it stung regardless. If there was any solace in the moment, this thought: we're never gonna do this shit anyway.

0100 hours, 15 September

The flames play tricks in the night. Behind us the fuel farm burns, dancing shadows as six elements of three or four men advance south through the cryo complex. My element hugs the west side, weaving in and out of containers. We advance until we reach the end of the complex; 20 to 30 yards away is that bunker. It's small, maybe ten feet long, five feet wide, camo netting above the back. Airstrikes hit it once before, but who knows if it's clear? I stare at the black under the netting, unnerved. Even my goggles reveal nothing in that space. I cover down behind a container and level my rifle at the bunker.

Paul whispers from my left. "I've got movement in that bunker, KU." We relay the info to the Brits. An element of Brits chops free to clear the bunker. I am relieved that none of my men are on it. From outside the complex a machine gun fires into the bunker. Then the clearing element lines up outside the bunker. They enter. The lead man gets inside. Two more enter, still a few outside. Shouting, then sustained automatic gunfire. The team exits, trailing smoke. When lead man entered, one of several insurgents at the back of the bunker threw a grenade. But it bounced back and detonated among him and his shithead friends. Lead man then squeezed his trigger until his rifle went dry. Somehow the Brits emerge without a scratch.

A few minutes pass. Elements bound past us to leave the complex. I watch the bunker; smoke seeps out the back. When it's our turn I run with two Brits. I make it no more than a few steps when I see flash from the bunker. A round tears into a barrier nearby.

"*Contact left,*" I shout as I turn, run behind a shitter, and back to cover. This is not the way to react to near contact. The standard operating procedure: turn to the threat and assault through. The Brits do my dirty work for me and clear back through the bunker to kill the rest. All told, five insurgents die in the bunker.

APRIL 2012

It was strange to lounge in the early Arkansas spring and listen to the pop-pop of gunfire from inside the shoothouse. Back in Alaska I supposed it was Easter. A time of year also known as "Breakup." All the snow finally melting away, exposing Anchorage at its ugliest: awash in mushy dog shit and graveled roads. Every morning, a dusty haze rising inside a temperature inversion until it could rise no more. I closed my eyes and saw it, flat across the sky, an apparition.

0130 hours, 15 September

I take a pull from a large arm bottle of water and pass it along. We are still outside the cryo complex, which continues to burn. Insurgent ammo in the bunker burns and cooks off, sending rounds overhead. We're headed back inside to clear two more areas. We stack again and move swiftly. Mine and one other element take the liquid oxygen area; Paul and Dan head elsewhere.

Moving amongst containers marked HAZARDOUS, we are one stray round away from a fiery death. I clear an office trailer with two other Brits. No Marine would leave a workspace in such disarray. Computer screens lie on the floor, lights knocked over and papers strewn as a child might. Before I exit I slap the door frame and say "Friendly." Exiting, I look down the barrel of a British rifle. The trooper behind it sees me, then points elsewhere.

I'm relieved when we finish and exit to line up behind some small barriers. We can see across the open ground to the north that ends with the Harrier hangars. It's a "pause in the action." Drink water, check your ammo, and take a deep breath.

I hear rotor blades overhead and have an idea. I lie on my back, my head against the barriers, and pull out my radio. I scroll through my programmed frequencies until I find RIGHTEOUS, the call sign for the Marine attack choppers. Pause.

"Any Righteous, any Righteous. This is Varsity One–Actual." Wait.

My radio comes to life. "Varsity One–Actual, Righteous. Go ahead." We exchange situation reports. They're about to hit five insurgents near the Harriers. They talk me on to the position. It's near a Brit vehicle. I request they hold off, pull the vehicle back, then clear Righteous.

"Roger, in hot. One minute." I advise the Brits, and we wait.

Streams of machine gun fire appear from the sky over the airfield. Over and over again the helicopters hit the insurgents. Cheers go up and down the line.

"Fuck yeah, mates!"

"Light 'em up!"

When it ends, Righteous says all but one look dead. Time for us to move out. We'll move on the road, using the vehicles for cover until we get to the Harrier area, then clear through the hangars. We line up and wait.

APRIL 2012

"Here's the deal, guys." My team stood in the barracks, jocked up. Brock's team had departed to exercise the same training mission. It was a Blackhawk Down type of scenario—worst case.

Helicopter down in an urban area, entrapped patients requiring extrication. Certainty of enemy presence. Within a minute of moving on-site, a town square with numerous avenues of approach impossible to cover, we were decisively engaged by role players playing Taliban insurgents. We took a beating for an hour. The men were anxious for payback.

"We're gonna act as a response force for the other team. Once they hit the objective and decide they need backup, they'll radio for us. We'll insert and it will be game on. Secure a perimeter and create some breathing room." The men beam because Brock and I worked this out without telling the instructors. Which meant the role players had no idea we were coming. "Whatever we got for ammo, bring it. Load every magazine you can."

The guys jammed mags with 5.56 rounds identical to what we'd carry in combat, save one important difference—the round was plastic, filled with paint. Travelling at a couple hundred feet per second, it would bruise but not kill, leaving tiny spurts of blue and yellow paint to mark hits.

My radio crackled: "Guardian 2, Guardian 1. Request response force insertion."

Time to go. We loaded two trucks and moved out. In the mock village a half mile away, twenty fake insurgents armed like us were wreaking havoc on the other team. The trouncing we took was fresh in my mind.

We took fire from a role player in the window of a building on the village edge. I flicked my selector from safe to full automatic. Raised my weapon, put the front sight post on the window. Then I squeezed the trigger and held it until my weapon stopped firing. The insurgent silhouette disappeared.

The staccato, sustained, jolted the PJ next to me. His eyes widened. "Did you just go full auto?" I reloaded.

"Yep."

He raised his weapon and did the same.

Once in the village, we secured a perimeter, and my team emptied magazine after magazine into diminishing waves of enemy. One fell to the ground after two of my men shot him. I shot him in the groin, and then his head. I heard a muffled "I'm down! I'm fucking down!" After twenty minutes the site was secure.

0230 hours, 15 September

There is nothing stealthy about the silhouettes of twenty troops walking up a road next to oversized diesel dune buggies. After the half-mile patrol I jump into a ditch with the command element. What I can see: The Harrier area is a half mile long and adjacent to the runway. One line of small shade structures for single aircraft parallels another row of large maintenance hangars. The insurgents cut a swath down the middle. Several Harriers have burned to the ground along with their shade structures. Smoke drifts along the ground. Every aircraft is either destroyed or damaged.

Klaxons wail into an empty night. Flashing lights warn us of a danger we hope has passed. It's a surreal picture, something out of a video game. Righteous is down to refuel and rearm, so we're on our own. Paul and Kyle chop to a team of Brits to take the hangars while Dan joins an element assigned the shade structures. The command element will take the leftovers. The teams move out.

A volley of gunfire. "Threat down," says Dan over the radio. Of the group of five Righteous shot up, Dan has put a round through the head of the sole survivor. Paul's team clears the first hangar, moves on to the second. My element moves up. A Brit calls out a large pool of blood at the door to the second hangar. My first instinct: wounded insurgent, one we didn't know about. The blood leads inside.

After Paul's team moves on, I have a moment to take a look at the streaks of blood leading through the hangar door. There is large pool of blood on the hangar floor. I step in the streaks as I enter the door, then consider. The hangar exterior is shot to hell, evidence of the helo gun runs and something else. RPG-scarring, small-arms holes in the walls, the blood leading inside the hangar: I replay it in my mind. The insurgents huddled and died at the concrete barrier—why would one drag himself inside the hangar?

An insurgent wouldn't, but one of ours would. I picture a Marine exiting the door to engage the insurgents. He is hit, bad. His buddies drag him inside while providing covering fire. Render aid. It's a large pool of blood, crimson on gray concrete, curdling and congealing in the dry night air. It's American blood, has to be. I walk out, careful to avoid the blood, but see my footprints in the streaks and realize the blood is on my soles.

Dan's element clears through the smoking wrecks and burned out shade structures ahead. When they reach the Harrier squadron building, Dan asks for the commander. A Marine major says, "I guess that's me. The commander is dead."

I arrive to find the roof of the Harrier building bristling with the silhouettes of Marines on watch. Tall concrete barriers surround the small building. The light inside is too much. I take off my helmet and cradle it in the crook of my left arm. My eyes adjust to the sight of any office on base, a dusty mishmash of office furniture furnished by the lowest bidder and what's been assembled by hand. I ask a Marine in full battle rattle for a phone, and he looks me up and down. For a moment I am self-conscious.

He points toward a desk. "Right over there, sir." I walk into an adjacent room, its television blank. Two armed Marines sit and regard my entrance vacantly. I give the ROC a status update, then hang up and ask the guys for the XO. The major Dan spoke to, a slim man with a shaven head, appears. I shake his hand.

"I hear you have a casualty."

"Yes. It was the CO."

"Where is he?"

"We've got him in a supply closet." He motions toward a door and opens it. Through the doorway, I can see the lower part of a body covered in a green wool blanket. I resist a need to walk into the room.

"I'm sorry. Fuck, I'm sorry." He regards me evenly, but says nothing. "Look, if you're worried about his body being in front of your men, I can get Pedro in here to evac his remains over to the hospital."

"No," he says, "That's unnecessary. We're not ready to let him go at this time."

OCTOBER 2012

During my post-deployment leave I barely left the house. I dragged myself out once a day to run in the crisp air, then called it good. Jen learned to avoid asking me about the deployment. I learned the art of angry, silent withdrawal.

Jen and I went to dinner one night at a popular restaurant/theater venue near our house. I dragged my feet getting out the door and we arrived too late to eat; she had to work an after-dinner event on the theater side. She was upset, then I was upset. We were barely seated when she had to leave me alone and withdrawn in the light and noise and jubilance of the restaurant.

I carried out food but ran into security for the show. I nearly choked the half-smile off the fat fuck who barred my way. I seethed my way to Jen, then erupted when I found the restaurant didn't include flatware with the to-go boxes. Jen finally told me to go meet up with Paul and some guys for beers. I walked through a light snowfall and drank with friends from a distance.

0400 hours, 15 September

It's over. At least it feels over. I take my helmet off behind a barrier and look down a line of aircraft hulks, the smoke acidic in my nose. One dead Marine, maybe one more. The blazing fuel pit in the distance: one mile, I estimate. One mile separates where tonight began from where it ended. If it even ended at all.

Paul and I look at the dead insurgents, who wear white sneakers, ball caps, and U.S. Army uniforms. RPG rounds protrude from their packs, belts of machine gun ammunition drape from their shoulders. AK-47 magazines. Grenades. Surgical masks hang from their ears. The dead men's faces are tinted green; cans of spray paint spill from one man's pack.

"They were huffing paint to get high," observes Paul.

The uniforms are complete, nametapes and rank present. Some even wear Velcro unit patches. God damn it all.

I want to do something inhuman, something strictly forbidden by the Rules of Engagement. I want to spit on their heads, now malformed and open. I want to empty a magazine into their grotesque angles of repose. I want them to burn, like their friends back at the bunker.

But instead I pause, Paul at my side. I spit on the ground. "Fuck you," I say. Then we walk away, carrying our helmets and rifles.

NOVEMBER 2012

We left Fairbanks and pulled into our Anchorage garage eight hours later, our newly adopted dog, Bonnie, in the backseat. A diminutive black-and-white border/shepherd mix bred to mush by an asshole who shot underperforming dogs in their kennels to make way for new talent, Bonnie was nearly feral from neglect when Carol liberated her; after two years teaching Bonnie to trust and obey humans, Carol agreed to adopt her to us.

The garage door was open when I let Bonnie out of the car, and she darted into the alley. She stopped when I called for her, then I called again: Come, Bonnie. She looked at me, then down the alley. Back at me. Then she darted into the brush at the alley's end. I called after her, louder. Panic squeezed my ribs. I shouted, pleaded, but she was gone.

I took off after her, a black dog at midnight. Me on foot, Jen in the car, we combed the neighborhood. Then I spotted Bonnie frozen under an intersection streetlight. I shouted and she bolted again. I sprinted after her, panting directions into the phone.

Ahead of me by two blocks, Bonnie slowed to a trot, hit a dead end, then stood foxlike in a front yard. She panted like a wild animal, her tongue curved up at the tip. I paused yards away. She was stiff, coiled. I took a step and she sprinted around the side of the house. I followed into a backyard that fell away steep and wooded. I slipped on some leaves and fell short of a fence that enclosed the yard. Jen drove in front of the house and waited. Bonnie had to be somewhere back here—be ready, I said, for her to emerge up front. Jen was armed with treats and a leash.

The brush stirred; a shape bolted along the fence, then stopped. Bonnie sat down uphill and stared at me. I approached, but she shifted and looked for an exit. I slowed and sat down. The incline was steep, slick with the detritus of autumn. I dug my heels into the earth. I smelled fresh dog shit.

For thirty minutes I spoke softly and inched closer. I understood her confusion and her fear. It's okay, I said. We're family now. Closer still. We are going to take care of you, I said. A few feet now. The fecal scent grew stronger. Jen and I—we're your new mom and dad. Arms reach. It's okay, I said, it's okay. I stroked her head while she panted and lay down. Then I wrapped my arms around her and picked her up. She had soiled herself and it spread from her backside up her tail. Now it was all over my jacket. I kissed her head and carried her up front, where Jen placed a collar and leash on her. I kept her in my arms while Jen drove us home.

0415 hours, 15 September

The Marines will send the commander to the hospital by ground. Dan will escort the remains, as he has countless times from the battlefield. He climbs into a British vehicle while the Marines carry the commander, covered and strapped to a backboard. Dan asks for a U.S. flag, and the xo returns with one. He climbs up into the truck with Dan, and they place the flag carefully between the backboard straps and the blanket covering the remains. I can't hear over the diesel engine, but the xo leans toward the commander's head. His lips move. His hand moves to the body. Then he returns to the other Marines. They watch in silence as the vehicle rolls away.

Dan rides alone with the remains to the hospital. Blinking in the sheltered fluorescence as the remains of Lieutenant Colonel Christopher "Otis" Raible enter the hospital, Dan stands inside the door. His chin forward, eyes ahead, he raises a salt-encrusted sleeve. He salutes while nonchalant hospital staff mill past.

It's time for Paul, Kyle, and me to go home. Brits give us a ride back to our little truck, abandoned where we left it in the light of the burning fuel farm. We unload, reload, and retrieve Dan from the hospital for the short drive back to the compound. Only the two of us in the back of the truck, the world is quiet and dark around us. Dan and I should probably be on our NVGs, scanning. Instead, I take my helmet off and slump in the truck bed next to him. Dan slaps my shoulder. "You all right?"

My mind is on loop, tugging at the threads of the past six hours. Two dead Marines. At least eleven dead insurgents. Hundred-foot fireballs. Harriers burned to the ground. Clearing the cryo complex. U.S. uniforms. Huffing paint. Warning lights and wailing klaxons. Shouting Brits and growling vehicles. Blaring radios and barking guns. All I feel is regret. Regret that I never fired my weapon.

Home after six hours, the guys see us enter the team tent and scramble to help. One of them looks at me, expectant, and asks how it was.

"Fuck." That's all I've got. I kit down. Someone asks me if I need anything, shoves a small cup of coffee into my hands.

"It's strong, sir. Just brewed it."

The four of us debrief, stories spilling out, questions, clarifications. Where to begin. We walk over to the ROC, debrief again. More spillage. Afterward I've got nothing left. I shower, change, and fall into the sleep tent. On my back in the darkness, I close a partition in my mind and fall asleep. If I dream I will not remember.

DECEMBER 2013

Jen and I were in the car when she asked about That Night. Weren't you guys put in for awards? My chest tightened. An ember flickered in my gut. Yeah, Bronze Stars with Valor. When will you get them? No idea, could be years. Who knows. Who cares.

She prodded further about That Night. My brow creased. I crawled into a place behind my eyes. My answers clipped. Blocks from home now. She asked something else. I refused to answer. She ought to know this shit already. Goddammit, stop asking me about it. We made a left, a sharp right, another right. Then right down the alley, and into the garage. My anger, unaccountable, drew my lips tight.

1300 hours, 15 September

After six hours I wake as if I never slept. The tent is hot under a midday sun. At the alert brief we learn the base is still in lockdown, but analysts have pieced a few things together. Fifteen total attackers breached the wire, one taken prisoner. You can still see the smoke rising across the runway. The brief concluded, I place my alert gear out on the helo and head back to the tent to eat an MRE.

I'm about to open the prepackaged spoon when my alert radio keys up. "Attention on the net. *Scramble. Scramble. Scramble.*" Goddammit. Dan, Matt, and I run into the ROC. Time is ticking. Intel gives us what they've got. Suicide IED at an FOB. Two Marines, godfuckingdammit, both Cat-As. Time to go.

We sprint out the door. The two alert helicopter rotors spin. The crew waves us into the cabin. I barely kit up before we lift off. We're over the fence by the time I unfuck myself and settle into the fifteen-minute ride. I am an endorphin smoothie pushed down the drain of exhaustion. Everything is too bright, too loud, too intense, too fast.

Then we're orbiting over the LZ. Two patients are ready for transport, littered and packaged. Our helo lands. We run to the litter teams, and while Matt and Dan work a patient handoff I lead the litter teams under the spinning rotors to load the patients.

Dan and Matt jump in, and as we close the cabin doors we lift off. Over the intercom, one word: "Buster." It means get us to the hospital as fast as you can. A patient will die if we don't.

Dan and Matt treat the Marines. We maneuver around the cabin, careful not to step on IV tubing or a wounded limb. It's borderline claustrophobic, deafening, chaotic. Can't stand up all the way, best thing to do is knee my way around and retrieve the medical supplies Dan needs.

Both Marines are fucked up, but at least they have their limbs. For now anyway. One of them is tubing fast. The other Marine, in better shape, rolls his head to the side. He reaches for his buddy's limp hand. His lips move but I can't hear what he says. His buddy responds with a subtle tightening, but his lips do not move in response. Then his hand falls away.

I see this, clap my hands for Dan's attention. Dan sees the Marine losing it and kneels down by his head. He pushes on his chest, shouts loud enough for me to hear over the turbines. No response. Goddammit, he's dying on us.

Dan pounds the Marine's chest with a closed fist and shouts again. Jesus, a little movement now. Fuck. Dan looks up at me. I can't see his eyes behind his sunglasses. There's sheen of sweat on his tanned face, drops run down his prominent jaw. He shouts something. What? He motions for IV tubing. I pull what he needs while he grabs a needle and draws from a vial.

I connect the tubing. Dan inserts the needle and slowly pushes a clear liquid into the tubing. He hands me the expended needle and I place it into a sharps container. He gets back into the Marine's face. I hear him this time.

"Come on. Stay with me, Marine."

The Marine opens his eyes. A bit of white, a sliver of pupil. It's enough for now. I check his vitals, write them on a strip of white taped to his chest. The pilots come over the radio.

"One minute out." The gunners look back and extend their index fingers to us. I stick mine up in return. I look out the cabin window, see the fence line of the base approaching.

I check the Marines to prepare them for the move. The Marine on the brink has a blast wound to one of his legs. At one point he had a tourniquet, but it was changed out for a pressure dressing by the time we got him. Pressure dressing protocol: pack gauze into the wound until no more gauze fits. Then wrap a dressing around the limb. Tight.

Between the tourniquet and the pressure dressing, the rest of his leg is mottled, a rising purple color. I recall I used to wrap strings or rubber bands around my fingers as a kid at school. I tightened them until my fingertips turned hard and purple, then released the strictures to feel the warm rush of blood return to the flesh.

We're about to land. We secure the patients, then we're on the ground and running them to ambulances next to the helo pad. We load the Marines, close the doors, and we're off for the thirty-second drive to the emergency room doors. When the doors open, hospital staff rush the patients into the ER. Matt and Dan talk to the doc, tell him what they know. The doc receives the info while assessing the patients, moving back and forth among a rush of multicolored scrubs.

I stand there, blinking in the white fluorescence, breathing in the chlorine. I feel out of place in my sweat-soaked uniform and kit. The doc scribbles notes then looks up: "All right guys, we've got it."

Dan and Matt head my way. We pause for a moment outside the flurry of activity. I feel shaky. Then we head out the double doors we entered.

DECEMBER 7, 2013

"Ladies and Gentlemen, please rise for the publication of the orders." The commander turned his head and said, "Major Komatsu. Post." I left where I stood next to Paul and Kyle, marching straight lines and turning crisp corners to join the commander in front of the flags.

Jen was in the front row, holding an iPad above the swell of our unborn child. I saw my parents on the screen, watching from their apartment in Ahmedabad, India. Behind Jen, rows of people here for the ceremony.

Matt Kirby read the citation from the podium. His voice rose and fell with emotion over twelve lines of text at twelve-pitch font. Mandatory opening and closing sentences. Somehow, it was all supposed to come down to this.

Then it was quiet. The commander and I turned to face each other. He pinned the medal on my chest. Spoke words of congratulations in low tones. Proffered the citation. Take. Shake. Salute.

We turned. Smiled for the cameras.

2200 hours, 18 September

It's been ten years since I last attended a ramp ceremony. There have been plenty of opportunities to see the dead off on the first of many flights to final resting places stateside. But I never went.

I need to be there tonight. Lt. Col. Christopher Raible and Sgt. Bradley Atwell, both killed in the attack, are going home. Protocol: The aircraft that will transport the caskets will sit on the runway, lights off and silent, aircrew inside and waiting. All on base are welcome to attend the ceremony: show up early, in uniform. Form two uninterrupted lines from where the ambulance will show up with the caskets, facing inward. Stand at attention. Salute the casket as it passes. Taps will play. The aircraft ramp will close. Then the formation will break up, and life will go on.

A thousand of us show up thirty minutes early to get into place. Paul, Dan, Kyle, and I walk over and settle into lines several people deep. We form up by the instinct of Day One, Basic Training. Arm's length behind the man in front, even with the man to your right.

The night is quiet when the ambulance arrives, caskets inside. All air traffic has been diverted, all ground movement on the runway silenced. Two caskets come out covered in flags, and a thousand people come to attention and raise their right hands in salute. The pallbearers carry Raible and Atwell past without a sound. Taps plays as the aircraft ramp closes. When it's over, we drop our salutes and walk away.

I walked alone through Arlington Cemetery on my last day in DC, headed to Section 60, Site 10217. The app on my phone showed satellite imagery of the plot. It was outdated, nothing but a bare patch of dirt. Skirting white headstones that stretched to the horizon, I arrived at my destination.

> Christopher
> Keith
> Raible
> Lieutenant Colonel
> US Marine Corps
> Afghanistan
> Aug 18 1972
> Sep 15 2012

I stood awkwardly in front of the lithochromed marble until I took off my backpack, and sat in the grass in front of his headstone. I should say something, I thought. But I couldn't think of anything to say. I tried to take a rubbing with a pencil and paper, but the pencil repeatedly broke through the paper. I found a thicker piece of paper and used a pen instead. It came out all right. I looked up at the sky, stared at the headstone some more. I listened to the traffic on the nearby Memorial Parkway. I took a picture on my phone. I stood and placed a patch in front of his headstone. Then I kissed my hand, placed it on his grave, and walked away.

The Long Goodbye

THOMAS SIMKO

I have too many texts from dead people. Too many. The last text
I ever got from Dominick was "Thx!" He was thanking me for
complimenting a tattoo design. It would be his last one, a grim
reaper tattooed on his chest over his one good lung. Even to
the last he hid his fear. He remained optimistic to his friends
and family, but I know he was scared. I use the phrase "good
lung" with a wide berth. He had maybe 20 percent use out of
it. Because of the lack of oxygen, he dipped in and out of sleep.
He couldn't play games. He couldn't really watch long movies
or movies he hadn't seen. Conversations were sometimes difficult. Those last months. I find it difficult to talk about them.

Every breath for him was a battlefield that took him back
to Iraq. He was a bad soldier, and I mean that. Sonofabitch
flipped a Humvee once. A Humvee. How the hell do you flip a
ten-foot wide, three-ton hunk of reinforced metal? One time
another private stole from his foot locker. Dom thumbed him
right in the eye, blinding him. The private got a discharge.
Dom got the shit details. That's what they did to bad soldiers
in his unit. They were sent into the worst places they could be.
It was the burn pits that did it to him. Those fucking Iraqis,
they'd burn anything. Garbage, plastics, dead animals. Uranium. Fucking uranium. Every time the air from those pits
filled him up, particles of burning uranium seared and cau-
terized holes in his lungs. The holes, over time, would expand.
The holes, over time, would kill him.

He limped on his cane from the kitchen to the bed they
made for him on the downstairs couch. He had a hard time

getting up and down the stairs to use the toilet, stopping to take breaks to breathe every few steps. Everywhere he went in the house a bundle of wires and tubes trailed him, leading from his mask to massive tanks of air, an oxygen content so high, Dom said, that if I had inhaled from his mask I'd be dead before they could call an ambulance. They were a constant companion, a constant reminder. I remember being afraid to step on them, worried that I might cut off his air supply. Even though I knew, at least intellectually, that I was being ridiculous, the fear controlled me.

I'd sit there and talk to him. Listen really. He'd tell me about shows he was watching, things he bought with all the money the military was sending him for his "disability," his plans for the future. It all seemed so ridiculous. He was going to buy a house, get his license back (he'd lost it after crashing his car when the blackouts started). He was going to live, long and happy, once the doctors fixed him up. After he got turned down for a transplant he still talked about those things, for a while. Even when he started on the morphine, he lied to us, told us it was no big deal like we didn't know it was the beginning of the death march. That's what they do, you know. Doctors aren't allowed to assist in suicides, but they certainly are allowed to prescribe ever-increasing amounts of morphine.

The fear drove me away from him in the end. I couldn't be there for his last breaths. I couldn't be there for the last push of the morphine pump. I couldn't be there when his mother, along with mine, undressed him, washed him, shaved his face, and put him in his fatigues. I left a part of me there, on that couch where he died, and I don't want it. If I could, I'd send it to the president. I'd send it the sergeant who sent him to the pits for the first time. I'd send it to the recruiter, who promised him a good job away from an abusive father and a neglectful mother, who traded him his shitty life for a long, painful death. He was so brave to be so scared and still pretend for us. So he'd text me, the last picture he ever drew, a knowing reaper, and a thank you.

What Happened Yesterday in Baghdad

RAUL BENJAMIN MORENO

Once, when I was young and intent on becoming a Texas cattle-man who also apprehended bandits, my parents commissioned a sepia portrait at the I-5 county fair. For about twenty-five dollars, families could select frontier costumes and stand inside a saloon as flashbulbs illuminated the scene. My mother, pictured wearing ostrich feathers and a brooch, refused to distribute the photo the following Christmas on account of whiskey bottles visible in the background. But the original has hung for years in our hallway back home. The visage of the boy at her side is somehow indelible: my pudgy adolescent jowls expressionless beneath a top hat, one small hand gripping a cane, the other pocketing a revolver. I hadn't examined it closely until recently. Then one August night, a thousand miles away on the Front Range, I saw what looked like the same boy online, in another portrait titled *Great Times Together*.

In this second photo, also in midsummer sepia but taken at a Mexican restaurant, sixteen Iraqi youths crowd against a pockmarked wall and a series of wanted posters. In the foreground four girls flaunt silk dresses. One of them grins as she holds up a burlap sack bearing a label: "10,000 GOLD COIN." Another cocks her head above a corset that pushes her chest toward the camera. The boys look even more ridiculous. White teeth and leering eyes pop out from a bandana masking the tallest. To the left a balding gentleman with a goatee raises his Stetson aloft. Three boys are brandishing pistols—one points straight at the photographer— and two others flash hand signs that might be mistaken, in the Denver suburbs, for a shout-out to the Latin Kings.

In the middle of the posse, buried in an overcoat and a wide felt hat, is a boy from Basra whom I'll call H. It is H. whose blank expression still frightens me a little, allowing my mind to transpose my own face. Below the photo, on Facebook, H.'s friends have written comments in Arabic. "Sincerely awesome," reads one. Another asks, "If a total stranger saw this photo, what would they think of you?"

Not long after posing for their portrait, H. and his friends were asked to don nametags and perform an Arabic ballad for a small American audience. We squat attentively in a circle, having agreed to become "conversation partners" for the Iraqis, who attend classes in the basement of Occupational Therapy, a brick building framing the entrance to one of Colorado's land-grant universities, where I teach writing. The students have arrived in the American West—after a week in Washington that featured seminars on "Understanding U.S. Politics," as well as the IMAX film *Deep Sea 3D*—by way of an exchange program sponsored by the U.S. embassy in Baghdad. A few years ago President Bush and Prime Minister Nouri al-Maliki announced the program at the White House, during the zenith of the sectarian violence that followed the American-led invasion of 2003.

On that Wednesday in July, as we gather for conversation in a room lined with tool belts and hacksaws, Maliki is back in Washington, taking questions in the Rose Garden. "Iraq has come a long way and it will continue to solve all problems," the prime minister tells the new president. "And there are so many problems . . ."

The signal for singing comes suddenly. Makeshift drums crafted from cardboard and cellophane appear from hiding, and H. begins beating out a fast rhythm that everyone but the Americans seems to know by heart. Seated to my right is a girl named M., with a birthmark in her left eye. She tells me, in a whisper, that the song narrates a story similar to *Romeo and Juliet*, about lovers whose affection is forbidden, and that it's a favorite at Friday potlucks back in Iraq.

Days later, when we meet for another dialogue, the Americans join in the singing—this time "Happy Birthday to You," in English and Arabic, for a tall, baby-faced boy. As the song's last bars ring out, the other boys rush forward to smother their friend in a hug. Meanwhile M., dressed in a long red T-shirt, has discarded her nametag ("I don't like nametags"). How old are you? Twenty. What do you study? Dentistry. Later I notice that, instead of a self-portrait, M.'s Facebook profile shows the cast of *Grey's Anatomy*. A status message she's posted there quotes Enrique Iglesias, asking about dancing and crying, asking if I would run and never look back. "And would you save my soul, tonight?"

I spent much of the Iraq War producing features for a big news network in Washington. I came to think of myself, during that time, as fairly knowledgeable about modern Mesopotamia and its bloody tribes. Many afternoons, just before airtime and depending on the week's toll from car bombings and street battles, I would become the voice of a wailing man who had just lost his children, a shop owner unable to stay in business, or a lawyer explaining the plight of a detainee. The translated words of these men usually came noted in scripts that take on, for producers, the immutable qualities of scripture: NEEDS ONE MALE V/O (voiceover).

Along with the sounds and pictures of war that crossed my desktop, there was also the lingering possibility that one day I would wind up in Baghdad as our bureau's producer. I am thankful, I think, that never happened. But in my mind Iraq remains a not-so-distant place. The men at desks on either side of mine were both sent. During one going away party, which felt more like a wake, we lavished our friend with hard candy, crackers, peanut butter, good luck charms, bourbon, and chewing gum. (He loves gum; it eases the stress, I imagine, of rock stars dying during graveyard shifts.) Finally, because it was hard to find in Baghdad, someone added a long, thick summer sausage. This producer returns to the little house by the Tigris every few months now. He complains of having to count cash—for the network's security guards, fixers, and cooks—in bundles piled high on his mattress. A photo posted online shows him playing Nintendo tennis with a veteran correspondent, her arms swinging high to return a volley. Even these days, Americans don't travel much in Baghdad.

The convoy enters a crowded neighborhood with houses close in on either side

30 //We got guys running in front of us //

The street is suddenly empty. Then . . .

26 "Small Arms! Holy shit. If you see fucking small arms fucking light em up" //

29 upsound shooting "goddammit, I can't see it" then fade under

The convoy takes fire from all sides.

UPSOUND SHOOTING

Staff Srgt Jimmy Whetsone says they were expecting something like this.

36 //I believe al-qaida has moved into that neighborhood, down in the

south neighborhood there they are starting to collect//

END HUMVEE SOUND

The first Iraqi I befriend in the basement of Occupational Therapy is F. She's seated at a table with four others, all young Iraqi men, and though we've only just met, she begins telling the story of her father's death. For years the man headed a bank in Alwiyah, a financial quarter of east Baghdad that once housed middle-class families. F. describes the city's neighborhoods as a daughter of Berlin or Buenos Aires might describe what is trendy and what is not; Alwiyah, it seems, has turned seedy and commercial. But she does this while blinking back tears. Her father's passing came during Iraq's first post-Saddam elections, in 2005. He had heart trouble, F. explains, and on voting day a curfew meant to protect polling stations also meant that she and her mother couldn't get him to a hospital. And so he died, at home, in their arms.

Recalling this moment smudges F.'s mascara. She apologizes with a little laugh. Her face, I begin to realize, displays a perfect clash of conservatism and coquetry: a tight black head covering hides everything but painted lashes, nose, and chin, but over the top of the covering she wears a black-and-white checkered flat cap, angled like Madonna's or Missy Elliott's. In less than a month, F. tells us, she will turn twenty-one. So I ask about the drinking age in Iraq.

"Well, people in Iraq—they don't drink, for religious reasons."

"Psssshaw!"

F.'s answer is interrupted by my online twin, H., who is seated across the table. The drummer boy from Basra has darting eyes and a fondness for football ("Sorry, soccer"). For a few seconds the girl and the boy chatter harshly in what sounds like practiced whispers. H.'s three companions, meanwhile, look uncomfortable. I ask F. whether she always argues with H.

"Oh, no, he's my friend. I like him," she says, glaring. Then, in Arabic, she mouths his nickname: "Mischievous."

H. ignores the teasing and tries to apologize for the confusion with the confidence of a travel agent. "Today you can do anything in Iraq you want," he says, scrawling his email address in my notebook.

Abdul Wahhab is a computer technician at the Trade Bank of Iraq. He was about 100 meters from the square when the white sedan exploded. He remembers two small helicopters hovering overhead—shooting into the square. He could see the flashes from the muzzles of their guns. Wahhab turned his car around and started weaving through the traffic to get away.

[Duration: 0'21"] <WAHHAB: I used my car horn and was shouting to the people go, go move okay and suddenly I use the middle mirror inside the car and I saw the armored cars

behind me.> [. . .] In his rear view mirror he watched the Blackwater SUVs closing in, swallowing the ground between them. Then he heard heavy thumps on his back windscreen. The Blackwater contractors were throwing water bottles at his car. Then it got worse.

[Duration: 0'26"] <WAHHAB: So suddenly there is something stop my car. When I turn around a saw a big car hit my car from the right side and the window of the front door it's broken. I feel my hands get broken, I know that they are shot me. So I open the door and drop myself in the street because I thought that they wants to kill me.>

M. is from Baghdad's Karada district. Track pants, a soccer jersey, and a baseball cap conceal the fact that he is studying medicine and will start earning money soon as a resident. His English is impeccable. He says that for most of the past decade his family has lived near the Green Zone, which can be both a good and a bad thing. The coming and going of Marines kept a lid on violence erupting in other parts of Baghdad. But in 2006, during the unrest that followed a Sunni group's bombing of the sacred Mosque of the Golden Dome, shells fell on M.'s house, then failed to explode. He spreads his arms wide to show me the size of the munitions. "Old shells," says the young doctor, chortling in a hollow-sounding way. "Those guys didn't know how to put them together." He pushes a pair of Coke-bottle glasses up the bridge of his nose. Neither M.'s parents nor his siblings were hurt, but the attack on Karada, intended for Americans in the Green Zone, pulverized spirits along with roof tiles.

Later, the teacher facilitating today's dialogue suggests that the Iraqis follow the example of Martin Luther King, Jr., that they promote an ethic of nonviolence among their countrymen.

"I'd just like to say one thing," M. interjects. "The last guy who tried that, who really represented that? His name was Imam Husayn, and he was murdered in front of everybody." (Legend has it that Husayn ibn Ali ibn Abi Talib, a Shiite grandson of the prophet Mohammed revered for opposing tyranny, was beheaded in the Battle of Karbala, in 680.)

(***SNEAK AMBI, MARKET SOUNDS AND GENERATOR, LEAVE UNDER***) IN BAGHDAD'S KARADA NEIGHBORHOOD, 30-YEAR-OLD KADOUM HUSSEIN WORKED IN HIS SMALL CONVENIENCE STORE AND SAID AS A SHI'ITE AND AS AN IRAQI, HE WAS GLAD TO HEAR THAT THE CEASE-FIRE WAS EXTENDED: CUT (ARABIC, NEEDS MALE V/O) We heard about freezing the Mahdi army activity for another six months. It's a good step and we bless it, and we congratulate Muqtada al-sadr for this brave decision. We hope it's a step forward to support national reconciliation between the Iraqi people and to achieve stability in this country.

OFFICIALS SAID SADR'S DECISION MAY BUY MORE TIME FOR IRAQ'S POLITICAL LEADERS TO COME TOGETHER, AND THE U-S SAID IT WAS READY TO INCLUDE MOQTADA AL-SADR IN THAT DIALOGUE. BUT SOME IRAQIS SEE TODAY'S NEWS AS AVOIDING JUST ONE OF MANY PITFALLS SCATTERED ALONG THE ROAD AHEAD.

Talk in the basement shifts to bribes. M. says that corruption is everywhere, especially in Baghdad. Just as in Washington or Denver, medical residents want to be assigned to major hospitals, not outlying suburbs. Test scores can get them downtown, but money also helps with placement. "I would pay, I would," he says. I ask if he could buy higher scores directly, but M. insists that's not possible now, because of reforms at the Ministry of Education. Still, everyone brought to this table by the U.S. embassy—M. in his track pants, a boy from Al Anbar with walnut-colored skin and a glassy stare, and A., from Irbil, with muscular arms decorated in tattoos—says they paid cash for a real Iraqi passport. One student quotes 250 U.S. dollars, others 400. "And it came back properly signed in three hours," someone adds. Paying less for the same document would mean waiting about eight months, they explain.

Who do you talk to for this?

"Anybody. They'll come to you," A. tells me. "I could get you one myself if you wanted." A. says he has been to Syria twice by bus to visit family. He also keeps in touch with Iraqis who have fled farther abroad—to Norway, Sweden, the UK, the UAE.

I push a bit farther: Could you get me an American passport? At this question the table falls silent. A. shakes his head.

THE PLANNING MINISTRY WAS A NIGHTMARE UNDER SADDAM, AND IT'S STILL BAD: CUT (ARABIC, NEEDS MALE V/O) Unfortunately, the problem is still happening, even after the fall of the old regime—the first thing is always the payoff. The official says how much are you going to pay me, then we can discuss the contract.

AS IT HAPPENS, THE PLANNING MINISTRY HAS ITS OWN BOOTH JUST ACROSS THE WAY. SPOKESMAN ABD ALZAHRA AL-HINDAWY SAYS CORRUPTION IS A PROBLEM, BUT IT'S A TWO-WAY STREET: CUT (ARABIC, NEEDS MALE V/O) I will not deny these problems, for sure there are corruption cases. Unfortunately there are some contractors who also want to get contracts illegally, so there is corruption from that side as well.

One Baghdadi girl named Z. feigns embarrassment at the talk of corruption. "You don't pay bribes to everyone," she says, stifling a grin. "Just to most people." Somehow, along with a number of other students here, Z. is celebrating a birthday. But she is also refusing to eat the sheet cake that the teacher has brought from the supermarket.

"We have a tradition that no one else can eat cake until the birthday girl does," explains the teacher to the rest of the class. All eyes lock on Z.

"I'm not hungry," Z. replies, crossing her arms above a black sequined blouse and rolling her eyes. (Later, over lunch, she is outed as a gifted pastry cook.)

As we depart, after shaking hands with the boys, I extend my hand to Z. and forget, for a moment, the gendered limits of physical contact prescribed by Islamic teachings, which today's meeting has already tested. Z. watches my hand as she might a viper weaving through the shallows. Then she leans forward at the waist, halting the snake's progress with a kind of samurai's bow.

Specialist major puts another piece of breakfast sausage on his hook. ACT: I TRIED BREAD AND CORN BUT THAT DIDN'T WORK AS WELL AS SAUSAGE.

Rumor has it the fish developed a taste for meat under Saddam Hussein because they were regularly fed with his victims. ACT: THEY SAID THEY HAD WOOD-CHIPPERS ALONG THE SHORE LINE OUT HERE AND THERE WAS BLOOD AND BODY PARTS IN THEM STILL.

Staff Sergeant David Pinney has heard the rumors too. ACT: CARP ARE CARP. THEY ARE GOING TO EAT ANYTHING I THINK PEOPLE STORIES GET A LITTLE, YOU KNOW. I DON'T THINK THERE'S ANYTHING TO IT. KIDS (LAUGHS)

Rumor also has it that these soldiers can expect another tour here in the future. Seth major hopes that is not the case. ACT: I REALLY DON'T WANT TO COME BACK AGAIN.

As one year at the network became two, then three, and finally four, it became easier—too easy, I think—to stride into wood-paneled studios and become a taxi driver bleeding from shrapnel in his back. Or an Iraqi police captain whose queue of recruits has just evaporated into dust. Affirmation of my "tracking" came in quiet little nods from engineers manning dials at the control boards. But certain characters, I came to find out, were better voiced by colleagues. The bearded editor upstairs, for example, would appear at my desk just before happy hour in Baghdad, after taking in a script, to become the voice of a cleric delivering a sermon. The red-eyed staffer with a house on the Bay, on the other hand, usually stood in for farmers. And the field producer, who rides to work on a skateboard, prefers insurgents.

Sometimes, late at night, frantic requests for voiceovers would come from someone working the morning show on the far side of the building. This person was usually a talented producer, but one who hadn't yet heard the Arabic screams or Kurdish whispers still trickling off the satellite dish of a correspondent on the ground. In these moments I became a little proud, I recall, of tracking voiceovers in just two takes. One full of the anger or agony that our script seemed to suggest. Another in a dull monotone, the kind of voice that could suffice, on deadline, for any kind of pain.

NIBRAS NASEER—A RAIL-THIN 18-YEAR-OLD—FLED IRAQ MORE THAN A YEAR AGO—AFTER HE SPENT 10 DAYS IN A HOSPITAL, HE SAYS, FOR INJURIES—THE RESULT OF SEVERE BEATINGS.

(doorbell—hot—and under—cross fade with kids sound) [. . .] U.S. SOLDIERS HAVE DISMANTLED A NUMBER OF TORTURE HOUSES IN IRAQ. IN PLACES LIKE THESE—FEW WERE SPARED, SAYS NASEER. INCLUDING AN 11-YEAR BOY. THE KIDNAPPERS ACCUSED HIM OF SPOTTING FOR U.S. SOLDIERS—POINTING OUT EXPLOSIVE DEVICES HIDDEN IN HIS NEIGHBORHOOD. THEY FORCED HIM TO ADMIT HE HAD HELPED THE AMERICANS.

Well, this little kid—they were beating him but not like us. What can you expect from a little kid, he was crying all the time.

What happened to the little boy? They took him out—and they killed him the same way—and I went crazy—I lost my mind.

AS NASEER TELLS HIS STORY—HIS SHOULDERS HUNCH SLIGHTLY. THE ONLY OUTWARD FLICKER OF EMOTION COMES WHEN HE RECOUNTS HIS UNEXPECTED RELEASE AFTER HIS FAMILY PAID A THIRTY-THOUSAND-DOLLAR RANSOM. HE HAS NO IDEA WHY HE IS ALIVE. OR IF HE WILL EVER GET OVER WHAT HAS HAPPENED TO HIM.

Our third and final morning in the basement begins with another circle. This one should form, explains the teacher, according to the hour at which the students went to bed last night. The glassy-eyed boy from Al Anbar shuffles to the far end of the line, says he didn't sleep until 7:45 a.m. thanks to a can of Monster energy drink. The room erupts in laughter. Most of the other students have clustered around 2:00 a.m.— the same hour that our campus's dormitories fall silent. But most won't say what kept them awake. An awkward silence sets in. Then, after some prodding, a Christian girl attending school in Irbil admits to a "complicated" interlude with R., a Muslim boy.

Again the Americans fan out among tables for conversations; this time I am joined by L., the student from Irbil, and another H., from one of Iraq's notorious western provinces. This H. wears severe, carefully-applied eye shadow that forms green butterflies at her temples. She talks longingly about Kurdistan, whose tolerance of minorities and religious differences "reminds me of coming to America." She describes a kind of magic, too, in walking Colorado streets with handsome boys like R. and not having village elders ask questions. Back home, H. says, she must tell the world "We're just friends." Her egalitarian wonder has been fed by literature. "I'm reading George Orwell—*1984*—and it's just like Iraq, just like Iraq," she tells me. "Also Salman Rushdie." I recommend *Fahrenheit 451* and she nods excitedly. "These are books where there's a political message, in the story, that you can't quite see, yes?"

L., meanwhile, longs for South Dakota. Years ago her Christian ("but not religious") parents managed to send her to a public high school near an Indian reservation, where the bitter cold reminded her of Kurdistan. I tell the girls about my grandfather's birth farther north, in farming country that lacked electricity. About the horse-drawn wagon with a woodstove that carried him to school, about the cold sermons in a white church, and about the day the first light bulb came to town.

Our conversation ends abruptly with the arrival to the basement of plastic babies—a dozen of them dressed in terrycloth. The Red Cross is sponsoring CPR practice. "I'm glad to know how to do this," says L., "but I could never do it in real life. Especially not with a baby!"

IN THE NEXT ROOM FIVE-YEAR-OLD ZAHRA HAS HORRIFIC BURNS ON HER THIN ARMS AND BACK. DOCTORS ARE TRYING TO SAVE HER ALMOST SEVERED LEFT HAND. SAJADAH HAMID READS HER STORIES.

Nat sound: her grandmother—(and continue ambi tail for next track)

SAJADAH, IN A TRADITIONAL LONG BLACK ROBE AND HEAD SCARF, EXPLAINS HER GRANDDAUGHTER WAS BADLY BURNED WHEN THEIR BAGHDAD HOUSE WAS HIT BY A BOMB.

(Arabic with English provided)

"She saved her sister from the fire and that's why her hands caught fire. Her sister died."

ZAHRA LISTENS INTENTLY TO THIS EXPLANATION. HER FACE BRIGHTENS WHEN ASKED HOW SHE IS DOING.

"I am comfortable here. They all like me here."

Tonight, as I page through some eight hundred scripts from features and interviews produced for the network, I am beginning to suspect that I know very little about Iraq. Except, perhaps, for that fact that so many thousands have been hurt, so many more love their homeland, and so few feel at ease. Take my new friends, for instance, the boys and girls who might be silenced or disappeared if they were named in an American essay. They have returned to Iraq to spend their nights posting messages online.

"Stop Killing Iraqi Christians," reads a Facebook invitation from one student.

"Colorado: How are you guys? Miss you so much." This from the tall, goofy-looking kid who told me he tosses fried bread over the walls ringing the Green Zone, in exchange for money.

"Miss you all. I want to see you," writes the girl named M. "How are you?"

"Miss you too," the boy named M. replies. "I feel so sad and devastated by what happened yesterday in Baghdad, although I still have my friends."

My other friend in Baghdad, the one with piles of cash on his mattress, is pushing a year in Iraq, all told, and sensing a kind of perpetuity. Early one Tuesday in September, with satellites blinking overhead, we tapped out a slow conversation.

1:17 a.m. Couldn't turn 40 in Baghdad or D.C. for that matter.

1:19 a.m. How's this shift? Any better or worse?

1:22 a.m. Well, the security situation is better. (Kind of—some good days, some bad.) But I am used to everything now.

1:47 a.m. Glad I caught you, man! We'll talk again soon.

1:48 a.m. Sorry I had to dip away. Let's please stay in close touch!

1:49 a.m. No worries, stay safe and keep the gum handy!

1:49 a.m. Gum is very important in Baghdad.

Some weeks later, with the incumbent prime minister talking up Iraq's security, two minibuses carrying bombs said to be assembled inside the Green Zone tore apart on crowded Haifa Street, outside the Ministry of Justice. The attack killed 155 people and wounded hundreds more. Then, in early December, another barrage: 127 killed, over 400 wounded, and the remains of suicide vehicles left smoldering outside three government ministries, including Justice.

But it was an ear-splitting Monday morning in January, with parliamentary elections looming, that nearly took my friend's life. This time the targets were hotel compounds frequented by foreign journalists, including the Al Hamra, which sits across the street from the little house by the Tigris; "an inelegant, 10-story wedge of concrete and glass," wrote one reporter of our compound's namesake. An Iraqi man working there told a colleague that shrapnel went through his chair by the window. "Luckily [I] wasn't sitting in the chair." Luck did not favor thirty-six people that day in Baghdad, and then half as many the following morning, at the city's crime lab.

As dawn breaks over a new decade here in the high country, my clock radio begins to murmur about an end to the war. I'm already awake, staring at *Great Times Together*, wondering how this friend and that one fared the night. I fall to wondering too, now, about what has become of the voices I left behind.

Zeh Mutaasif Yum

MICAH FIELDS

Someone had made a mistake. Somewhere, in that brilliant and complicated train of communication, in the churning mess of government decision, someone had been wrong.

We had been sleeping when it happened. We couldn't hear it from our cots, but were soon dispatched, on our feet and into that July day, in Afghanistan, in air that felt like a continuous blast of jet exhaust in your face. We were filing west down a dirt road, all eight of us, leaving only a few to man the outpost. We were walking toward a drop site.

At some impossible altitude, undetectable except for a low growl in the clouds, a pilot had been looking down from his upholstered chair, had seen everything, and had suspected a dot on the road for something malicious, which had then been relayed to someone else, and then someone else, and so on, becoming a more dramatic and imposing dot with each rung of command, until the dot, hardly seen by anyone, became the enemy. It became, inevitably, through the handling of various officers, a distilled point of evil itself. It needed to be killed.

It took only moments for this to happen. It took less for the dot, not an IED implanter but an eight-year-old getting water from a ditch, to vanish from the pilot's screen, leaving only a cleared circle on the earth. I have seen bombs drop from a distance, which is to say that I have seen a place on the ground go from not exploding to exploding in an instant, and despite what happened afterward—the walk out there, the seeing him on the road in pieces, the inability to explain to his father why, why, was getting water so threatening?—he did not feel it.

At fifteen I worked at a veterinary clinic. It was my first job, and the act of earning was liberating for me. I could now buy the fresh-baked cookies sold at lunch in the cafeteria, some CDs, and an accordion of condoms that sat uncomfortably expiring in my wallet past graduation. I wore hospital scrubs and learned from the technicians how to administer fluids subcutaneously to a cat, for example, and scooped shit from a patch of grass in the back. On Fridays a man would come for our weekly euthanizations. He would carry them from the freezer in the basement, load them into a white GMC van, and take them, I guessed, to be burned. I would help with the especially large animals, and we carried them up the stairs like a loveseat, or a coffee table, minding the corners and repositioning at doorways. They were draped in foggy white trash bags, stiff with rigor mortis and cold. I remember thinking of them not as dogs, not as Great Pyrenees or wolfhound or mastiff, but as furniture, stuff to be moved. Like a plank in my hands, they became invisible after death.

There had been training, in Hawaii and California. There had been the firing of practice rounds, the rehearsing of hand grenade lobbing—like a baseball!—and fire team rushing to bunkers with plastic targets. There had been talk of death, of killing, but mostly the silent and individual imaginings, fantasies, little movies of heroism we played in our heads, movies where we prevailed, perhaps slightly wounded but intact and proud and celebrated, on some false battlefield. It is the kind of contrived self-assurance that has driven some terribly evil forces, I now know, but we dreamed them.

We learned some Pashto and Farsi, quick phrases that sounded awkward on our midwestern and southern tongues. "Wadarega!" meant stop. "Wadarega yaa dee wulim!" meant stop, or I'll shoot you. "Chup sha" meant shut up. Though we quickly forgot them, it didn't matter. They were meant for fighting men. They were meant for warriors, American action figures in some Mexican standoff, not us. So we walked around not talking to anyone, adolescents in body armor, not knowing anyone's name, or where we could get some Pepsi, or why their son's body was now half a body, smoldering, actually smoldering, on the road near their house.

We would search in our military phrasebooks, looking for some instruction, some way to manage what we couldn't understand, but it wasn't there. Like our childish desires to be heroic, manly, the simple act of feeling, communicating, had been stripped from our world. We were in some bigger machine. We were in a place where one man could sit in the sky, kill someone, and send us, a squad of recent high school graduates, armed with our government-issue travel guides to Afghanistan, to explain it.

I remember this day not as some convenient war anecdote, but as the day our movies stopped. That day Afghanistan, war, our lives, became its own slippery kind of monster in our brains. The obscured shapes in those bags suddenly became paws, a tail, the sagging jowls of a Great Dane. It was the first time I had seen a body part by itself, and I stood there, scrambling for interpretation, sifting through the useless demands for obedience. We had learned everything that didn't matter; how to scrape carbon deposits from the little chambers in our rifles, how to make our beds, folding the sheets at forty-five degree angles. We had been taught how to order a mortar strike. We had not, however, under any circumstances, been taught to apologize.

Chai Party

JONATHAN BURGESS

The Science of War

The blast of arid heat hit me square in the face the moment
I stepped off the plane as I struggled a bit under the weight
of my three bags. I straightened my back, tried to maintain positive control of my rifle, tucked my chin a bit, and
engaged my legs as I willed one foot in front of the other. I
surveyed the barren desert through the shimmering heat
and dust in front of me. Unintelligible shouts came from the
enlisted leaders, but I couldn't discern where they were or
what they were saying through the cacophony of the C-130
engines and the military vehicles nearby. Our company of
infantry Marines landed at Camp Leatherneck, Afghanistan,
in the early summer days of 2009. It was my second deployment, and I was only twenty years old. I had left behind my
wife, who was also a Marine, in Southern California pregnant with our first child.

We settled into the area, aligning our cots and establish-
ing guard duties, and got an orientation to the camp's facili-
ties (with strict instructions to avoid the female-heavy areas).
Most of us shaved our heads within the first couple of hours.
The entire company slept on old metal and canvas cots under
the same giant tent. When I first laid eyes on it, I thought of
fumigation tents and the old southern tent revivals. The grow-
ing sense of madness, restlessness, I felt probably germinated
from the constant presence of dust and sweat in, on, or around
anything and everything and pervaded all of my senses.

The Suck

The usual culprits: boredom and homesickness set in. We were thankful that our leaders left us alone, with the exception of the necessary and understandable control measures typical of military life.

"Stay hydrated, and keep your cot area squared away," the company gunny would say.

"Aye, Gunny," we'd respond. They were likely just as bored and uncomfortable as we were, and there was a resulting banality to our daily schedule. Once, this lull in rigidity afforded me a rare opportunity. I sat on my dust-laden cot, drank water, and loosened my boots. I stared at a two-sided laminated photo I carried in my cargo pocket. One side was one of my favorite snapshots of my wife, Kelly, and the other side was a three-dimensional ultrasound printout of my unborn son, Dominik. It looked as if he was smiling at me. I smiled back as often as I could.

It didn't take long for the usual din of heavy metal music, laughter, and rifle and machine gun parts to crescendo to a roar early every evening when the sun returned to its own trench to fight another day. The card games started, and we enjoyed a steady influx of energy drinks (oh, the joy of half-sized Rip-Its "tactically acquired" from the chow hall!) and tobacco into the company area. Hardly any of us had ever experienced combat, but all of us were itching to go farther down into the Helmand River Valley for a taste. We daydreamed, joked, and speculated about killing the enemy. As the expression goes: when all you have is a hammer, everything looks like a nail.

The senior leaders, enlisted and commissioned, must have picked up on our restlessness and sense of urgency, because the games soon began. Uniform, grooming, and weapon regulations became more strictly enforced. Aaron Cardenas, or "Cardy," kept a close eye on me but not like the higher-ups. He was a veteran of the battles of Fallujah and Ramadi and had weathered two deployments at sea just to get back to combat.

He had taken a special interest in helping, and I had, in some strange way, taken a special interest in helping him. Cardy had a twin named James, but I was one of the few who could tell them apart. He was a short, squat, unassuming Marine with a kind of ethnic ambiguity about him. He hailed from Monterey Park, California, and always offered me an "Al Capone" cognac-dipped cigarillo at certain momentous occasions. He moseyed over from time to time in the tent to talk about Terminator, the movie *Platoon*, or guns; or to ask me how I was doing and to see if I had my gear and my team in order.

The company began discussing the mission at hand, the terrain in which we would be operating, the enemy and his resources, and our objectives and goals. The tacticians among us loved every second of it, but I—being at the bottom rung of the leadership ladder—just wanted to take my fire team into the bush and run through walls to kill bad guys. In retrospect, our immediate motives could have been loftier or more profound; but we were there, we were responsible for each other, and we were going to kill anyone who offered opposition.

The planning began, though, or at least in a way that was visible and immediate to me. The maps went up, the notebooks came out, and little terrain models in the sand littered the area just outside the tent as smaller units rehearsed concepts. We soon started patrolling with weapons across the base, which took just over half a day to accomplish while carrying a full pack and wearing body armor. The load was eighty pounds or more. It was especially apparent what was needed and what was not when we received our full ordnance allotment just before we pushed out into enemy territory, "Indian country," where we would live out the rest of the deployment. The ammunition list, at least for myself, consisted of two hundred and forty rounds of 5.56mm rifle ammunition, twelve rounds of 40mm grenades for my grenade launcher, four 60mm mortar rounds for the mortar team traveling with us, several smoke and fragmentation grenades, and flares. In other words, our packs got heavier but morale improved.

Batter Up

It wasn't long before a sergeant major and a general (I recalled their names as well as they recalled mine) came down to see us. That's how we, the grunts at the bottom, knew it was getting close and getting serious. This meant we were in for an over-the-top and obligatory pre-combat motivational speech. There was the usual shouting, knife handing, and boisterousness that we hoped the enemy could somehow hear miles away from the base. We were coming for them, and we wanted them to know it. We wanted them to be ready. We wanted a worthy opponent. We wanted a good fight. The order was given, and we commenced with more planning and training. Soon we were told to pack up the bags we wouldn't get until later in the deployment when we had cleared a safe area. Cameras and phones had to go into the bags as well, and the only things left were our armor, weapons, and the packs out of which we would soon be living.

Word had already started getting around about little skirmishes with the enemy here and there, and we couldn't go more than a day or two without hearing rockets being launched from another part of the base. The base increasingly ceased any and all external communication in something commonly referred to as "River City." No phone calls, emails, video calls, or letters could leave. Fortunately, I had already said "goodbye for now" to my wife and various other family members. Then the time came to stage the entire unit on the airfield at the other end of the base.

We were going to launch in the dead of night; so we waited around with our packs and armor all lined up in neat rows just a hundred feet or so from the helicopters. We chatted, took pictures for posterity's sake, smoked cigarettes, and milled about the area looking for our buddies in other companies within the battalion. I found a friend of mine, David Baker, perched on top of a dirt berm conversing with several British soldiers. I joined in, and we joked until the glow of our cigarettes became the only indicators of our presence there on our little dirt island of normality. Someone said through the darkness, "I wish I was where I was when I was wishing I was here." Everyone laughed.

I looked at David's silhouette and said, "Man, if I ever make it out of this place and manage to get out of the Marine Corps, I'll dye my hair green."

Everyone laughed again. David said, "Promise?" Several months later, I would hear David died in a cornfield after stepping on a landmine set by the Taliban.

Before I wandered back over to my squad's staging area, I traded 40mm grenades with one of the Brits. I gave him some sort of parachuted flare, if memory serves, and he gave me one of my most prized possessions at that time: a 40mm red phosphorous grenade. It took a place of honor on my armor and would be reserved only for the most special occasion.

Once I returned to my team, I approached my squad leader, Aaron Denning, and told him there was a folded American flag in a large plastic bag at the bottom of my pack. I trusted him with my life and would have followed him anywhere. He was the young, stout-hearted kind of Marine, a man's man. There in staging area I squinted through the dusk sunlight at him, and he squinted back, the usual five o'clock shadow threatening his clean-cut appearance. With as little melodrama as possible, which was a feat for me in those days, I asked him to take the flag from me if I died and to give it to my son. He gave a firm reassuring nod and said, "No problem, brother. I promise." He raised a pack to his face and pressed a Marlboro between his lips, and we left it at that.

The Art of Survival

We filed in and sat on the hard seats shoulder to shoulder with our packs and weapons on our laps or between our legs. The high-pitched whir of the helicopter engines assailed my ears. The smell of fuel, body odor, foot powder, and Copenhagen Long Cut tobacco pervaded my nostrils. There was a soft glow of round green circles when we lifted off as men started turning on and testing their night vision monocles one last time.

The midflight signal came from a dark, helmeted silhouette to make our weapons ready and a brief roar of shouting followed. I flipped my night vision monocle down over my left eye and looked across the green interior of the compartment at my friend and fellow team leader, Josh Ibanez. He ripped his rifle's charging handle to the rear chambering a round, slammed a 40mm grenade into the breach of his grenade launcher, and slapped the butt stock of his rifle. I laughed in spite of the churning in my stomach. I swallowed what felt like a large ball of cotton and looked over at my teammates. I raised my left thumb. The three of them responded in kind with a thumb up or a raised fist.

I felt the helicopter plunge deeper into the darkness. I kept waiting to hear the sound of bullets peppering metal, but it never came. We touched down, and everyone stood up to file out. I stood as well, but the weight of my pack sent my small frame careening right onto my face in the floor. I panicked as I saw boots walking away from me, but I flipped up my night vision monocle, braced myself on the metal floor, and tried to stand. Claudio Patino, one of our snipers, pulled me up from the floor and shoved me forward. He had a hard, clean-shaven jaw and a warrior's gaze. I felt his face over my shoulder as he shouted into my ear, "You okay, bro?" I turned, gazing into the abyss at the end of what felt more like a subterranean tunnel than the inside of a helicopter. I turned my face back and shouted over my shoulder, "Yeah! I'm good, man! Thanks!" Patino would die in a bold and selfless act several miles north of that place in a gunfight eleven months later.

I stepped out into the black void without knowing where my foot would land. I sank immediately into about five feet of water falling forward yet again, and Patino landed on top of me. I panicked again, but Patino pulled me up a second time after swimming his way to stable footing. I had become acquainted with Patino a bit at the base but not well enough to create all this extra work for him. I wound my arm around his, pulled myself up letting go as soon as possible, and raised my weapon to an alert position. I swore under my breath. If survival was an art, I was dabbling in the abstract.

As we waded through the flooded field, I straightened my helmet and flipped my night vision back onto my face. I caught sight of several men darting through a tree line just outside a nearby compound. I considered shooting them but couldn't see any weapons in the mix. They were gone as quickly as they had appeared, prompting me to lower my rifle halfway back to the ground. I trudged onward and started scrambling to find my Marines and corpsman. We managed to reunite and reorganize in the chaos of the rotor wash from the helicopter as it lifted off leaving us there in black, muddy ditches. We spread out and formed a large circular perimeter, and a preternatural quiet settled through the ranks. I caught myself missing the dry, barren desert as I kept sinking into my grassy, muddy position. Aaron Denning came around and told us the plan was to wait for daylight just a few hours away before we began the push north. Until then we were supposed to take turns sleeping. Half of us went to sleep first while the other half stayed up. As Aaron crept away into the night like a heavily-armed Cyclops, I thought to myself: *No one in his right mind would, or even could, go to sleep right now.* Someone from another platoon began snoring almost like a whisper in the darkness to my right.

The Push

The next morning we rose from the wet field soaked and pining for a gunfight, and we started walking. The sun crested the tree-lined horizon and prompted the onset of humidity and temperatures above the nighttime norm of ninety-five degrees Fahrenheit to hover without mercy around one hundred twenty. The night and following dawn had been quiet, but I wasn't convinced. We moved from one flooded field to another, avoiding the usual, natural routes of travel, which were likely booby-trapped or prime ambush territory. We shifted under the weight of our packs and strolled along through the flat, grid-like fields in a wide formation. The sun began a slow boil as we crossed an open field to a tree-lined ditch filled with stagnant water. My point man and my automatic rifleman moved into the open field on the other side of the ditch.

Three eruptions of dirt just a few feet in front of their boots halted us in place. As I felt a rush of blood to my face, my mind recognized the three snaps in front of us to be bullets. I scanned the most likely direction and source but couldn't see anyone. "Get down!" I yelled at the two of them, simultaneously motioning with my hand to Doc Welsh, the corpsman beside me. The four of us slinked into the concealment of the trees and took cover in the ditch as a few more pop shots rang out. I got on the radio and informed Denning that we were being shot at by an unseen enemy and asked if we could engage. Another squad leader, Daniel Avalos, spoke out over the same frequency, "Did you just ask if you could shoot back?" I felt my cheeks flush and tugged at my body armor. Daniel was one of the few experienced combat veterans among us and one to be emulated. He had fought in Iraq a few years earlier.

I spotted movement in the far tree line just behind the ledge of a low dried-mud wall across the open field. I raised my rifle just as Joshua Ibanez shouted, "He's got a gun!" Josh launched a 40mm grenade at the target as I decided against the rifle and slipped my left hand down to the trigger of my grenade launcher. I already had the range in my mind. Apparently Josh and I weren't the only ones with the same idea. Two other grenades were launched, and all four impacted the enemy position in quick succession. Debris flew in every direction as a violent concussion broke the morning stillness yet again. Nothing remained when the dust settled. We picked up and pressed on.

Just a few moments later, after clearing a neighboring compound, we were invited inside a gentleman's home for a bit of chai tea. After having an early morning gunfight in his backyard, we all sat around sipping tea in the floor of this man's home and erupted into fits of giggling at the absurdity of the situation and our surreal morning. I moved from room to room surveying the mud palace as our commander sat on the floor conferring eye to eye with the generous host and his family with the help of an interpreter. I noticed ornate rugs rolled and precariously stacked in one room from floor to ceiling. There were hefty white bags of some sort of grain stacked high and deep in the next room. A couple of women dressed head to toe in burkas huddled with five small children in a far room. One woman gripped the shoulders of a small child at her feet, the pair gazing at me with a mixture of fear and curiosity in their eyes. The child wore a small cap, dirty rags for clothes, and a thin pair of durable looking sandals that seemed homemade. Some of the other children were squatting alongside the second woman. Their nervous mumbling among themselves contrasted sharply with the buoyant, inviting tone of our host.

I seem to remember the gentleman brought out several clear glass cups—some with a short, thick stem and base—and served hot chai tea from a polished metal kettle with a wooden handle. He looked around at the rough dozen of us and to our hands to see who had a glass. The corners of his mouth dropped and his forehead tightened a bit before he went back into another room with the interpreter and returned with more cups. It hadn't occurred to me then, but he was more nervous about following an ancient custom than about the dirty, armed Americans in his living room.

We had retained a cursory amount of the cultural education mandated by our commander before the deployment, and a portion of that was the prehistoric honor code by which the Pashtuns had lived for centuries. It was called Pashtunwali, and that gentleman was following it to the letter, providing us shelter and sustenance as we were pursuing and had been pursued by our shared enemy. It was the only shred of civility for miles, and I had no idea how to behave. I had come prepared to perform like an animal, but I found myself dumbfounded at the cultural contrast, the difference between preconceptions and reality. However, this was the same code that would later allow the local Pashtun tribe to exact revenge on us for the unfortunate death of a young boy named Mahmoud, killed during a nighttime firefight.

The quiet and civility didn't last long, and we soon moved on, finding ourselves in a few more gunfights. I was more comfortable roaming through a field single file with bullets impacting the dirt in front of our patrol than I was in our former host's home. Another platoon nearby spent a few moments of their afternoon getting hammered by enemy machine-gun fire. We all fought well, and the enemy was—from a strategic perspective—running away from us. They didn't want to fight us. At least they didn't want to fight then or there. We moved a few dozen miles over the next few days, and the absence of clean water and food soon became just as dangerous as the cowardly Taliban fighters in the area. We still hadn't been able to get a substantial resupply; everyone was hungry, dehydrated, filthy, and tired.

The sun hammered the top of my head and the back of my neck from its position in the cloudless sky, unforgiving in the lush humid landscape. We moved from tree line to tree line, in and out of compounds, and I pined for shade from the exposed open fields. I became a bit dissociated from my limbs and stared down at my mud-soaked legs a few times, wondering how they were moving. I wasn't particularly amazed or impressed with myself, but I looked around at my brothers and willed myself to not let them down, to keep moving, to be as inspiring to them as they were to me. Once during a movement to try to help another platoon in a firefight Cardy, my team, and I skirted the outside wall of a tall mud compound. As we reached the corner Cardy stopped and said, "Wait, wait, wait. Burgess, do you see that? What is that?" We all looked left out at the open green field as if on cue. There stood what appeared to be a big coyote or a wolf. "Is that a fucking jackal?"

Cardy asked me over the mound of gear on his left shoulder. "That's a fucking hyena," someone said behind me. We turned back to the corner and headed on about our business.

At night we would stop for a few hours of rest and lie in a prone position, all together forming a circle. We placed claymore mines several meters in front of us in avenues by which the enemy might approach, and we took turns sleeping. Lapsing into a coma didn't seem so far-fetched at that very moment. The soft, high grass lapped at my face and all about my exposed arms just below my crusty folded sleeves, and the soft mud and flattened grass made a nice bed. I kept looking at my three teammates occupying concealed positions nearby, hoping they were okay, hoping they were resting but ready. The end of my watch never seemed to come fast enough.

Every day for about a week we walked. We stopped here and there if we got shot at, found explosives or mines, saw something suspicious, or wanted to search a compound because of certain pieces of intelligence relayed to us. But we walked on. I heard from someone that we had walked about 32 miles in five days, interspersed with fighting and what were essentially battlefield errands. One day, after a little skirmish, we stopped to regroup and redistribute ammo and water. I sat between a wall and a tree-lined wadi with Cardy. He passed me a cognac-dipped cigarillo. He told me—in his own way—that he didn't look like it, but he was having the time of his life. We didn't speak for a while, even after the cigarillo, and listened to a little sporadic gunfire in the distance. It stopped after a bit, and we just sat there, aching, trying to savor the smell and taste of the cigarillos, our weapons just within arm's reach.

There were moments when I kept walking, with my full Alice pack on my back and my body armor, and I wasn't quite sure how my feet were moving, but we walked. Sometimes I felt detached or dissociated from my own body in a strange way. I wasn't Catholic or even particularly religious at the time, besides having CATHOLIC stamped on my dog tags, but there were times when I wondered how Jesus had managed to walk to Calvary carrying the cross. I thought about his feet and the hard cross on his shoulder. That's it; nothing else. My feet and shoulder hurt too.

The sun was merciless on my head, neck, and hands. I still tasted the salt the corpsmen had come around to shove in our palms and tell us to eat one night after we had run out of clean water. My muscles constantly ached, not just from the load, but from pivoting, scanning, examining my surroundings, and watching my team. Once, when we finally stopped, we pulled our week-old socks off, and most of us had white sheets of dead skin on the bottoms of our feet. Johnny Castro, our platoon sergeant and consummate Texan, was an Iraq veteran; he told us to suck it up and to stop being dramatic. "Change your socks; it'll go away. Quit being a bunch of bitches," he said. We put our socks back on and kept walking. I wasn't supposed to look tired or be tired, but my bones shook under the façade. I was so tired I was angry. I wanted to breathe smoke and walk through mud and shoot my grenade launcher. There were times when I considered turning to the side of the hot moon-dust road to launch a high-explosive 40mm round into a compound just because the men were standing outside staring at us, always staring, gaping, and gawking, and I hated it. Were they gathering intelligence? Were they scouts for the Taliban? Was I just the first American Marine they had ever seen? Later, after I had injured my back, gotten a concussion, and had to return to the United States, I was enraged every time someone stared at me. I even snapped at my wife for a loving gaze.

Outlaw War Garden

The landscape began to seem less beautiful, the smell of smoking meat made me feel wild, and I wanted to choke every rooster and goat within a kilometer. We usurped a Taliban commander's compound and made it our patrol base after the long walk. We called it Patrol Base Outlaw. I believe our lieutenant named it, but I could be wrong. It sounded like something he would call it. Greg Kosh was a tall, fit, blonde frat-boy type with no time for the weak and no room for the stupid. Our radio operator, an Alabama native named Gary with a constant dip in his lip, had to show him how to skin and clean a goat. I respected Kosh and would have followed him anywhere too. It was a strange thing to never get along well with someone I would have died for.

Fortunately, the Taliban commander and his family had maintained an excellent garden—in addition to their healthy supply of explosives, cannabis, guns, opium, and heroin—full of ripening tomatoes, watermelon, and cucumbers. We had our own supply of drugs and explosives, but we lacked a reliable food source. Coalition forces, presumably the army or Marine Corps, had dropped our resupply in the wrong location a few days before. The compound was more like a compound-within-a-compound. There were a few layers between the outside world and the center.

The house sat on the edge of a grid-like farm area much like the rest of the prominent real estate of the neighboring villages. The walls were a light-colored mud and straw composite so thick that even rockets had a difficult time penetrating. Oddly enough, the roof was made of several strata of straw mats on wooden beams parallel to the ground. It was an uneasy thing to set up a sandbag and machine-gun post on top of it. There was a cooking area with a stone oven and dry storage, where the interpreters made naan bread to go with the goat or chicken and rice meal we had once. There was a large covered chicken coop with several chambers. The garden was outside this interior compound that housed the bedrooms, cooking area, chicken coop, and goat stall. There were goat paths alongside a single outside wall that led to the ninety-degree angle formed by two tree lines and a wadi. On the opposite side, a wide-open field of corn and a single dirt road skirted by a stream led to the village market.

There was another chamber in this second layer alongside the garden that didn't house anything in particular, and this is where we had to dig and dig and dig with small shovels to make a bathroom. Even when we finally had some makeshift stalls and barrels with bags for the waste, we still had to burn our own human waste. The smell lingered everywhere and with everything.

On our way out on patrols, Marines would occasionally stoop and pluck a fresh cucumber. I did this once and took a big bite right out of the edge. The watery juice ran down my beard and muddy elbow. It finally overpowered the burning feces and smelled like fresh produce from a farmer's market back in Southern California. I could have died happy right there in a mortar attack or something. I shoved my wet hand back into my dusty glove and walked about twelve kilometers that day. My shoulders and legs didn't hurt so bad, and Daniel Avalos and I built a shower a couple of days later. The shower, about a month overdue, wasn't nearly as good as the cucumber.

We operated on shifts shared among the platoon's three squads. One squad had to stand post around the patrol base, one had to go out for long patrol up to 14 kilometers away, and one squad stayed in the innermost chamber of the compound as a "quick reaction force," or QRF. That QRF squad was also supposed to sleep because the shifts rotated indefinitely, and that would be their only chance to rest. In other words, there was no bedtime; operations were continuous, and eating and maintenance were concurrent.

The house had four rooms with curtains for doors, but the two hallways intersected and were open to the outside breeze. Once, I was resting while my squad was on an QRF shift, but the sun was high overhead. I decided against the broil and opted to go inside to bake. I established a little sliver in the breezy hallway as my bed, covered my face to block out the flies and stench, pulled my pants down to my ankles, and tried to sleep. I noticed movement through the fabric of my tan shemagh, and pulled back the veil.

I saw a group of Marines huddled around one person carrying something outside. They were snickering a little and mumbling to each other. The Marine in the center, called Crum, had something in his hands. I tried to lie back down, but my boyish curiosity got the best of me. I decided to go join in the entertainment just as someone came trotting back to the group with a small cup and a shiny metal urn. I could smell the fuel in the cup. Several of the guys chuckled at the new development.

Crum fumbled the mouse he was holding but didn't take long to recover his prey. He dropped it into the urn, and the mouse ran round and round, scratching and clawing. I was the only one not laughing, but I felt a little numb inside. I was recovering from a bad illness that had given me a fever of about 104. I stood there watching over someone's shoulder as Crum pitched the urn side to side and jabbed at the mouse inside with his K-Bar knife. "Do it, do it," he said, not looking up. A corner of his mouth stretched toward his ear, and sweat dripped down his nose.

It seemed like the hand holding the cup of fuel didn't have an owner in the mangle of bodies. The hand doused the mouse in fuel, and Crum popped a match into the urn. Bright orange flames pierced the edge of the rim and reflected off the metal. From my stance about a meter away, I could hear the tiny squeaks and the sound of claws on metal. "That's fucked up," someone said through strained laughter. The whole group was laughing and taking turns tapping the urn. I stood there in my flip-flops and tan camouflage pants, crusty lips parted, brow tense. I felt my stomach turn a little as someone tapped the urn with their boot and the charred mouse rolled out onto the dirt.

Crum knelt down and sawed at the mouse's neck, but the tail end kept flipping over. Someone knelt down beside him and pressed their bayonet against the body while Crum sawed the head off. It didn't take long, but I felt like I had been standing there for longer, silent. After he painted a rodent blood piece on the ground, Crum impaled the mouse head with the tip of his knife and held it up in front of his face. He spotted me on the other side of the mouse head and stood up to face me. His lips curled back across his jagged teeth, and he extended the mouse head toward me. I glanced at his tattooed, shirtless, lanky body and at his outstretched arm. I looked anywhere but the mouse's head, and said, "God, man."

He chuckled to himself as I turned away to lie back down in the hallway. I smelled burning feces and body odor, and I tasted my own sweat. I tried to go back to sleep, but I kept thinking about a boy someone had shot in the head a few days earlier and the mouse head on the tip of Crum's knife. Night came before I was ready. I took my post anyway. I passed the garden on my way out. But I wasn't in the mood for fresh vegetables. All the good stuff, the ripe fruit, had been yanked out anyway.

A Bridge to Nowhere

JASON ARMENT

It was a few weeks after General Petraeus canceled Echo Company's suicide mission. I thought about what happened while I sat on post staring at a dozen decrepit buildings and a parking lot. In Baghdad the Mahdi Army had shot rockets from a borough nicknamed Sadr City into the Green Zone. The president of Iraq threatened a Marine invasion of Shia cleric Maqtada al-Sadr's stronghold. Echo would have been the main element to roll into Baghdad and punch through the guts of Sadr City. The densely populated suburb promised small-arms fire from thousands of enemy combatants, withering blasts of roadside IEDs, and hidden snipers using fifty-caliber rifles. I'd have taken many of them with me in blaze of glory: fifty-cal thumping, eyes wide, screaming like a banshee before I disintegrated into a cloud of blood and pulp. But it didn't happen. Instead higher scrapped the doomed mission.

I had half an hour left standing watch outside the small sandbag pillbox. I tried remembering how much time Echo had left in country. The desert was so hot out I couldn't remember what month it was, much less the day of the week. The thermometer on post read 120 degrees and rumor had it close to 140 degrees around noon. As the temperature soared time blurred.

I kept thinking about how I might go home without killing anyone, how I might not be a *real* Marine unless I took a life. I obsessed over it in the free time that being Battalion Quick Reaction Force (QRF) allowed me when I wasn't stuck on post. All QRF did was sit around and wait to get called out to either rescue a downed vehicle (this happened often) or roll up to some place where Iraqis were doing something they shouldn't with the willingness to kill everything we saw (this happened a few times). I thought about it while I walked to the chow hall. I thought about it while I jogged around the dusty base of Habbaniya. I thought about it while I showered, while I jerked off, while I called home, while I wrote letters. I felt like a fraud when I would one by one slide the rounds out of my magazines and then pull the plates off the bottoms to let the springs relax; this was important to do so they would function properly when I needed to kill someone.

I guessed maybe "need" was being used with a little stretch of the imagination, but it was quite possible to take a life completely in bounds of the Rules of Engagement. As QRF we utilized roadblocks whose main purpose was a show of our presence to the population. Roadblocks interrupted traffic, and this confusion was increased when Marines tried to keep Escalation of Force protocol straight in their heads—one hundred meters out utilize the Dazzler, a laser, to signal to the cars to halt, at fifty meters fire a warning shot into the deck; after that the vehicle was pretty much fair game, depending on its speed and whether warning shots were put up the front to the windshield and then onto the drivers head—while trying to direct cars off the road to pull fingerprints, or check IDs. Some Iraqis got more confused than the Marines, and others were too fed up with a scorching commute to comply quickly. Killing someone might not be a need, but depending on the day it could be done easily.

I threw rocks at a camel spider skittering across the road in front of my post as I ruminated, managing to break one of its gangly legs before it disappeared under a vehicle. Unofficial doctrine of the moment was to shy away from engaging vehicles because things weren't "hot," and not temperature-wise. Things weren't "hot" as in there wasn't enemy activity that involved Marines taking small-arms fire on a regular basis. Somehow "hot" didn't take into account the numerous raids on smaller bases, like Forward Operating Base (FOB)

Viking a few miles to the north, or things exploding in Fallujah that didn't have any business exploding. If there weren't
rounds pinging off walls around you or shrapnel screaming
into your Humvee's ballistic glass, you didn't really have much
to worry about, or so we thought. I figured it was the indiffer-
ence of complacency.

Finally the internal debate had worked itself out enough
that I brought it up to my team leader, Rose. He was beside me
flicking water from his CamelBak hose onto a nearby Humvee,
watching the dark spots of water turn lighter and then disap-
pear as they evaporated in seconds. Duties on post included
making sure the vehicles weren't broken into and stopping
anyone who looked suspicious from coming through the parking lot to our barracks or the neighboring unit's barracks. Our
barracks were two buildings that had been acquired when
U.S. forces seized control of the base. Habbaniya was an old
base left over from the British occupation of Iraq in the fif-
ties, a base that we shared with the Iraqi army. They had a
habit of letting themselves into our trucks and borrowing our
gear without returning it, so we watched the vehicles. The sun
had finished blazing for the day and was now on the steady
descent down the western sky. In a few hours the stars would
spell out strange constellations.

"So I've been thinking, in a few months we will probably
go home," I said, then took a long drag of my cigarette. "You
know, barring us getting blown up or something."

"Let me have a smoke," Rose said. His arms moved deftly
in his body armor as he caught the pack of Miamis—generic
Iraqi cigarettes. They cost about a quarter a pack, or five bucks
for a carton. Even then we paid double the normal price. The
tax didn't bother me. I made more in a month then most Iraqis
could dream.

Rose didn't normally smoke, but whenever a Marine started
off a conversation on post with, *So I've been thinking,* it signaled a time when having a cigarette to hide behind might be
a good idea.

"I signed up to go to war and kill someone, among other things. I think we all did," I said. I idly kicked rocks as I spoke, the tip of my boot barely touching the ground as I leaned way back in one of the few unbroken chairs that had been dragged out from the post.

"Yeah, I think most of us expected to kill somebody. You don't exactly join because of how great it sounded to sweat in the desert, or how you watched a movie about war where they wasted their lives doing nothing."

Rose's eyes were hidden behind the dark blue Oakley ballistic glasses, helmet in his lap. He looked straight ahead, puffing on his cigarette with all the gusto of a novice smoker. Pausing for an extra beat between puffs, Rose tilted his head at me and said "Don't go to jail."

That was all we said. If I wanted to kill someone Rose just wanted me to be sure that it was justifiable, or at least justifiable enough that it wouldn't get me thrown in the brig.

All of our careers we had been told that at some point we would extinguish the lives of young men much like ourselves. Many of us had gone through basic training with drill instructors who were veterans of the invasion. They hadn't been gentle about the harsh realities of pulling a trigger on someone who was just going about their business, how even children might become targets. Realistic training exercises had shown there would be times when the safety of the squad dictated someone die that didn't have malicious intentions. The risk of allowing a car or personnel near a checkpoint was always real. Any car could be a Vehicle Borne Improvised Explosive Device housing multiple 155 artillery rounds that would kill a handful of Marines. Whether or not this would make me a "bad" person didn't cross my mind. Good and bad, right and wrong, they were just mirages in the desert. Iraq existed away from them; out here life was too hard and death too sudden for such notions.

"I'll try not to end up in the brig," I said as we stood to go to the chow hall.

Two Marines came out to relieve us from post. As they trudged nearer their gait seemed to slow, as if they were reluctant to accept the fate of having to sit through another few hours of watching their lives slowly tick away. By the time they made it out Rose and I were smoking new cigarettes and wore sour looks dripping sweat. The sinking sun was still scorching. Some of the bats in the palm trees stirred the air, although they wouldn't come out to hunt insects clustered in the glow of street lights until the night was well under way.

"Holy shit, take for fucking ever. Seriously," I said, flicking what was left of my cigarette at the nearest Marine's face.

"Watch it, motherfucker," Smith said as he casually batted the burning butt out of the air. "You put out my eye and they'll send me home, and then you'll really be in some shit!"

Smith was a big corn-fed Marine with blue eyes, a prominent jaw line chiseled from granite, and bulging biceps. He stood a little above six feet, which put his face quite a few inches above mine. Behind him was Huelete, wafer thin compared to Smith's bulk. Huelete looked like some college kid with dirty blond hair that had somehow wandered into a recruiting station and then ended up in desert with the rest of us.

"Holy shit, it just took you eight minutes to walk less than forty meters." Rose said. His voice took on the wounded pride of a Marine that has been around for a while and knows when some of the junior Marines aren't pulling their weight. "I don't know how in the fuck that's even possible."

"Fuck off, that's how that's possible. It's not like you guys don't make us wait for you to relieve us," Huelete said as he sparked up his own smoke. Huelete and Smith were both part of Assault, another squad that made up Weapons Platoon with Machine Guns and Mortars.

"You Assault men are always such martyrs. Speaking of," I said with grin slowly spreading across my face. "Huelete, wouldn't that God of yours want you to get out here extra early so we could have time to really enjoy the chow hall?"

Smith and Huelete started chatting as Rose and I walked

away from post and down the road to the chow hall. We ate and joked around with other Marines from our company. The chow hall was able to accommodate several hundred people. The servers were Indian men and women hired from a company that sold long-term labor. Much of the personnel on the base had been contracted out from elsewhere. The guards at the chow hall and at the internet cafe were Ugandan army, many of whom had seen action during some of the brutal conflicts in their country—they had the scars to prove it. The workers who helped run the internet cafe were temporary Indian labor, while the sanitary workers on the base were Americans. All mercenaries here to get a piece of war's spoils.

The atmosphere of the chow hall always seemed phony. The fobbits—as those who never left the base were referred to—always in clean, crisp uniforms; officers with spotless pistols hanging from the newest tactical holster. Other times there were Marines from beyond the vast Al Anbar province, and they might not have had a haircut or a shave in days, if not weeks. Their faces were dirty and their uniforms stained. Marines like me had shitty fades for haircuts, swollen muscles from alternating eating chow and pumping iron, and attitudes that turned from dark humor to something much more volatile.

As I walked under the palms on the way back to the barracks the bats braved the light, darting out and snapping up insects. The sun threw its last rays over the black horizon, making the trees cast long shadows on the rocky sand of the base. A hot, dry breeze was blowing, but not hard enough to kick up sand or dust. Terrible lung infections could take hold from exposure to winds that carried debris; there were health hazards in the sand, fecal matter from animals and chemicals from the war. A light breeze would allow breathing with an uncovered mouth without too much risk.

I started planning as I walked back to the parking lot by the barracks. If I was going to smoke someone at a roadblock I might get a chance tomorrow. We were supposed to set up between Habbaniya and Ramadi, the next major city to our west. Following the rules of engagement was imperative, and that meant adhering to the different tiers of escalating force. I figured it was lucky I was a turret gunner behind a fifty-caliber machine gun. It would make the work a lot easier.

I stopped by my vehicle in the parking lot in front of the barracks. My knees creaked and my back ached as I hauled myself up the side of the MRAP. MRAPs looked like SWAT trucks on steroids. The vehicle weighed around twelve thousand pounds. Its hull came to a V at the bottom of the vehicle, made of heavy reinforced armor so if we got hit by multiple 155 rounds buried in the ground it wouldn't tear us apart. But I'd heard stories that it didn't take much more than five to eight thousand pounds of explosives to flip an MRAP, and when that happened pretty much everyone died. Personnel would bounce around inside like jelly beans in a can, and the sharp edges of gear, guns, and the inside of the hull would split you to pieces. If the bouncing didn't get you the flipping upside down and burning to death would; there was no way to crawl out from under the gear. I imagined it felt akin to getting in a tumbling dryer after dousing yourself with gasoline and lighting a match. I tried not to think about it, but it visited me in nightmares.

Sweat poured down my face as I pulled myself up onto the side panel, and then finally onto the top of the truck. The little food I had just eaten in the chow hall threatened to come up, and my back throbbed. The deployment was wearing me down, making me old, but I had to press on. I hopped into the armored turret behind the fifty cal and checked the few things to make sure it would fire properly tomorrow. Rooting around the inside of the truck turned up a bottle of lube that I used to douse the bolt of the weapon. I inspected the ammo in the box attached to the large gun, making sure there was no rust, and quickly cleaned off the film of dust that had accumulated since I had checked it last.

Climbing back out of the turret and on top of the truck I became afraid someone would see and know. I thought about it for a second as I checked the barrel of the weapon to make sure it was screwed in properly to the receiver. I checked my weapon often, much more than the average Marine. Even if someone did see me they wouldn't think it strange. I lit a cigarette. I felt better behind the smoke as I sat crossed legged, the truck's hot metal surface making my ass feel like it was on fire.

Rose walked by, laughing with a group of Marines staying in barracks close to ours. He glanced at my truck and saw me sitting on top smoking like the desert heat was making me smolder. The ember on the tip of my cigarette turned my glasses to squares of fire with each puff they reflected. Rose didn't say anything, or call out, he just looked sad. We locked eyes for a moment, and even though we were only a few meters apart I knew that if I got up at that moment and ran to embrace him I would run forever. As close as we'd become from deployment this came between us, like some kind of gulf. It wasn't that Rose found killing distasteful or wrong. As Marines we'd been taught that blood made the grass grow. But the decision to pull the trigger on an innocent was like jumping off a high point into a body of water. The first few steps off the ledge to start the descent marked the beginning of a fall that was solitary. Rose couldn't join me in the journey. It wasn't that kind of war, not for us anyway. Maybe taking lives didn't come between brothers in arms during the invasion, when everyone was slaying bodies. But this wasn't the invasion, this was the occupation.

I crawled off the truck and wandered over to the designated smoking area. The fifty-caliber machine gun was ready, but it was a precaution. Because of the requirements of escalating force I would start the engagement with my M-16. Usually I had my Beretta nine-millimeter pistol at the ready while I was in a turret; the smaller pistol was easier to maneuver. I needed to transition quickly between the warning shot and engaging the driver's head with my rifle. Going from pistol to rifle would be hard in the turret behind the large fifty-caliber. Using the fifty seemed like overkill, and the transition from whatever weapon I used for warning shots to the fifty would take time. I'd heard sometimes Marines would use the fifty for warning shots and skip the rounds off the road into the vehicle. The round would skip off the deck and into the cab, bouncing around and causing multiple casualties. I needed the kill to be a careful application of force, not the act of some turret gunner who lost his mind and sawed a vehicle in half with a machine gun.

I lit a third cigarette as I thought, unsure if I was becoming lost or disoriented in all of the jargon, protocols, and procedures. I would have to hope for a good field of fire when I set up, which would be a lot of luck. Getting a bad driver could be a show stopper. It could fall in my favor that we would be doing a joint operation. The added chaos would bring opportunities. There wasn't much else to do but wait. I knew my rifle was ready, and my pistol. I didn't know if I was ready, but I felt ready. After my fifth smoke my lungs seemed like they were filling slowly with tar so I went inside and lay on my rack.

The barracks themselves were buildings used for businesses prewar. There were three big rooms on the first floor and three big rooms on the second floor, along with a few smaller rooms. The bigger rooms were used to house a squad, and called squad bays. Machine Guns squad had around fifteen people in it. We lived on bunk beds that were only a few feet apart, and kept all of our belongings either underneath them or overhead on storage shelves we'd nailed to the walls. Three window AC units ran constantly. Their low hum gave the illusion of quiet. But if I sat very still I realized it wasn't quiet, but brooding—a sensation I had felt in midwestern forests before a storm. My bunk was the lower one, transformed into a cavern by nailing standard issue blankets on all four sides. I drifted off to sleep and woke to the sound of Marines getting ready to head out on our operation.

We didn't do patrol briefs, or any kind of briefs anymore. The Standard Operating Procedures were borderline fictitious in how they thought events would unfold in anything but a maelstrom of hate and discontent when a Marine went down. Eighteen-year-old kids in turrets would be expected to watch their friends get shot, listen to them die over the radio, and then remain calm instead of turning powerful weapons on everyone that wasn't a friendly. We all knew what would happen if a sniper popped a turret gunner's head, or if an IED made Swiss cheese of a vehicle; mass chaos would ensue. People would shout into the radios and shoot at everything in sight. We hadn't so much stopped caring to do patrol briefs as we'd lost our imagination.

Going through the vehicle and gun checks flew by, *Gun up! Truck up! Let's roll!,* and before I knew it we were rolling through the front gate, *Echo Four you are cleared and good to go,* and leaving the wire. It was a scorching hot day, just like all the rest of the days that summer. The sands would burn your eyes if you stared too long. The breeze was hot and coarse, carrying with it dust and sand. I tried to make myself comfortable in the sling the turret had for a seat. We were moving quickly along a main supply route toward wherever the roadblock was to be set up. It turned out to be a bridge in the middle of nowhere.

We set up on one end of the bridge, facing some of our gun trucks across it so they could use the bridge as a fatal funnel. Some trucks faced the other way down the road, the way traffic wouldn't be allowed to pass through at all. This traffic would just back up for the next few hours. I stood on the sling, pushing my head out above the top of the turret. Lounging back, using my gear as a buffer between myself and the hard edges of the turret's armor that came up about a foot and a half all the way around except where the gun faced outboard, I smoked and watched the setup.

"Hurry up, Marines, we don't have all day!" Sergeants screamed into the desert with eyes wide, tendrils of spittle quivering between their teeth.

My MRAP was the main truck blocking traffic from advancing across the bridge. Granted, we weren't actually blocking it, but we were parked just to the side of the road facing down the bridge, meaning our fifty-caliber was doing the same. This would be enough to stop most traffic from advancing. The corps had been controlling the Al Anbar province for a while and it was readily understood that noncompliance could get you killed. Twenty or so meters in front of us was a Humvee from the other unit that had tagged along. I didn't know who was in the turret, but he was behind a 240 Bravo medium machine gun. From what I could tell from watching him pick his nose and joke around he didn't seem like a killer. On the other side of the road, right across from the vehicle that belonged to the other company, was another Humvee. This Humvee belonged to Echo, and the turret gunner was Larkin, a member of Machine Guns. Larkin was dependable, and had been the point man to my second man quite often during the first half of our deployment when we did foot patrols.

Flicking the smoking butt out into the wasteland, I dropped down into the MRAP. I glanced around the inside quickly, then grabbed my rifle. I turned to close the open back door of the truck to see Terrones looking in at me.

"Hey, I think you are supposed to be in the turret," Terrones said.

He looked exhausted, having ridden in a Humvee with no air-conditioning. Terrones was a Mexican and we were about the same color since I got so bronze in the sun, but there was enough dirt on his neck to make a dark ring. The breeze carried enough debris to coat a sweaty person in a few seconds; I was thankful to be stuck in a turret.

"I was just grabbing my rifle," I said.

Terrones hustled off to help signal vehicles across the bridge so that drivers and passengers could be hauled out and have their irises and fingerprints put into a database. I rose back up in the turret, rifle first. It was a squeeze until I situated the rifle to the side of the fifty-cal. The action was just getting under way, with Marines signaling cars forward and pulling them off to the side of the road at gunpoint, then extracting the occupants. After watching for a few minutes I realized how badly it had been set up, and how confusing it was to the Iraqis.

There was nothing on the other side of the bridge to let Iraqi drivers know what was going on. Essentially they came up on the bridge doing anywhere from fifty to sixty-five miles an hour, saw my truck with the fifty pointed at them, and slammed on their brakes. After stopping they would either be signaled forward and get their identifiers harvested, or they would be waved through the roadblock. There were two vehicles ahead of mine with Marines in turrets that were signaling people forward across the bridge, and it was confusing not only to the Iraqis but to the Marines waving them forward as well. The Iraqi drivers were having a hard time seeing the two Marines. The haze of dust cut visibility to about thirty meters. The situation was optimal, I decided, blowing dust out of the optic on my m-16 that magnified things four times and allowed for easy aiming through the luminescent chevron floating inside.

I waited and chain smoked. It was kind of like all the other mind-numbing times I had sat in a turret and waited, except this time there was a purpose. The breeze picked up and brown haze filled the air. Beneath me and off to my right was where Marines took Iraqis to get their fingerprints and iris scans. From what I could hear it was a slow and tedious process. The machine that took pictures of the iris wasn't in a box and didn't have a shroud; meaning that the blazing desert bore down on the person trying to look into the machine. More than once I heard a Marine tell someone to "just hold your eye open," and it made me chuckle when the Iraqis protested about the sand in their eyes.

About forty minutes had gone by when a beat-up red car didn't stop at the other side of the bridge. Instead it kept going, doing about fifty miles an hour. The bridge spanned about sixty meters, and a fourth of the way across the driver must have sensed something was wrong, slowing to twenty or so. My body went cold and mechanical as I grabbed my rifle from beside me and steadied it on top of the fifty. I tried pressing the butt stock tight into my shoulder but couldn't get it seated comfortably. My body armor kept getting in the way. The stock felt cold against my cheek as I peered down my optic.

The driver was a middle-aged man in a business suit with a lousy haircut and deep wrinkles creasing his face. The desert had left a heavy mark. His eyes were flashing back and forth from one Humvee to the next as he slowly approached our side of the bridge. The Humvee in front of me from the other company had its turret gunner waving the man back. At least that's what I thought he was trying to tell the driver by jumping up and down and flailing his arms wildly. Larkin, across the road, was waving in a vain attempt to get the driver to stop moving and focus solely on him. Neither one of them did much but ensure the driver would continue forward with a confused look on his face.

I centered the glowing chevron on the man's face. His eyes darted wildly. He signaled to the two Marines with his hands. I put my finger on the trigger and moved my thumb downward in a sweeping motion as I had countless times before to take the gun off safety and move the fire selector to single shot, but I didn't feel anything. Canting the weapon to the right I glanced down quickly and saw that at some point I'd switched the rifle to single shot already. Oftentimes things like this would happen; my body would go through an involuntary response and I'd operate on autopilot. The fire selector switch looked alien when I glanced at it, like it had never been there when the rifle was first designed but was slapped on by someone who wanted to neuter the weapon. My brow furrowed for a second as I struggled to remember if I had ever seen it there before that very moment.

When I looked back into the scope the man was beginning to dart his car to the left, toward the Humvee in front of me. The turret gunner was yelling, "No, no, no, stop!" over and over. Larkin had his rifle out but didn't look like he was going to use it anytime soon, except maybe to neutralize the Marine across the street from him screaming incoherently. The driver brought the car to a stop for a second, but the kind of stop all three of us could tell was just a stutter. He kept going. He did it again, and I started to put pressure on the trigger.

The man looked frightened. He couldn't understand what we wanted him to do. I couldn't tell where he worked, but from the way he dressed it wasn't outside or with his hands. He probably had a family somewhere, kids and a wife. I was cleared to kill him though. I could "smoke" him, as the saying went, and he would have been like smoke; there one second and gone the next, leaving behind a corpse. I would explain how he failed to stop, how he continued across the bridge and defied both of the forward Humvees when they waved for him to halt. For all I knew the car had 155 rounds in the back and he was going to ram a Humvee.

I couldn't take the chance. That's what I would say. I'd talk about how I feared for myself and my fellow Marines, how the fog of war set in when the first Humvee's turret gunner had started to act like a child, causing communication between all three of the vehicles blocking the bridge to cease. I had to end the threat the man in the car represented. The shot would ring out, his head would snap back, a fine pink mist would cloud the back seat and his rear windshield would be covered in the black and red gelatin of brain matter. Somewhere his wife and kids would be completely fucked. We'd have to pull his car off to the side of the road and take care of the body.

I'd like to say something along the lines of "I couldn't do it" or "I didn't have it in me," but that would be a lie. I could have done it, and I did have it in me. It would have taken just a few more pounds of pressure on the trigger and the world would have one less Arab. It's not that simple, of course; I'd be dealing with the aftermath of it every day, and the fact that it wasn't a "righteous" kill would probably haunt me. My dreams would be filled with that man and his family. I'd hear his wife weeping, their children sobbing. Maybe I'd run into him again on the other side, if there is anything over there.

What stopped me was the realization, *This guy is just trying to go to work.*

When that realization hit me, the world stopped for a second. Not the way the world stops when your heart skips a beat, but the way it stops when the concussion of a nearby explosion hits you, or when the shriek of rockets fills the air; when everything is done moving, the little snow globe of reality frozen with the suspended snow looking like sand and there is nothing else but stillness. I recoiled back in the turret, the back plate of my body armor softly thudding against the Humvee's metal. It was a completely original idea, new and pure. I had never thought it before about anything or anyone in my entire life, not just the words, but the meaning and everything they represented. I felt that man's struggle to provide, thought of the commute and how shitty it must have been, knew his frustration in not being able to make ends meet, saw him at the table with his wife and children talking about how they would have to tighten their belts to make it through the troubled times.

I carefully put the fire selector back on safety. And then double-checked that it was on safe as I watched a couple of Marines haul the man out of his car and slam him on the hood. The guy babbled some stuff I didn't understand and an interpreter hustled over. As I watched the scene I unloaded my rifle, slowly pulling the magazine out, racking the bolt back, and catching the round that popped out in my hand. Pushing the round back into the magazine, I wondered if I should feel sick, I wondered if I should feel anything. I checked my rifle over once more, looked at the man getting sternly talked to, and threw it down into the truck.

"It's your lucky day," I muttered as I stared at the Iraqi man being released to continue his commute. I wondered how much longer he would be tied to this world and if he would depart from it at some other checkpoint or roadblock in the future.

I spent the rest of the operation sitting in the turret smoking. There really wasn't much for me to do if I wasn't going to do my job. Ignoring the rules of engagement in order to avoid engaging civilians was a weird paradox. I considered that maybe things were just broken over here. Maybe Iraq really was never-never-land, as some people joked. What were we supposed to do? The person in the turret behind the gun would most likely be pay grade E-2 or E-3, private first class or lance corporal, and fall between the ages eighteen to twenty-one. The worst part was eventually the car would be a VBIED and I'd watch a Marine get blown out of the turret and slide around on the pavement in his own blood as he tried to get back up.

"Not today?" Rose shouted up at me as he walked by to jump in his Humvee as the roadblock got ready to leave.

"It was close," was all I said. It was all I needed to say. He gave a single nod in understanding before closing the Humvee door. He stared out of the ballistic glass at me for a second, then down at his hands.

The broken telephone poles, sand dunes, palm trees, Iraqis, and time all rhythmically passed us as we headed back to our barracks at Camp Habbaniya. I felt numb. The kind of numb you feel when one of your appendages finally starts to wake up. I tried to think back to the point when I'd first gone numb. Maybe it was when I had first rationalized pulling the trigger on someone? How long ago had that been? Years. I thought about the Iraqi man who hadn't stopped, whom I'd almost murdered. I tried to envision the family he may or may not have had, how his wife reacted to another story of Americans hauling him out of his car, how his kids would deal with the tension.

I imagined my own father driving to his job at Pioneer, getting stopped by the military, almost shot, and then hauled out of his car; or I tried to at least. I couldn't really imagine it because it was such a foreign idea. The phantoms I could conjure up in my imagination were something that would have filled me with anger and hate if they ever manifested in the real world. We created "terrorists" by the dozen with our pointless little roadblocks, I was sure of that. Years later I would try to look back and envision myself in the turret, gazing out over the top of a truck, deciding whether or not a commuter was going home that day. I couldn't. It wasn't possible, because things like that were only possible in Iraq, or other war zones where the "rules of war" collided solidly with reality and left a mangled wreck for kids to navigate while keeping as much of themselves intact as possible.

There wasn't really anyone there to talk to about the way I felt, and I knew it. Maybe Rose, but it wasn't that easy. No man is an island, but we were all peninsulas, and we were all going through the same shit. It would have been like one drowning man turning to another and saying, "Would you please pass me a life preserver," only to hear back, "I don't have a life preserver, you fucking idiot, that's why I'm drowning." There wasn't anything any of us could do about it but try to get back home in one piece, but it was going to take more than that. Our survival was linked more to our humanity than our bodies.

When I hit the rack that night I didn't have any dreams; those would catch up with me years later. For the time my mind was burned out from thinking and my eyes hurt from the sun. I would have plenty of time the next day to ponder how "God, Country, Corps" tattooed on my arm conflicted with what we were doing.

I didn't think about it the next day, though. I just fell back into the routine of preparing for combat and being constantly ready to leave the wire. I didn't want to kill a man anymore. I didn't want to kill anything anymore. That isn't to say that I wouldn't, or wanted to not kill a man; I just didn't want to actively seek out the confrontation. I was content with letting violence come to me. It surrounded me. My entire life revolved around it. I didn't see how it wouldn't eventually find me. I could only hope that maybe one day some other kid would pass me up in his rifle's scope. I wondered if it had already happened.

The next day I felt at peace. I felt alone.

Wilderness

BENJAMIN BUSCH

My commanding officer was missing. The message came ten years after our tour in the war. He had retired and was fishing alone on a lake in Canada. Search parties went out. Then he was found.

It's hot as I drive away from home. The funeral will be tomorrow, 737 miles to the cemetery, eleven straight hours. I leave late and head into night, Michigan letting me go. On a route around Toledo, the asphalt is so new the rollers are still parked along the shoulder. Streetlights reflect off the smooth pitch as if it's moist, that oily-licorice look of a surface too slick to steer on. I was in charge of repairing roads in Ramadi, filling bomb craters and clearing trash. I never saw a clean street in Iraq, a country where tar is so close to the surface the Sumerians used it as mortar for their bricks.

But that's not what comes to mind right then. I'm already adrift.

It's midnight and my drive is just beginning, even though I'm three hours into it. I haven't been to a military burial since 1996. I was only out of the Corps for two months when two birds collided over Camp Lejeune, North Carolina, an attack helicopter rising into a troop transport killing twelve of my Marines. My departure had been so recent I hadn't even been replaced, and my seat in the Sea Knight fell to earth empty. I imagined the fuselage ripped open by Cobra blades, all of us cut to pieces, sky and swamp sprayed with blood. But I was home with my wife trying to see suburban America as a place I could live in.

We bought a small house in College Park, Maryland, just inside the beltway, and I paced the yard like a pen. I had lost a sense of direction, unable to recognize myself out of uniform. Standing in the honor guard with my peers, my sword drawn, our Dress Blues keeping us stiff, we buried a lieutenant in front of his fiancée. Their wedding was planned for that weekend and friends had all gathered to celebrate. They stood shocked and quiet. There was almost nothing said. It was May. I joined a reserve unit a week later.

I scan the channels for rock stations and they blare in and fizz out, overlapping with talk shows and commercials. A few minutes of AC/DC and then they're gone like their century, signals making their way into space with our casualty reports and radio checks. All of the urgent messages and calls home just noise that passed away. A sign for the Toledo Zoo stands strange in the dark web of roads and ramps, a conquered hinterland now barren of animals and trees. Before we deployed, my co named me Lone Wolf because I was often on my own, drawn to the fringe. Our small detachment didn't lose a man in 2005. I was the only one wounded. I remember him rushing into the casualty center as I was attended to. We'd been in Iraq for two weeks then. A decade ago. There's no distance kept in time. It was last month. It was every day, the Euphrates opaque, barely moving past, dense with dust and sewage, no fish striking its surface and no way to see its bed. It boiled, churning rather than flowing, the current indiscernible. No one swam. It was known to pull people under and keep them for miles.

I was sent to swimming lessons for years but found ways to never really learn. I didn't believe it was a physical act I could master and it kept me wary of the pool, where drowning happened. Somehow I remained completely dauntless in the river, the shore always near enough, the current sensible, pressing me, bulging against my waist. The pool was chemical. It burned my eyes and smelled nothing like water.

I failed the swimming merit badge test at Boy Scout camp.

We did laps within lanes of roped floats in a deep block of lake. The odd formality of the evaluation returned me to the panic of water taught as danger. I took some in my lungs and coughed myself helpless. Quitting hurt as much as learning I could die in a pond.

The base is still eight hours away but my hair feels long. I may have gone feral since the war, like when I was young. I'm an expatriate returning to Quantico, Virginia, where I became a Marine. I spent years there. I think about the zoo, its absolute captivity. I understand a little how it must be to live in one. All those rules and boundaries and waiting for a gate to be left ajar. It's hard to be an outlier, to get to the outer reaches. It's harder to come back.

An ad hisses for Kiss touring later this summer. The first album I ever bought was *Love Gun*, from a yard sale across the street in Poolville, New York. The cover was incomprehensible and compelling. There was no gun, and I didn't understand the innuendo for years. I joined the Kiss Army. Then I bought the *Destroyer* album as another collection was sold. Records were part of garage sales back then, a dollar or two each, especially as guys began buying tapes to play in cars. "Detroit Rock City" was the hit on *Destroyer* and still plays in southern Michigan all the time. The song ends with a car crash. It comes on at midnight as I drive and the beat takes me back to Poolville, to me before I knew anyone who died. Before war was more than just stories I'd heard. Music takes me to the water.

In the Sangerfield River, which curled around my town, yellow leaves in the stream signaled the end of trout season. Foliage dropped and moved past, suspended and spinning, pressed like scabs onto stones and logs. The river had cooled, and I waded through it to the deeper pools where I hoped a worm might still be noticed. I rarely used silver lures, though I had a few. I preferred the hook. I rubbed worms in leaves to marry their scent as if they fell from trees.

I ventured upstream from the ruins of a dam that once

powered textile mills and saws. It was fished-out near the village, but no one walked this far up and I considered it undiscovered country. In truth, the area had been well trafficked for two hundred years by boys with poles and men with guns, natives with arrows and nets before that. But I'd never seen any of them. Rediscovered country was almost as good.

As I threw in my line, I tamped the clay bank to form a place to stand in the thinning shadow of an old willow tree. An oak trunk lay below the surface and I had mapped how the water was sucked under, carving a pit patrolled by trout. The bait would have to follow this path or fish would know it to be bait. The river struck its stones, the sound of static between stations, a solitude of water, the hushing of a crowd. I hummed rock songs.

Three o'clock in the morning at a rest stop near Youngstown on the Ohio/Pennsylvania border and people are sleeping in their cars, seats back, windows fogged with air conditioning. The humidity smokes halos around the light poles. Toll plazas are the loneliest places despite people pulling up with their windows rolled down. At this hour the roads are bare. I'm searching for a radio signal and still not thinking of Iraq.

I push past Gettysburg in the dark, markers noting where fifty thousand soldiers died, then bend through the Virginias. I shave off my beard in a gas station bathroom. I wonder, as I approach the gate to the base, if the Marine guard will turn me away. I'm a civilian now. A savage. I look wrong, like a terrorist, on my driver's license. This is tribal territory and I am unrecognizable, my sixteen years shorn and starched impossible for him to see in me. I sit straight and want to apologize. I want to confess that I feel less complete now than I did when I belonged here. I'm missing too, but no one is looking for me. I'm Lone Wolf. The guard waves me through.

The service is at eleven hundred. I have a few minutes to buy a small eagle, globe, and anchor pin for my lapel, change into my suit at another gas station, and line up at Quantico National Cemetery to follow the hearse, the heat over a hundred degrees. I speak of him as my CO, not as a civilian, not as someone who became someone else or was anyone before. Most people wait sealed in their cars, engine fans laboring to keep passengers cool.

Headstones stand in rows draped over the rolling knolls, their perfect geometry revealed and warping as I pass. Someday, if there's anyone left, they'll uncover this cemetery, Arlington too, all the dead in their uniforms, and try to make sense of them. Four hundred thousand and counting, like the terra cotta warriors of Emperor Qin, the fired clay slow to shatter back into silt. We are so quick to be soil, embalmers doing their best to preserve us for . . . for what? Rediscovery? The pharaohs of Egypt have been uncovered, looted by thieves and archeologists, displayed in museums to be viewed as nothing more than dead. And here's one more, found in a lake at peace. We all go missing when we die. Is it right to find us?

Marines carry the casket to a small brick-pillared committal shelter and we gather around. Only a few make it into the shade, the rest lit bright and squinting. I sweat fast into my black suit, my thick hair dripping at the tips, the sun unavoidable, and I finally think of Iraq. I thought the war would be on my mind the entire trip, but it wasn't. I looked at yellow lines and charcoal hills, tried to stay awake. I wandered and forgot. I had no music in Iraq so I don't return there through songs. I remember Iraq as static.

A priest reads some passages, dust to dust, and no one is invited to say anything about the man in the coffin, the one who survived the war and died fishing alone in a boat. A heart attack. Fell, drowned, and drifted for a day, gone wild, lungs filled with lake. He was fifty-eight and two years from receiving military retirement pay. His family will get nothing. Nothing but a plot in a line on a slope. Taps plays its haunting notes. His wife cries quietly. I haven't slept in twenty-eight hours. My suit is soaked.

Then it's over, a line forming to shake hands and offer brief embraces, a folded flag presented to his widow. The day stretches, heat bridging the desert to the hole they have dug. We held memorials in Ramadi for our dead, but we didn't bury them there. They went missing from us, taken away to be laid in graves while patrols went back out, one man short. We're a naval service, so every seat in a bird, truck, or ship is known as a "boat space." Mine plunged into a swamp without me. They recovered an empty boat on a lake, my co's watch still in it. That's when they knew. I want to be found alive or never found at all.

At the Basic School, on the far side of base from the cemetery and twenty-three years ago, we jumped into a pool from a fifteen-foot platform. Full gear. Abandon-ship drills. We struck the deep end of the vat with our legs crossed and resurfaced, hands first, splashing furiously above our heads. The purpose was to puncture a hole in imaginary fuel burning above us if our ship had been sunk. These were lessons from World War II. Our backpacks served as life preservers and we kicked our way forward while sweeping the water aside, palms facing out. It seemed absurdist and, though we went about it very seriously, we sputtered and flailed like drunks, lumps of wet woodland camouflage bobbing on packs swollen with clothing in Ziploc bags. It looked like the reenactment of a disaster. Helmets slid over our eyes, rubber rifles hung from our necks, and our boots dragged like stones tied to our feet, all of us trying to push the water out of the pool.

I had to come in on days off for remedial instruction in the crawl, which I had already taught myself to do badly, my head up and arms wheeling the way teens escape sharks in movies. The precision of our technique was examined closely. In war water would be hostile territory, every ship sure to be torpedoed. I wasn't concerned enough that any of this was possible. Lungs full of air, my dead man's float was measured at eleven inches underwater.

I never wore a watch when I was a kid. The sun told the time and I was usually late getting home. I never worried, as my parents did, about drowning. In the bright noon I tied a wet maple leaf by its stem eight inches above the hook to serve as a sail. It joined the swirling camouflage. Filament pulled over my finger from the reel so I could feel the action. I was stalking while standing still, almost holding my breath, the line unwinding. Leaves trapped in the flow pressed under the fallen oak and surged on the other side as if spilling up from beneath the earth. My pilot leaf was lost in the billowing wreckage, uniquely indistinguishable, and the line went lax as the bait circled the pool. I can see myself then, hunched on the shore watching the reflection, waiting for the dull golden flash of a trout strike, hunting the frontier. Being there in the sounds of fall, I was in the space that still grows around solitude. My co found this one last place, heard the call of the wild, listened to the water, went all the way.

I drive on as dirt is shoveled over him, through the Wilderness battlefield, and find it noted only by a plaque. It's strange to see a sign beside wilderness that says it's wilderness. Like a sign in a city for a zoo. They still find bones here, men forever lost in the woods. The radio is on but I'm afloat on the road, forest on one side, the Euphrates on the other, past ads for caves cut open for tourists, squares of pasture and lawn, all the found places marked, fenced and named, rain dropping so thick people are pulling over, the highway ahead blurring into cloud. I think of the funeral as the sound pounds the windshield and roof. Rest in peace, sir. I want to know what the water told you.

Warplay

BRIAN LANCE

War is infinite nuance. War is the universal story of human suffering and yearning, transcending cultures and languages, as told by Tolstoy. Told by girls and boys, Jews and goys. War eats with many mouths. War chews sirloin, lamb, rice, grape leaves, liver sausage, haddock, and challah. War is the encapsulating event of the entire human experience. We love war. We love in war. We hate war. We hate in war. We bear war. We bear in war. We bring war home, sit together throbbing on Kansas porches watching the bobbed-hair high school girls hold hands. Sleep with war in brass four-posters, Murphy's, cots, the banks of trout streams, stretchers, gutters, mud. Wake with war in all those places, the aftertaste of aperitifs in our air, clouds of chlorine gas. Wake in clouds of Chanel, or third-world knockoff scents mixed with the sweat and secretions of other pilgrims, seeking solace on the come-stained sheets of war's matron saints. Or maybe that's just the clawing of life on leave. Wake from the sear of habu sake. Wake amid a Guinness Stout–soothed night shading all remnants of home and whoever there waits. All the requisite hallmarks of rest and recuperation. War repeats.

War whispers in between Top Forty tracks. War rides in our backseats watching over our shoulders. War reaches up front and steers our cars, blind and reckless. War prefers halted traffic, the kind that leaves us no choice but to wait, to think, to suffer some more, to pretend we're not, to pretend we are. War loves headwork, lingering in cubicles. War qualifies us for benefits we might do better off without, or fear we don't deserve. We marry with war bearing brass rings at the altar. Raise children with war rumbling in our backyards, the backs of our minds. War slaps spouses. War draws blood and tears and blank stares. War shackles lunar cycles, sequesters serotonin. War digs trenches in Flanders and the Somme, tunnels in South Vietnam, our neighborhood woods where we ran, sticks for swords, sticks for rifles, sticks to reflect the human race to create, maim, kill, create. War builds shacks and shanties, hootches and bunkers, spiderholes and Green Zones, McMansions and malls. And war penetrates them all, through and through, like the walls, no, bulkheads of tall ships. But war remodels as well as it storms and sails. War soils and sweeps.

War hangs heirlooms on walls. A machete from the Mekong. A sailor sword, tight-link gold chains binding the stingray skin grip, golden leaf, and leviathan hilt, and the myth of a job never done well enough to match its neighbor the machete. War shelves the sands of Iwo Jima, charcoal black, stowed in a Del Monte jar—specialty selected fruit in syrup. If the victors reap the spoils, is the villains' shit luck passed onto them? Believing otherwise helps despite the clicking beads of history's fingered rosaries clicking Chosin, Khe Sanh, My Lai, Mogadishu, more and more until there are no victors or villains. War fills manila notepads with sketches of martyrs. War fills frames with martyrs too. Fills frames with discharge papers, with papers preventing the purchase of the guns once carried. Fills books with lies. Fills books with truths. War wrestles the dealers of definitions into submission. War prefers metal to concrete. War forges bronze, silver, gold, brass, and those other mysterious alloys dangling from nylon ribbons. Alloys pinned to puffed chests, alloy pins stuck in sunken chests, alloy sixpenny nails piercing the six-foot planks of pine sea chests. War teaches us to wear them. War teaches us to toss them into grand canyons, suburban storm drains, reflection pools, cheering crowds, closets. War teaches us to send refrigerators and trash to Davy Jones, tease his reach with oil. War plunges donkeys to death in Smyrna, places them in power in America. War carries things and drops things.

War is a human fascination, a point of constant and unavoidable fixation in our collective consciousness like fucking and faking. War fertilizes poppy fields and paddies with shit and flesh, synthetics and things ferrous. War fertilizes the history and fiction of mankind. War fertilizes masterminds, writers, and otherwise. War fertilizes the richest human fantasies, peace among them. War writes its own histories through puppet hands, masterminds, and otherwise. War writes and writes and War—

The Gift of Our Attention

An Epilogue

JOHN WHITTIER-FERGUSON

Toward the end of the eighth book of the *Odyssey*, Odysseus—unnamed stranger and guest at the court of Alkínoös—breaks down in tears as he listens to the harper Demódokos sing of the fall of Troy. Odysseus himself had asked that Demódokos tell this particularly harrowing episode from the ten years' war, but the horrors so vividly summoned by the poet leave the warrior sobbing as he sits beside his host, the king. Alkínoös bids his harper cease, noting that the "theme has not been pleasing to all here," and yet he turns then to this sorrowing traveler and asks a provocative question:

> Tell me why you should grieve so terribly
> over the Argives and the fall of Troy.
> That was all gods' work, weaving ruin there
> so it should make a song for men to come!

We might take these words simply as offered comfort: there is a pattern to the sacking of a city, its ruin "woven" by the gods who design our losses and give shape to our anguish. There are plans even for the broken walls, the burning roofs and towers, the dead and wounded we humans leave behind us as we go about our business of making and unmaking our worlds. But Alkínoös doesn't stop at consolation. His second sentence implies another, stranger explanation for the gods' work on earth: they weave our ruin, with our wholehearted help, in order that we have subjects for our songs. What more exalted occasion for those songs than war? Were history ever actually to end, were we allowed to live in some golden age of unbroken peace, our harps would soon fall silent; we'd have almost nothing to recount, no more stories to tell. It's a thought that occurs even to the benevolent, aging Rev. John Ames, in Marilynne Robinson's *Gilead*, as he considers what the angels sing about in heaven: "In eternity this world will be Troy, I believe, and all that has passed here will be the epic of the universe, the ballad they sing in the streets." Here on the mortal earth is where the plots are and will remain, and it's in the narratives from our wars that those plots become especially consequential, the stakes especially visible, our interest in the outcomes (with life and death held so clearly in the balance) more vivid than it is for ordinary tales. I imagine you will have found this to be true as you've read through this collection, with each new paragraph in so many of these stories threatening to turn suddenly toward some terrible surprise.

But these narratives from our modern wars present us with a twenty-first-century quandary: what shapes might our songs of war take if the antagonist is not Hector but an IED; if the enemy is not so much a state or a fortified city as it is a noun—"terror"—or a loosely networked and perpetually changing assembly of factions spread across a region without being confined to any single nation; if the vehicle that carries our narrator into battle is not a chariot or a steed but a Northrop Grumman B-2A Spirit—a "stealth" bomber designed to be, as Jason Armagost puts it in the opening contribution to this volume, "a whisper in a very noisy, very dark room." I have watched a post-mock-combat interview with pilots of F-15s who were in combat with an FA-22 (the "stealth" fighter), and there's not much of a story to tell. One of the F-15 pilots offers a laconic summary of the encounter: "I could never see them. I never knew that they were there. And I died." Those of you who've seen *Restrepo* will know that one of the eeriest things about that documentary is that we never catch even a glimpse of the enemy, though the soldiers at FOB Restrepo are under fire throughout the film. Or hear this crucial moment from Paul Van Dyke's "A Sliver of Blue" in this volume, when the Humvee he's driving during his deployment in Iraq triggers an IED:

> I found a spot to enter the ditch that looked like it would be relatively smooth. The front end of the Humvee dipped into the trench, then launched skyward in a single violent, chaotic heartbeat. I slammed chest-first into the steering wheel with enough force to bend the steering shaft. The steady rumble of the engine was gone. My ears rang and it felt like I was swimming too deep underwater. The windshield was black and warped, in some places melting. Everything happened so quickly that I couldn't put anything together.

Even when he does recover sufficiently to name, five paragraphs later, what caused everything around him to come apart ("IED. Our truck blew up"), there's only the scantiest story to build around this cataclysmic event—no bomb-throwing Gavrilo Princip or sheer Pointe du Hoc to describe, no explanation for what part this smooth spot in the ditch played in the war's larger plans on either side (how many sides are there, exactly, to this war, these wars?). The bomb was there, one can infer, because that spot was the most likely entry point any one of us would have chosen if we were trying to find a path back to "Supply Route Uranium"—not because the ditch was valuable ground, not a named or even a numbered hill, some piece of land to take or hold or turn to our use. As he moves into the heart of his narrative, which might be summarized as "the storyteller escapes, with agonizing difficulty, from his burning Humvee," Van Dyke insists that we not read his sentences as though their sequence built a larger structure: "I can remember quite a few details, but coherent war stories are a myth." "It is hard," Van Dyke tells us at the end of his story, "to draw meaning from hitting a blind bomb under a railroad bridge where no trains run while looking for a sniper that doesn't exist." The sentence, set in the position where we expect to find, if not a moral, at least some kind of conclusion, carefully accomplishes almost nothing as it summons its central nouns ("bomb," "bridge," "sniper") only to under-cut or negate each one. "The IED was terrible, but unfortunately not every nightmare teaches a lesson."

The wars that we'll still be fighting, it seems likely, long after this book has gone to press, are not the first to be named theoretically unnarratable. Theodor Adorno had already thrown up his hands in despair in the fall of 1944, as he tried to measure a war too big and too various to comprehend:

> The Second World War is as totally divorced from experience as is the functioning of a machine from the movements of the body, which only begins to resemble it in pathological states. Just as the war lacks continuity, history, an "epic" element, but seems rather to start anew from the beginning in each phase, so it will leave behind no permanent, unconsciously preserved image in the memory. Everywhere, with each explosion, it has breached the barrier against stimuli beneath which experience, the lag between healing oblivion and healing recollection, forms. Life has changed into a timeless succession of shocks, interspersed with empty, paralysed intervals.[1]

This sounds uncannily accurate as a description of conflicts in our own day, but in important respects it's wrong about World War II, which remains our most narratable conflict of the preceding century—"The Good War" as Studs Terkel reminds us—the story of evil defeated, our tactical and strategic goals comparatively clear, America triumphant. Not, of course, that each U.S. combatant came out of Europe or Asia with well-shaped war stories or that the individual experiences of any war arrange themselves into wholes, but the Second World War itself stands as an indispensable narrative pillar of "the American Century." In 1942, the outcome of this war unknown, Robert Frost could gesture in artfully general, morally obtuse, martially simplistic terms toward our manifest destiny and war's place in our rise to power, arguing that we made America "ours" through sacrifice—our blood (and the unacknowledged blood of those we slaughtered in "our" own and others' countries) underwriting the story told by our gifts of violence:

> Such as we were we gave ourselves outright
> (The deed of gift was many deeds of war)

A young nation without a catalogue of wars lies fallow, almost empty of meaning, scarcely realized, innocent of art and lacking consequence ("The Gift Outright").

This faith that war produces meaning and is the activity by which we fashion our homeland worked on a grand scale in the early 1940s—indeed it was crucial to the psychology of general mobilization—but by the time Frost delivers "The Gift Outright" again to the American people and the watching world, in January 1961 at John F. Kennedy's inauguration, the poem will poorly fit the coming decade and its war already long in progress. The confusions of our involvement in Vietnam— alluded to in this collection's title, recalled regularly by analysts of our wars in Afghanistan and Iraq—require another writer to do them appropriately hallucinatory justice. We might turn to Michael Herr's *Dispatches* (1977), which opens with the author, exhausted at the end of a day in Saigon, staring at an old map of French Indochina—"a marvel, especially now that it wasn't real anymore." As a boy Conrad's Marlow had sought out blank spots on maps of the world for their promise of exploration and adventure; some six decades further on, Herr knows that the maps he inherits are useful for decoration only, for dreamy musings, and for confirming that we're lost:

> It was late '67 now, even the most detailed maps didn't reveal much anymore; reading them was like trying to read the faces of the Vietnamese, and that was like trying to read the wind. We knew that the uses of most information were flexible, different pieces of ground told different stories to different people. We also knew that for years now there had been no country here but the war.[2]

That last phrase does not describe the land as the Vietnamese know it, any more than the accounts collected in this volume

give us the countries of Afghanistan or Iraq as their own people experience them. Herr's inherited map has always been
an outsiders' affair, never really accurate to what it claims to
represent, "made in Paris," its geopolitical divisions long outdated, its colored shapes "laying a kind of veil over the countries it depicted." But it perfectly captures the psychological
geography of late-modern wars—wars undeclared and interminable, concluded without being finished, tending to unmake
rather than create shapely stories.

War's vaguely realized "enhancement," trumpeted by Frost
in 1942 and 1961, has its more modest, more literal reflection
in the journalist J. Malcolm Garcia's "A Promise to Keep." Realizing that, in his four visits to Afghanistan, he "had never given
anything back to the people who had told me their stories,"
Garcia works for a few hours with a man building a house in
an empty field outside Gardez, in Paktia province, not far from
the border with Pakistan. He returns by bus to Kabul the next
morning, considering his tangible contribution to the recon-
struction of this nation: "I thought of the man and his incomplete house and the remains of blasted walls around it. . . . I
stared out my window and wondered how long my section of
wall would last, my small mark upon the land." We discover
diffidence regularly in these stories—a sign sometimes of
deliberate narrative failures and also a mode of accounting
(these authors share a rigorous, often ruthless capacity for
unflattering self-assessment). "We had learned everything that
didn't matter," Micah Fields ruefully concludes, as he recalls
some martial-sounding phrases in Pashto and Farsi that he'd
memorized in training. Those tough-guy tokens—"Stop or I'll
shoot you!" "Shut up!"—prove impossible to take seriously or
say out loud in Afghanistan, "so we walked around not talking
to anyone, adolescents in body armor, not knowing anyone's
name, or where we could get some Pepsi, or why their son's
body was now half a body, smoldering, actually smoldering,
on the road near their house." In his closing two sentences
Fields shows us how a confession of inadequacy can become,

too, the sign of a grown-up's moral reckoning: "We had been taught how to order a mortar strike. We had not, however, under any circumstances, been taught to apologize."

But the voices in *Quagmire* are not all lowered in humility or apology. Wrath remains as central to these newest wars as it has been since it commanded pride of place in the first line of the *Iliad*. Gerardo Mena rails against a Marine staff sergeant who ran from a blast that killed another Marine. Mena would have all who read his short, violently focused piece bind our anger firmly to his own, thereby helping to cauterize the wound that one man's fear inflicted on the body of the Marines' phalanx. "Go fuck yourself," Mena begs that we say together to the dishonored sergeant: "It should've been you." "I can't feel anything unless I'm angry," says Rebecca Kanner's bodybuilding brother, back from Iraq and living now, it seems, only to eat and lift and compete. This account from a heartbreakingly worried and supportive sister promises us, in its last scene, that we have by no means arrived at a conclusion: "He waits until my father and I gather around to step on the scale: 202 pounds. 'Do you need to get much bigger?' my father asks. 'Yes,' my brother says." Bobby Briggs's sardonic "Service with a Smile" forces a bloody war story into the broken frame of a Sunday brunch in Baton Rouge. Briggs's narrative lurches toward the corpse of an interpreter whose body has been severed at the waist by an RPG. Arriving at this dismembered focal point, Briggs pauses: "'I'm not really sure how to end this story. I guess that's it.'" The civilians, gathered on this October day for "the Ole Miss game," are unable to stitch the brunch back together: "I could tell the story didn't go over well. The mimosas were wearing off, and I felt like I was on an island. Lizzie [Briggs's friend] looked at me with eyes that said 'What did you just do?'"

Anger exfoliates in this story, spreading from the mistakes made leading up to the mission that cost the interpreter his life, to the frivolous football fans, to the incompetent waiter who can't get even the simplest tasks right, to the storyteller himself, who has ruined part of another day. The selections in this book tend to grow more rather than less complicated as they conclude, and unfocused or overmastering emotion often explains why. Consider Nicholas Mercurio's "Lucky," which culminates in a medical clinic in Afghanistan, where Mercurio, surrounded by critically wounded patients, slips into the fantasy—at once completely understandable and horrifying—that this abundant evidence of trauma is not quite real or, rather, not "realistic" as it would be in movies and on TV: "The blood was too red, impossibly red. . . . It looked fake, a high-fructose fraud cooked up for some low-budget production, which, in turn, explained the bad acting." Mercurio turns, for a moment he won't soon forgive, into a media critic, before shifting to self-laceration: "The war-wounded in this scene portrayed pain that was too immediate, their delivery too diffident, to be believed." Better actors would, no doubt, perform their pain more coherently, with greater authority. The enormity of this thought immediately precipitates its corrective, which then turns against itself: "I started worrying that I might be fucked up. Then I started hating myself for selfishly wondering if I was fucked up while people around me were legitimately fucked up." The recursive anguish of this story stains its title. All those not dead, or maimed, or bleeding out (the narrator included) are "lucky" but, as Mercurio's roommate points out, referring to a surviving driver sitting dazed in a chair (his vehicle has just plunged some sixty feet off a bridge into three feet of water): "I don't know man. He's gotta live with this."

As do all of us reading this collection with the attention it deserves: each of these stories constitutes an artful, urgent, disturbing cry for our efforts of comprehension. The distances we have to travel (to fall?) to live with the voices in *Quagmire* are daunting enough that we might need to recall the provocative encouragement offered by Phil Klay, in his *New York Times* Opinion piece from the winter of 2014. Klay argues that civilians and people in the military must attempt to hear voices from the other side of the great divide war opens up in our social landscape. We must not allow the impasse of "I could never imagine what you've been through" to prevent any of us from at least making the attempt to undertake that imaginative labor:

> Believing war is beyond words is an abrogation of responsibility—it lets civilians off the hook from trying to understand, and veterans off the hook from needing to explain. You don't honor someone by telling them, "I can never imagine what you've been through." Instead, listen to their story and try to imagine being in it, no matter how hard or uncomfortable that feels. If the past 10 years have taught us anything, it's that in the age of an all-volunteer military, it is far too easy for Americans to send soldiers on deployment after deployment without making a serious effort to imagine what that means. We can do better.

We come soon enough to see, as we give each of these storytellers their due, that this means we will have to undertake some version of a primal journey, still called by the name the ancient Greeks gave it: *katabasis*—the descent into the dark place where the dead lie or remain unquiet, the world underneath the routine occupations of most days, that final hole in the ground. Near the beginning of *Dispatches*, Herr realizes his reporter's work—the job of making a place for others' narratives in his writing—has extended disconcertingly beyond his brief as he'd first conceived of it:

> I felt so plugged in to all the stories and the images and the fear that even the dead started telling me stories. . . . However many times it happened, whether I'd known them or not, no matter what I'd felt about them or the way they'd died, their story was always there and it was always the same: it went, "Put yourself in my place."

At the conclusion to his record of deployment, Matthew Komatsu brings us with him to Arlington Cemetery, where those voices might be more audible than usual, but where almost all words feel beside the point. Only the simplest information retains its dignity:

> Christopher
> Keith
> Raible
> Lieutenant Colonel
> US Marine Corps
> Afghanistan
> Aug 18 1972
> Sep 15 2012

Komatsu would make an offering ("I should say something, I thought. But I couldn't think of anything to say."), and that offering is a few acts of silent attention and a final gesture of inexpressible, perfect intimacy that confirms the connection and the distance—nothing closer, nothing farther away—between the living and the dead:

> I looked up at the sky, stared at the headstone some more. I listened to the traffic on the nearby Memorial Parkway. I took a picture on my phone. I stood and placed a patch in front of his headstone. Then I kissed my hand, placed it on his grave, and walked away.

Thomas Simko, in the wry lament that opens his sketch, "The Long Goodbye," gives us the dark-comic version of this poignant, unrealizable interchange: "I have too many texts from dead people." Though Simko means this complaint literally, recording the final "Thx!" from a veteran named Dominick who died from exposure to toxins at burn pits in Iraq, it resonates figuratively, too, as do so many details in this assembly of war stories. Reading Simko's first sentence, I think of Odysseus and his meeting in Book XI with the "blurred and breathless dead" gathering at the bloody votive pit for their impossible conversations with a living man. And of T. S. Eliot, admonishing us not to forget the voices that have made us what we are: "Someone said: 'The dead writers are remote from us because we *know* so much more than they did.' Precisely, and they are

that which we know" ("Tradition and the Individual Talent").
It was Eliot's assertion—a reminder that I have been repeating to students in my classrooms for decades now, the most
succinct defense of historically informed study of the humanities that I know—that also came to me as I read Armagost's
essay, "Things to Pack When You're Bound for Baghdad."

In his B-2A bomber, on the 20,000-mile flight to bomb
Saddam Hussein's palace, Armagost carries with him, in addition to toiletries and spare clothes and a payload of some of
the most destructive nonnuclear weapons on earth, "a bag
of books and journals." And he names each one of them, in a
two-page homage that recalls for me Tim O'Brien's famous
lists in "The Things They Carried" as well as Leopold Bloom's
inventory of his library in "Ithaca." There are no ironies of his
mission that escape this thoughtful author, whose essay's med-
itative balance weighs these carefully chosen books (all read,
all known, all tested for their profundity and power) against
the violence he's bringing to Baghdad. Closing in on his target, precisely on time, all his instruments working perfectly,
his two-billion-dollar "roving black hole of electronic emissions" invisible to his earthbound victims, Armagost prepares
to return an aggregation of human shelters to the elements.
He is, in Eliot's phrase salvaged from the Blitz, "the death of
air" ("Little Gidding"): "A few hundred miles northeast lies a
city that will soon spit fire and become fire." He is aware that
the incandescent terror he dispenses is capable of engulf-
ing him, too—"If I am shot to earth, my library will burn in
a Heraclitean fire"—and that, however much he craves and
is sustained by his airborne library, he cannot measure his
effect on the course of civilization in the moment of his acting: "Who can forgive Julius Caesar his 'collateral damage'
when Alexandria burned?" Walter Benjamin would not surprise him with his insight that civilization and barbarism are
woven together, the warp and weft of history.

After his bombs have fallen and the air war has been officially
designated "victorious," Armagost interrogates his mission:

There are unclaimed dead through the buried bunkers and desert landscapes of Iraq ... Babylon ... Nippur ... Ur ... Uruk ... Iraq. How many dead? In the aftermath of the air war, some now may be mine. Bodies disintegrated in holes below once lavish palaces, terrorist camps, command centers, and barracks. How to think on these things?

It was at this point, as I followed Armagost on his journey, that I recalled lines from Randall Jarrell's poem from the Second World War, "Losses":

In bombers named for girls, we burned
The cities we had learned about in school—

I have long admired this poet and this poem, but it now seems to me, after I've read Armagost's restless, thoughtful essay (which is itself the answer to his pressing question—"how to think on these things"), that Jarrell's lines rely for their undeniable effect on a cheap, ironic shot, or a collection of such shots: the planes' cheesy names not even worthy of repeating; the implied shallowness of the airmen's knowledge of whatever it is they're flying over and destroying; the slight condescension in that last phrase about school; the narrative gambit whereby Jarrell allows himself to speak for this boyish, destructive cohort. Indeed these easy disparagements are made easy precisely by turning individual, actual pilots into "we." How often, since 9/11 and the wars that have followed, I have heard and sometimes joined in comparable attacks on the political narratives that have been attached to those wars and which perform the same generalizing sleight of hand (on the positive rather than the negative side of the ledger)— "operation infinite justice"; "operation enduring freedom"; "MISSION ACCOMPLISHED." This book you hold is not interested in these literally incredible brandings. It gives us instead a gathering of people—named, sometimes confident, often uneasy—trying to tell us about what these wars have meant (and failed to mean) in their lives. They work as writers at a local, utterly embodied level. I have spent this past year as a visiting professor at the Air Force Academy, and my seniors this spring term, a week away now from being commissioned as second lieutenants in the air force, are aligned in sensibilities and thoughtfulness with Armagost rather than with Jarrell's imagined "we" or some collective operational tagline.

In one of the many rituals at the Academy that mark this consequential transition from students to officers, the English Department held a banquet for its graduates a couple of weeks ago. After the meal and some short speeches, the seniors were called to stand before their teachers and their younger peers. Each cadet was then named, and his or her field of duty and first posting were announced to us all. I was in the midst of reading this collection at the time, and I couldn't help thinking of the wounds these stories present to and inflict on their readers. Graduations of any kind are poignant, especially for the older and more settled among us, our thoughts variously compounded of hope and concern, veering between Miranda's "O, brave new world" and Prospero's "'Tis new to thee." The problems of narrative form that I discussed near the opening of this essay are essentially the challenges of shaping a life, and I found myself earnestly hoping that each of these young men and women will find attentive listeners in the years to come, even though some of them, especially those most directly engaged in our wars, will become mired in experiences that refuse the consolations of plot but nevertheless require articulation.

Sympathetic listening, however, even as we embrace Klay's ardent call for imaginative, empathetic attention, should test us in ways for which we will be unprepared and cannot really plan. There should be an urgency attending our efforts at receiving these stories; we should be shaken by the voices in this volume. Unfortunately, the manifold complexities and confusions (narrative, political, military, historical) of the wars that are the subject of this collection, and the distances that separate most of the United States public (and most of the readers of this book) from the volunteers in our armed forces, mean that it is often a challenge even to figure out what it is we're supposed to listen to from those who have come back from these modern wars. All too often our puzzled outsiders' positions make our attempts at attention devolve into something akin to (though, we can hope, less awful than) the conversation sketched with lacerating satirical force by George Saunders in his story, "Home," published in *The New Yorker* in 2011. Mike, the narrator, a veteran who's now back in the nation he's been somehow fighting for, meets two young clerks in a store:

"I've been away a long time," I said.

"Welcome back," the first kid said.

"Where were you?" the second one said.

"At the war," I said, in the most insulting voice I could muster. "Maybe you've heard of it?"

"I have," the first one said respectfully. "Thank you for your service."

"Which one?" the second one said. "Aren't there two?"

"Didn't they just call one off?" the first one said.

"My cousin's there," the second said. "At one of them. At least I think he is. I know he was supposed to go. We were never that close."

"Anyway, thanks," the first one said, and put out his hand, and I shook it.

"I wasn't for it," the second one said. "But I know it wasn't your deal."

"Well," I said. "It kind of was."

"You weren't for it or aren't for it?" the first said to the second.

"Both," the second one said. "Although is it still going?"

"Which one?" the first one said.

"Is the one you were at still going?" the second one asked me.

"Yes," I said.

"Better or worse, do you think?" the first one said. "Like, in your view, are we winning? Oh, what am I doing? I don't actually care, that's what's so funny about it!"

"Anyway," the second one said, and held out his hand, and I shook it.

These confused young men are "sweet," Mike thinks, "Not a line on their faces"—"kids" who are about Mike's age. And they're trying to keep things straight, to show this soldier respect, even if they possess between them nothing but the most meager collection of clichés and unconsidered opinions. There is only one other character in the story who knows where Mike has been and what he's been through, and that's because this other young man was deployed to the same mysterious, memory-haunted place ("Al-Raz") as Mike. They don't tell each other stories because they don't need to:

> I asked the first guy if he remembered the baby goat, the pocked wall, the crying toddler, the dark arched doorway, the doves that suddenly exploded out from under that peeling gray eave.
> "I wasn't over by that," he said. "I was more by the river and the upside-down boat and that little family all in red that kept turning up everywhere you looked?"
> I knew exactly where he'd been.

We cannot simply tick off a complementary list of telling details as we dwell on each of the contributions to this book, assuring the authors that, if we were not quite *there*, at least we were close by. But we can try to register the full weight of these others' voices—preserving in our attempts the humility to acknowledge that there's much we're missing; knowing, too, that there's a respite for every storyteller in distances: something to be cherished in the fact of a world of separate consciousnesses distinct from each small, perceiving, unsettled "I" that's been shocked into storytelling. Language itself, always inadequate, always essential, is summoned and shaped by those distances.

Roused from his weeping by Alkínoös's invitation to identify himself and tell the assembled company who he is, Odysseus spins out the "years of rough adventure" that followed after he sailed from Troy. He speaks for a considerable length of time, so much does he have to say. Alkínoös was right when he connected loss to song. Odysseus at last closes the circle of his narrative, arriving at how he came to Phaiákia and this banquet in the great hall, and his conclusion leaves his audience still, silent, and spellbound. Alkínoös, as wise in the ways of receiving stories as he has been in explaining the motivations for their telling, rouses his court to bring gifts to this man who has lost everything on his long journey back to Ithaca. The compensatory generosity of the Phaiákians—hospitality on the grandest scale—restores to the dispossessed warrior some measure of the riches to which he is entitled by virtue of his fame, his valor, and his station. Their generosity serves, too, to remind the members of Alkínoös's court that they are whole and sound, that they possess enough to give liberally to this stranger they have come to know. We have in this volume stories from those who have been far away from home. Let our tributes be the gift of our attention.

Notes

1. Adorno's grim assessment is focused primarily on the Holocaust, as the rest of this section of *Minima Moralia* makes clear. And he is, of course, correct in many respects about this war and the scale of its losses, its destruction, as many later histories demonstrate. I'm simply interested here in how World War II is successfully turned to narrative account, both during and after the war itself.

2. Herr's phrase is no more accurate, it need scarcely be said, to the experience of the Vietnamese people than Frost's assessment of America being "unstoried" before White settler-colonizers came to these shores. For a corrective collection of views about Vietnam, see "The Other Vietnam"—a two-part series from the *Michigan Quarterly Review*, Fall 2004 and Winter 2005. See also the recent (2017) attempt, controversial though it was, by Ken Burns and Lynn Novick, to narrate the war in Vietnam from many sides.

Contributors

Donald Anderson has been editor of *War, Literature & the Arts: an International journal of the humanities* since 1989. He's editor, too, of *aftermath: an anthology of post-Vietnam fiction*, *Andre Dubus: Tributes*, and *When War Becomes Personal: Soldiers' Accounts from the Civil War to Iraq*. His collection *Fire Road* won the John Simmons Short Fiction award. His most recent books are *Gathering Noise from My Life: A Camouflaged Memoir*, *Below Freezing: Elegy for the Melting Planet*, and *Fragments of a Mortal Mind: a nonfiction novel*. See www.donaldanderson.us.

Jason Armagost, an Air Force major when this essay was first published, is now a major general. The most recent book he took to combat was Seamus Heaney's translation of *Beowulf*. He read portions of it in the left seat of a B-1 while orbiting fifteen thousand feet over the middle Euphrates River valley as the ISIS Caliphate fell in February 2019. Small arms fire and people everywhere. "In off the moors, down through the mist beams, god-cursed Grendel came greedily loping." A note in Latin in the margin. Red ink. *Auribus teneo lupum* . . . twelve tick marks. One for each bomb that day.

Jason Arment served in Operation Iraqi Freedom as a machine gunner in the USMC. He's earned an MFA in creative nonfiction from the Vermont College of Fine Arts. His work has appeared in *Iowa Review*, *Rumpus*, ESPN, *The Best American Essays 2017*, and the *New York Times*, among other publications. His memoir about the war in Iraq, *Musalaheen*, stands in stark contrast to other narratives about Iraq in both content and quality. Jason lives and works in Denver. Much of his writing can be found at jasonarment.com.

Bobby Briggs is a U.S. Army officer who is currently teaching composition and literature at West Point. He also serves as the officer in charge of West Point's Creative Writing Forum. Bobby has a BA in legal studies from West Point and an MA in literature from the University of Mississippi.

Jonathan Burgess was born and raised in South Carolina, where he resides with his wife, four children, and a giant schnauzer named Titus Andronicus. Jonathan is a Marine combat veteran of the war in Afghanistan. He holds a BA in English and an MFA in creative writing. His work has appeared in *Catholic Exchange*, *O-Dark-Thirty*, and *Blood & Thunder*.

Benjamin Busch is a writer, filmmaker, and illustrator. He's the author of the memoir *Dust to Dust* (Ecco), and his essays have appeared in *Harper's* and the *New York Times Magazine* and on NPR. His poems have appeared in *North American Review*, *Prairie Schooner*, *Five Points*, *Michigan Quarterly Review*, and *Epiphany*, among others. He teaches nonfiction for the low-residency MFA in creative writing program at Sierra Nevada College, Tahoe, and he lives on a farm in Michigan, where he shovels by day and writes at night.

Teri Carter writes about politics for the *Lexington Herald-Leader* and the *Washington Post*. She lives in Kentucky. Find her at: tericarter.net.

Brian Duchaney holds a BA and an MA in English from Bridgewater State University. He is currently working on his PhD at Boston University's Editorial Institute. His dissertation is a scholarly edition of John Steinbeck's World War II dispatches written for the *New York Herald Tribune*. A ten-year veteran of the U.S. Army, his memoir about his military service, published by WLA, was nominated for inclusion in *The Best American Essays of 2014*. He is also the author of *The Spark of Fear*, published by McFarland. He currently teaches at Bridgewater State University in Bridgewater and at Curry College in Milton, both in Massachusetts.

Micah Fields is from Houston, Texas. He's written for WLA, the *Oxford American*, *Gulf Coast*, *The Baffler*, *Columbia Journalism Review*, *Sonora Review*, *Hayden's Ferry Review*, and elsewhere. He holds a BA from the University of Montana and an MFA in nonfiction from the University of Iowa. He received the *Oxford American*'s 2018–19 Jeff Baskin Writers Fellowship, an Iowa Arts fellowship, and the AWP Intro Journals Award in nonfiction. He served as a Marine Corps infantry rifleman from 2007 to 2011 and is a combat veteran of deployments in Iraq and Afghanistan. He lives in Helena, Montana, and his book about Houston and its story of development and storms is forthcoming from W. W. Norton.

J. Malcolm Garcia is the author of *The Khaarijee: A Chronicle of Friendship and War in Kabul* (Beacon, 2009); *What Wars Leave Behind: The Faceless and Forgotten* (University of Missouri Press, 2014); *Without a Country: The Untold Story of America's Deported Veterans* (Skyhorse, 2017); *Riding through Katrina with the Red Baron's Ghost: A Memoir of Friendship, Family, and a Life Writing Stories* (Skyhorse, 2018); and *The Fruit of All My Grief: Lives in the Shadows of the American Dream* (Seven Stories, 2019). Garcia is a recipient of the Studs Terkel Prize for writing about the working classes and the Sigma Delta Chi Award for excellence in journalism. His work has been anthologized in *Best American Travel Writing*, *Best American Nonrequired Reading*, and *Best American Essays*.

Jordan Hayes is a veteran of Operations Enduring Freedom, New Dawn, and Resolute Support, where he served in a number of leadership positions and as an embedded advisor to the Afghan National Army. He currently resides in San Antonio, Texas, with his wife, Whitney, and their children, Henry, Francis, and Marigold.

Rebecca Kanner has two novels published by Simon & Schuster: *Sinners and the Sea: The Untold Story of Noah's Wife* and *Esther*, which was chosen by *Library Journal* as one of the Best Books of 2015. Rebecca holds an MFA in fiction writing from Washington University in St. Louis. Her writing has won numerous grants and awards, including Minnesota State Arts Board grants in 2013, 2016, and 2019. Along with other authors, including Michael Cunningham and Joyce Carol Oates, Rebecca is featured in *Truthful Fictions: Conversations with American Biographical Novelists*. She teaches at the Loft Literary Center in Minneapolis. You can learn more about her, and find links to selected stories, essays, and videos at www.rebeccakanner.com.

Matthew Komatsu is an Air National Guardsman, veteran of Iraq and Afghanistan, and WLA nonfiction editor. He graduated from the University of Alaska MFA in creative writing program in 2017, and his work has been anthologized in *The Kiss: Intimacies from Writers* (W. W. Norton, 2017) and *The Spirit of Disruption: Landmark Essays from The Normal School* (Outpost19, 2018.) This essay does not represent official policy or position, but you can keep up with him on Twitter (@matthew_komatsu).

Brian Lance, an MFA graduate from Western Connecticut State University, is also an alumnus of the Yale Writers' Workshop. He served nine years in the U.S. Navy, both as an enlisted sailor and as an officer. His work has appeared in WLA, *Electric Literature*, *Salt Hill*, *Akashic Books*, and elsewhere.

Alyssa Martino is a writer and editor in Brooklyn and originally from Boston. She has an MFA from the University of New Hampshire.

Gerardo Mena is a decorated Iraqi Freedom veteran. He spent six years with the Reconnaissance Marines as a special amphibious reconnaissance corpsman (SARC) and was awarded a

Navy Achievement Medal with a V for valor for multiple acts of heroism while under enemy fire.

Nicholas Mercurio is an active duty air force public affairs officer currently assigned to Secretary of the Air Force Public Affairs, the Pentagon. He holds a BS from the U.S. Air Force Academy, an MA from George Mason University, and an MMOAS from the Air Command and Staff College, where he was also a Distinguished Graduate and received the Commandant's Award for Academic and Research Achievement. His work has previously appeared in the *Journal of Veterans Studies*, *Small Wars Journal*, and Air University Press's *Wild Blue Yonder*. The views expressed herein are those of the author and do not represent the official position of the U.S. government, U.S. Department of Defense, or U.S. Department of the Air Force.

Patrick Mondaca served in Baghdad, Iraq, with the U.S. Army in 2003. He won the Waterston Desert Writing Prize in 2018 and the Monadnock Essay Collection Prize in 2020, and his writing has appeared in the *Washington Post*, the *Globe and Mail*, *USA Today*, and other publications. He lives in Clinton, Connecticut.

Raul Benjamin Moreno is an English professor at Clark College in Vancouver, Washington, and has been teaching writing, literature, and journalism since leaving the other Washington in 2008. He holds a PhD in English from the University of South Dakota, where he focused on creative writing and edited nonfiction for *South Dakota Review*. Raul's previous work has appeared in *The Normal School, Hobart, Quarterly West, The Millions,* and *Drunken Boat*. He lives in Portland, Oregon, and is currently at work on a collection of short stories and other prose.

Nolan Peterson is a U.S. Air Force Academy graduate and a former Air Force Special Operations pilot with deployments to both Iraq and Afghanistan. Now a journalist, he returned to the Afghanistan War in 2013 as a war correspondent for United Press International, reporting from the front lines while embedded with U.S. and Afghan combat units.

Thomas Simko lives in Allentown, Pennsylvania, with his daughter, Arianna, and their cat, Miles. He has published and presented in both creative and scholarly fields, is a graduate of the Wilkes University MFA program, and is a professor at Lehigh Carbon Community College. He is currently seeking representation for his first novel, *Annaliese and the Chalk Doorway*.

Paul Van Dyke deployed to Iraq (2006–7) as part of Charlie Company 2/135th Infantry, and is the recipient of the Purple Heart medal. His work has appeared in *O-Dark-Thirty*.

John Whittier-Ferguson is a professor in the English Department at the University of Michigan, where he's been since 1990. During the academic year 2017–18 he served as Distinguished Visiting Professor at the U.S. Air Force Academy. His most recent book, *Mortality and Form in Late Modernist Literature*, was published by Cambridge University Press in the fall of 2015. He is the author of *Framing Pieces: Designs of the Gloss in Joyce, Woolf, and Pound* (Oxford University Press, 1996), and coeditor, with A. Walton Litz and Richard Ellmann, of *James Joyce: Poems and Shorter Writings* (Faber 1991).

CPSIA information can be obtained
at www.ICGtesting.com
Printed in the USA
LVHW110532120821
694453LV00005B/5